'92

To Alan
With much love from
us all.
Ding, Pie, Elizabeth. Kate
and William
xxx

Down Your Way

BRIAN JOHNSTON'S

Down Your Way

Methuen London

First published in Great Britain 1990
by Methuen London
Michelin House, 81 Fulham Road, London SW3 6RB

Copyright © 1990 Brian Johnston, Anthony Smith and Victorama Ltd

A CIP catalogue record for this book
is available from the British Library

ISBN 0 413 18540 0

Photoset by Rowland Phototypesetting Ltd
Bury St Edmunds, Suffolk
Printed in Great Britain by
St Edmundsbury Press Limited
Bury St Edmunds, Suffolk

Contents

Illustrations

Foreword

I should like to emphasise that *Down Your Way* was always a team effort. It was a small team, admittedly – just the producer, recording engineer and myself. I was merely concerned with the interviews on location. Although I was consulted and my suggestions sometimes accepted, it was the producer who chose where we were going. And he or she always tried to ensure that we covered geographically the whole of Great Britain every year.

Once the six interviews had been recorded my job was finished until the following week, but the producer had to edit the six interviews for time. We usually recorded about seven to eight minutes, which had to be cut to between four and six minutes depending on the length of the music chosen. This too had to be slotted in at the end of each interview and cut to 'come out' after about one and a half to two minutes.

So you will understand that the quality of the final product depended entirely on the producer's skill and judgement. I would like to place on record my thanks and appreciation to them all. My main producers were Phyllis Robinson and Richard Burwood in London for three years. And then, when the programme production moved to Bristol, Tony Smith headed the team which from time to time included: Carole Stone, Sarah Pitt, Jill Marshall and John Wilson.

I hope they will all approve our final choice of interviews and that they will share my happy memories of countless journeys around Great Britain. One thing I'm sure they will agree – we did have lots of fun!

Introduction

20 May 1987 was both a sad and a happy day for me – sad because after fifteen years I recorded my final *Down Your Way*, happy because it came from Lord's Cricket Ground, my next favourite place after my home. This was the 733rd programme, and when I arrived at Lord's I was touched to see that the Grandstand scoreboard was reading:

Total 733

Last man 733

That made my day, and incidentally is the highest score ever recorded on that board, the previous highest being Australia's 729 in 1930.

People still ask me why I decided to stop, and whether I now miss the programme. Well, I took over from Franklin Engelmann the week after he died in March 1972. Since then I had enjoyed fifteen very happy years. But I began to get a bit fed up with all the travelling, and also felt it was unfair on my wife Pauline. Remember, except for the last two years the programme went out *every* Sunday, fifty-two weeks of the year. Latterly the Controller of Radio 4 had decreed that all programmes like ours should have a six-week rest every year.

Even so, because I had to bank some programmes to cover my holidays, I still had to go off *every* Wednesday at midday and return on Thursday evening, or Friday evening if we decided to record on two days instead of one.

So it was a fixed date in my diary, and I lost count of the

number of social engagements Pauline had to refuse because I
would be away. Just before Christmas 1986 I reluctantly decided
to look around for a suitable date to finish. I found that I had
recorded 712 programmes compared with Richard Dimbleby's
300, and Franklin Engelmann's 733. I then had the idea of copying
what John Francome the champion steeplechase jockey had done
in 1982.

He and Peter Scudamore were battling it out for the most
winners ridden in that season. Peter Scudamore was ahead in the
table when he fell and broke a collar-bone, and was told that he
could not ride again that season. John Francome continued riding
and gradually began to catch up with Scudamore's total. One
afternoon he reached the magic figure and, although he had
been booked for more rides, immediately announced that he was
cancelling all his rides for that day, and for the rest of the season.
He felt that as Peter was unable to compete it was unfair to go on,
and far better for them both to be equal champions.

So unashamedly I did the same thing with 'Jingle' – as we
called Franklin Engelmann. I added up and found that the third
week in May would be the final date.

I have never regretted my decision, but of course I *do* miss the
programme – not the travelling but the people and the chance of
seeing more of our beautiful countryside. I interviewed about
4500 people and it was a privilege and a joy to meet them all.
Forget what you read in the papers about murders, rapes, drugs,
muggings and so on. There are still millions of *good* people who
don't make the news. I was always amazed to find how many
people were caring for others, looking after the sick and the less
well off.

These were the people who talked to us about their city, town
or village. They told us about themselves, their hobbies or strange
jobs. What was so nice was that they all seemed to enjoy it and
to be proud to represent their community. I am also grateful for
the warm welcome and friendship which they gave to the *Down
Your Way* team wherever we travelled in the British Isles. I so
often thought after leaving a place, Well, that's another six friends
I have made.

People are kind enough to say that they too enjoyed the programme, and that the new version is not the same. No, of course
it isn't. It is in a completely different format, but still under the

same title. Instead of myself as the solo presenter the BBC invites celebrities from all walks of life to host two programmes, and to choose their two locations themselves. Inevitably these are connected with their childhood, schooldays or places where they lived or worked. So the emphasis is very much on the presenter, with the people interviewed helping to jog his or her memories of the place.

In *our Down Your Way* we tried to portray each place as well and as fairly as we could through the mouths of those interviewed. It was my job to stay in the background and to try to draw out from the many marvellous characters we met stories and anecdotes, and of course information connected with the place or themselves. They were the important people. I was merely the link between them and the listeners.

There have been other changes too. They have dropped our signature tune – Haydn Wood's 'Horse Guards Parade' – and those interviewed are no longer asked to choose their piece of music. I always thought this was one of the most delightful ingredients of the programme. You never knew what anyone would choose (though *we* had to check just before the interview in order to make sure that the BBC Record Library had the request in stock). A bishop might choose the Beatles or a dustman the 'Moonlight Sonata'!

All this does not mean that the new version is not a good programme to listen to. But it's not *Down YOUR Way*. I am sorry that my suggestion that it should be called *Down My Way* was not accepted. It would be a truer description of what the pro-gramme now is.

With all the information that we had gathered over fifteen years, it was inevitable that when we had finished our thoughts should turn to putting everything down on paper. Tony Smith, who was my main producer over the last twelve years, undertook to try to begin what was obviously going to be a mammoth task. Imagine listening to hundreds and hundreds of tapes, picking out bits you wanted and then transcribing them all on to paper. He was assisted by Clive Dickinson and together they soon realised that if we were to cover all the places we had visited the book would become a vast tome of several hundred thousand words and would take years to produce. So this book is a compromise.

The interviews were made over a period of fifteen years and,

although all the details were correct at the time of original recording, some circumstances have inevitably changed during the
intervening period. We have done our best to bring these up to
date where appropriate, but where we have been unable to do so,
my apologies to those concerned.

It is not a guide book or a travel book. It is a collection of the
most interesting and unusual things we heard, covering a whole
range of subjects: history, architecture, ancient ceremonies, traditions, unusual customs, forgotten crafts, jobs and pastimes, as
well as the orgins of a good many well known phrases. We have
done our best to cover the United Kingdom, but are very conscious
that we have had to leave out hundreds of places and stories
which we would have liked to include. There is a wealth of
material still untapped.

However, we hope that what we *have* chosen will inform and
amuse you, and give you a feel of what a great nation we still are
and how lucky to be the heirs to such a rich legacy.

The South-West

1   Chapel Porth, Cornwall.

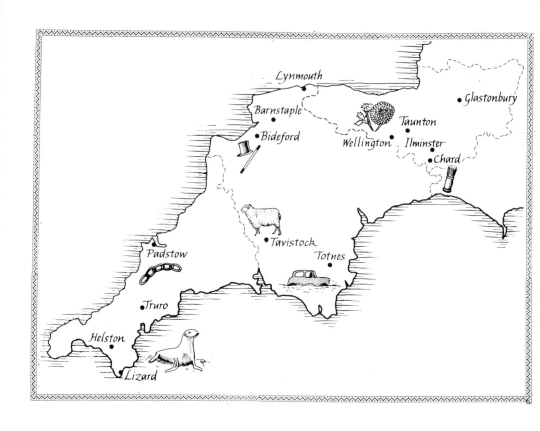

Ever since the age of seven I have had many happy memories of Cornwall. We used to go to Bude every summer for our holidays and later lived there for ten years or so. And I still go back when I can – partly to visit my parents' grave in the nearby village of Stratton.

I'm afraid food plays an important part in my recollections. After bathing in what was usually a very rough sea we always had saffron buns or cake, and I still relish the taste. In the afternoons we used to go by a wagonette drawn by two horses to some delectable place for tea. It might be the old water mill in Coombe Valley, Morwenstow or Crackington Haven. Sometimes it might be by boat up the canal to Wonnacott's farm. The end product was always the same – splits and cream.

The beach naturally played a big part in our lives. We kept white mice and used to dig trails, tunnels and bridges in the sand, and then let the mice loose. It used to attract large crowds, who watched them scampering in and out of the tunnels and over the bridges.

In the summer there was cricket on the edge of the cliffs. It was very windy and favoured the slow leg-break bowler who could bowl high into the wind. The cricket also shared the ground with the tennis club. This caused quite a scene once when my stepfather, trying to avoid being run out, flung himself forward with his bat, just inside the crease (so he thought). To his horror he was given out – the line he thought was the crease turned out to be the base line for the tennis.

In the winter we would hunt with the Tetcott, a small farmer's hunt. The ground in the valleys was marshy and, as in Ireland,

there were banks instead of hedges. They were difficult to nego-
tiate as the horse had to jump on to the top, pause and then drop
down the other side. If the bank happened to be narrow the horse
would sometimes end up with his tummy astride the bank, which
caused quite a few problems for its rider.

Since those days, I have been back to Cornwall many times.
My eldest brother used to live at Port Isaac and Truro, and we
took our children on holidays to Treyarnon Bay and Polzeath.
For me the main attraction of Cornwall is the magnificent Atlantic
coastline with its scenery and views, towering cliffs, large sandy
beaches and giant Atlantic rollers pounding against the shore.
The interior is largely without character except for its winding
narrow roads and steep hills.

Devon, by contrast, has a far wider variety of scenery and
countryside; it is, of course, a far larger county. As a boy or young
man I never lived nor even stayed in Devon. I always seemed to
be driving through it or popping over the border to visit beauty
spots like Dartmoor, Hartland and Clovelly. But in school holidays, and when on vacation from Oxford, it provided me with
some of my happiest cricket. Tavistock was the scene of my
highest cricket score, when I made 79 playing for Bude.

I also used to play at Mountwise in Devonport for the Mount
Cricket Club run by an enthusiastic colonel, Bobbie Burlton,
and consisting mostly of Royal Navy officers. But my happiest
memories were undoubtedly at the little village of Bridestowe,
where the present Lord Carrington's father lived and had a small
but beautiful little cricket ground with a small thatched pavilion.
The club was called Millaton and consisted of retired clergymen,
doctors and solicitors who during the holidays invited one or two
young people like myself to join their team.

There are many other places too – like Dartmoor and Exmoor,
Plymouth, Torquay, Exeter and Dartmouth. The variety of scenery
and breath-taking views of Devon are never ending and it must rate
as one of the most beautiful counties in Britain. Oh, and I nearly
forgot. Devonshire Cream! Don't ask me the difference between
that and Cornish, nor which I like better. They are both delicious!

Somerset was another county through which I used to drive
regularly on my journey to and from Cornwall, and when at
Oxford I had an Austin Seven which I bought second-hand for
£17! Although it was slightly longer, I used to favour going via

Taunton on to the A4, instead of the more easterly route via Honiton, Wincanton and Andover. I used to time my journey so that I could lunch and have a slight rest at the Castle Hotel in Taunton. Remember that the 240-mile journey from Bude to London in my car took something like eight hours! Anyway, luckily the Castle is still there and better than ever.

During my time with the BBC I have of course done commentaries from the County Ground at Taunton. But I first went there way back in the twenties to see Somerset play Yorkshire. It is sad that the only thing I can remember was that Abe Waddington and Maurice Leyland refused to give me their autographs. It taught me a lesson which I pass on to all young autograph-collectors. Never ask cricketers for their autographs when they are on their way to lunch. They may have been chasing around the field for two hours, they only have a forty-minute interval and their thoughts are on their stomachs.

The longest stay I have had in Somerset was during the late summer of 1940 when my battalion was stationed at Castle Cary. At that time I was still in charge of the motor-cycle platoon. We had a lot of clapped-out second-hand machines and I, as commander, sat in a side-car which had obviously been used to take the family to the seaside. If the Germans invaded the south coast it was the job of my platoon to drive down the A35 to Weymouth and send a despatch-rider back as soon as we sighted the enemy. Looking back now, it was ridiculous. We had no radio, no armour on our vehicles and only a few rifles slung across the shoulders of my gallant motor-cyclists. Just imagine what *would* have happened had we met the advancing Germans head-on! Luckily it never happened, but it very nearly did.

Since then on my *Down Your Way* travels I travelled the length and breadth of Somerset with its cider and pretty villages. It is a friendly county, and during our *Down Your Way*s we have always received a very warm welcome.

Thirteen hundred miles due north from a given point on the coast of Spain you reach dry ground once again on the tip of the LIZARD PENINSULA, the most southerly point in Great Britain, an ideal place to start a *Down Your Way* tour of this fascinating island.

Our visit coincided with the first snow they had seen there for five years, which, though blotting out some of the spectacular scenery, did give us a chance to concentrate on some of the less well-known aspects of this remote and intriguing corner of the country.

Very few precious minerals have been found on the Lizard, not that this seems to have affected its settlement; the first monks to arrive were building their monasteries in the 'meneage' lands as early as the ninth century. Following the Crusades, leper colonies were created all over the peninsula, which according to one theory gave it its name – leper/Lizard.

At the point where you would actually climb ashore if you had made that voyage from Spain you would find the flagstaff of the lighthouse which, apart from welcoming you to these shores, serves the more practical purpose of dividing the Atlantic from the English Channel. Looking out to sea, the great ocean lies to its right, the Channel to the left.

St Keverne, the Celtic missionary who gave his name to one of the Lizard's villages, may have cursed its inhabitants' rather frosty reception by ensuring that no precious minerals would be found within the hearing of the church bells, but he obviously overlooked the future importance of one mineral which is unique to the Lizard – its serpentine stone.

Talking to Harry Curnow, who had been a stone turner since the age of fourteen, I discovered this beautiful green rock with gently coloured mineral strains running through it. It is a hard rock, not quite as hard as Cornish granite, but hard enough to work even with the help of tungsten-carbide tipped tools. For the most part it is dug up by hand from the small deposits found in the twelve miles from Lizard Point at one end of the peninsula to Helston at the other. Today Harry and several other villagers in Lizard create small decorative objects and everyday household bits and pieces like ashtrays, bowls and table lamps, which they sell during the holiday season.

As well as the obvious attractions the Lizard has to offer – its sandy beaches, fishing coves, tiny inlets and generally mild climate – holidaymakers can find dozens of unusual places to visit and things to see. Anyone wandering round the churchyard at St Keverne, for instance, can get an idea of how terrible shipwrecks must have been in earlier centuries. Two hundred victims from one wreck alone lie buried there.

On the wall of the church there is a plaque to the 'St Keverne Blacksmith', Michael Joseph, a man who took on Henry VII single-handed in 1497 after the King tried to impose yet another tax on the already impoverished Cornish. With a band of followers Michael Joseph marched all the way to London, only to be summarily defeated by the King and executed at Tyburn. 'I will always be remembered,' he said as he went to his death, and he is. Every year a small ceremony in his honour is still held.

No one interested in wildlife could fail to be captivated by the Cornish Seal Sanctuary that Ken Jones and his wife started in the village of GWEEK on the River Helford in 1972. There they operate a rescue service for baby grey seals, washed from their winter breeding grounds by high seas and gales. Taking the place of the mother seal is no mean feat. The babies are born three feet long and weighing thirty pounds. In two and a half weeks, though, the baby's weight increases to four times that level. After which she leaves it to fend for itself. The eighteen-day-old, 120-pound baby seal is the only mammal on earth that has to learn to catch its own food, which is where Ken and his wife play such an important part.

2 Ken Jones with a one-week-old seal pup outside the Seal Hospital.

Many baby seals never survive beyond their early weeks and, of those that do, dozens are injured in storms and can't catch food even if they knew how to. From bottle-feeding with emulsified fish for the severely undernourished 'patients', Ken moves to pushing whole mackerel down a baby's throat, teaching it to take fish as it has to in the wild. Once this has been mastered the rapidly growing seal (they consume ten mackerel a day each) moves to the final stage of the sanctuary's work, taking mackerel in one of the pools, before being released fit and well to lead a normal life in the open sea.

Up behind St Keverne, on top of Goonhilly Downs, stands the Goonhilly Satellite Earth Station run by British Telecom, a sight to remind Lizard people that their home has as much to do with the present as the past. Telstar, which I remember vividly coming into operation in 1962, is now old hat. Today's satellite, hanging 23,000 miles up above the equator, carries 12,000 telephone calls at a time to destinations anywhere in the world from the west coast of the Americas to the Gulf States in the Middle East. There is also a television receiver that handles 800 programmes a month, and a service to shipping in the Atlantic.

Anyone who has seen Goonhilly's dished aerials must wonder why they are so large – ninety feet across in most cases. Apparently it's to do with the intensity of the signals a satellite sends. The aerials need to be that size because the signals can be very weak, so weak in fact that they've been likened to the amount of heat we'd get from a one-bar electric fire pointing at us from the moon!

Eleven miles up the A3083 from the Lizard is the market town of HELSTON, a port in Roman times, I was surprised to hear, but now cut off from the sea by the bar sands that have been thrown up in intervening centuries near Porthleven two and half miles away.

Bob Fitzsimmons, who became world heavyweight boxing champion in 1897, was born in the town, but Helston is probably best known for its ancient Furry Dance custom, which is the focal point of civic celebration every year on 8 May.

The origins of the Furry Dance are ancient, probably pre-Christian, I learned from Edward Cunnack, the long-serving Chairman of the Stewards responsible for organising the dance. 'Our primitive forefathers expressed their deepest emotions in rhythm,' he explained, 'and the emotion expressed on our festive day was unquestionably the joy of the triumph of spring over winter, of life over death, of light over darkness.'

Why the 8th of May, I wondered?

Mr Cunnack reckoned that we have the first Christians in the area to thank for that. Far from dismissing the primitive dance they witnessed, they saw it as a way of expressing the same triumph of light and the coming of light which inspired their own religion. All they did was to link the dance with a saint's day, and they connected it with the Feast of St Michael, who is Helston's patron saint.

Familiar as I was with the tune (it used to be quite a popular request on *Down Your Way*), I didn't know the ins and outs of what happens during the day.

The day of celebrations begins at half-past six with the church bells summoning the town to a special service of Holy Communion. Half an hour later the Early Morning dance gets underway. This was formerly the dance of the retainers, Edward Cunnack said – domestic servants who for the rest of the day would be waiting on their employers. Today their place is taken by the young people and some older ones who aren't available for the rest of the day, the men dressed in grey flannel trousers and cricket shirts and the girls in summer dresses.

At half-past eight begins the Hal-an-tow, which really means 'haul on the rope' – after an old sea shanty. This involves going out into the woods to collect branches of sycamore and beech which are brought back into Helston to be paraded through the town accompanied by the singing of the fine rumbustious song with its chorus: 'Summer is a'come, oh; and winter is a'gone, oh!'

In 1928 they started the children's dance in Helston which has been enormously popular ever since. 'You find now that there are nine hundred children dancing at ten o'clock, and they really are a lovely sight,' Edward Cunnack told me.

The high point of the Furry Dance is reached at the first stroke of midday when the Principal Dance begins. This is the one in which the dancers dress as they would for a Royal Garden Party, with grey toppers and morning coats for the men and gorgeous hats and dresses for the ladies. Lily-of-the-valley is worn as a buttonhole, symbolising purity and chastity. In days gone by this was the dance reserved for the gentry, several of whom had town

houses in Helston to which they would invite parties specifically
for the Furry Dance. Now it's an invitation dance for about 120
couples. Exactly as the town clock strikes twelve the first dancers
lead off through the doors of the Guildhall, dancing through the
narrow streets, through shops, through houses, through banks,
through gardens – dancing processionally in sets of four.

3 The Children's
Dance on the
Helston Flora Day.

The last dance of the day begins at five o'clock and used to be
the one held for the 'employing tradesmen' of the town. Today
just about everyone joins in to round off a memorable day.

I had one final question – the name 'Furry Dance', where did
that come from? 'From a Latin word, *feriae*, which means "a
patronal feast",' the Chairman of the Stewards assured me.

When I arrived in Helston by taxi the first thing pointed out to
me was the pub that brews its own beer, the Blue Anchor in
Coinage Hall Street. They've been brewing their beer (Spingo
beer) here since the fifteenth century. Brewing 115 gallons at a
time, they have to brew up to four times a week during the
summer. The Blue Anchor is one of only a tiny number of pubs
that brew their own beer, though it has the distinction of brewing
two of the strongest in the country. The best bitter was reckoned

by those who know about these matters to be the second strongest in Great Britain, while the special brew prepared at Christmas and Easter took pride of place as the strongest of them all.

Whereas Helston ceased to be a port several centuries ago, TRURO, the administrative capital of Cornwall, still operates as a port, though with nothing like the volume of trade it had until the Great War. Truro lies at the head of a surprisingly large waterway, comprising the Fal and Truro rivers, which flows into the Carrick Roads and the sea a dozen miles away. We saw a number of very large ships lying at anchor during our trip down river in the harbourmaster's launch – two of them over 38,000 tons, he told me. This is one of the largest and most important lay-up ports in the country, offering inexpensive, sheltered, deep-water moorings when ships aren't employed at sea. It is said that the Carrick Roads are a barometer of world trade: when there are laid-up ships and things are going well in the Truro area, the situation is bad for world shipping – and vice versa.

The river is a good deal wider than I had expected, 400 or 500 yards in places, widening out just below King Harry Ferry into the estuary and the Carrick Roads. The action of the tide means, however, that there is only water in the heart of Truro for about four hours. This and the silting up of the river have brought an end to most of the city's coastal traffic.

With trees coming right down to the water's edge, the approach to Truro by river provides a lovely setting for the cathedral, the first to be built in England since St Paul's Cathedral in London. Work started in 1880 and lasted for thirty years. From the outside its main features are the four spires, the largest of which is 250 feet high – the same number of miles to London going the old way from Truro.

Travelling northwards from the city you come to the fishing port of PADSTOW, famous for its May Day 'Obby 'Oss with its voluminous black skirt and fearsome witch-doctor's mask, and also the home, we discovered, of a very unusual form of wood carving.

With one of the West Country's most up-to-date net and twine-makers, Net-Tec Limited, based in Padstow, you might wonder what need there was to carve chains from a solid piece of wood. As I found out, though, the need for the work was charity.

Up a narrow lane leading from the harbour past the Old Customs

House we found Bill Lindsey, once the operator of the ferry across to Rock and in his retirement the creator of some of the most intricate wood carvings I have ever seen. Among the love spoons, anchors, ship's wheels, candlesticks and heart-shaped clocks, all of which had been created by his own hands, lay one of his chains, each link beautifully worked and from a single piece of timber. The longest, he told me, had 253 links, which took three months of painstaking work to carve. But how, I wanted to know?

4 Bill Lindsey with one of the wooden chains and other items
he carved to raise money for charity.

Starting with four grooves in a cross, Bill worked with a coping saw, tenon saw, small knife, file and finally a pointed junior hacksaw blade (which he used to separate each link) before finishing each off with sandpaper. It's a delicate business, particularly when you get to the end grain where the links are weakest. But all the links I saw had a perfect regularity: two inches long, one and three-eighths inches in diameter and about a quarter of an inch thick.

Bill's time and patience were obviously well rewarded. By

being sponsored for so much per link, or by getting people to guess the length of his finished chains (in anything from rods and perches to centimetres and millimetres!) he alone had raised £4500 for two local medical appeals. St Petroc, Padstow's sixth-century patron saint and father of the Cornish saints would give his hearty approval, I'm sure.

The spirit of the sea is ever present in this part of England and TAVISTOCK, just across the river Tamar in Devon, is the birthplace of one of England's greatest seafarers, Sir Francis Drake.

His father had been a shepherd to the Russell family, who became the Dukes of Bedford, and I had assumed that Drake had learned his sailing in Devon. It seems, however, that the Russells and their shepherd took the same side in one of those arguments that they always seemed to be having in days gone by about the form the Prayer Book should take. As a result they left Tavistock and Drake senior ended up as lay preacher on a hulk in the river Thames. While father ministered to sailors, Francis was apprenticed to a bargee and became captain by the time he was eleven years old, when the bargee died and left him his ship. So his sailing was learned on the Thames.

Another misconception about Devon's famous son that I'm sure I share with lots of other people is that he was knighted by Queen Elizabeth. Apparently this wasn't exactly the case.

Clive Cunnell, who was giving me this brief lesson in local history, explained. 'When Drake returned from his circumnavigation of the world, Queen Elizabeth went to meet him, accompanied by the French and Spanish ambassadors. Turning to the French Ambassador she said, "Have you got a sword?"

' "Yes," he answered.

' "Then dub him," commanded the Queen of England.'

In the Queen's Head in Tavistock, I conducted what I think was my most public interview ever for *Down Your Way*. Farmer John Doidge was holding court. He was in his eighty-eighth year and had started farming in 1918 with thirty acres. 'I mind,' he said, 'when beer was threepence a pint.' He had greeted me, pint in hand, with a song: 'Browny Ale, Browny Ale, thou art my darling. Oh, it's thee that makes me wear these ragged clothes, but if I can only get thee to my nose, ten to one down she goes.' And indeed, down it went, quick as a flash.

Farmer John had clearly enjoyed every minute of his life, which had not been without adventure. He said he'd been stolen by gypsies when he was a baby. Some people had said it was to spite his father, who had summonsed them for sheep stealing, but he thought they really wanted him to improve their breed. I wished him many more happy years in Tavistock. 'Can't expect many more,' he said, 'besides I'm beginning to wonder what I've got to answer for.' The crowd in the bar egged him on to sing 'Paper Roses'. He wouldn't, but suggested I came back at closing time.

Across Dartmoor, overlooking the river Dart itself, TOTNES is the birthplace of another famous Devonian, Charles Babbage. Babbage may be less well known than Drake but he is every bit as influential, for it was he who designed a calculating machine early in the nineteenth century which was the forerunner of the modern computer. As a mathematician and a Fellow of the Royal Society, Babbage began work on his machine around 1830. He soon ran into difficulties because the techniques for making the intricate parts he required weren't fully understood at that time. If they had been he would undoubtedly have succeeded. Nevertheless, he is regarded as the father of the computer and the Totnes Museum celebrates this achievement in its Babbage Room, in which you can see a number of exhibits donated by the big computer firm ICL that trace the development of the computer from Babbage's pioneering work to the present day. Apart from the Science Museum in South Kensington, this must be one of the very few comprehensive exhibitions of the evolution of the computer in the country.

There's a motor museum in Totnes, too, with a collection that ranges from Rolls-Royces to an Austin Seven. The one that caught my eye in particular was an amphibious car made in Germany in the mid-1960s. I must have sounded a little sceptical when I asked if it was effective in the water.' They're capable of crossing the English Channel,' the museum's owner, Richard Pilkington, assured me. 'We certainly followed the Tall Ships Race out from Plymouth one year and were out for several hours.'

The doors are completely watertight and only the wheels and brakes are in the water. There are two big propellers under the tail which are more or less hidden, and with the car fairly high off the ground they never have any problems on uneven roads.

Up in the north Devon port of BIDEFORD we came across the Supreme Magic Company which had more than a few surprises, as one might imagine. Edwin Hooper, the founder, manager and inspiration for the company, gave us a guided tour and showed us some of the 16,000 tricks he markets – without giving away any of their secrets, I hasten to add. This isn't the sort of firm that sells its goods to all-comers. It restricts its customers to recognised magicians, though this isn't as limited as you might expect. The company has some 30,000 magicians from all over the world on its files. Many of them are professional performers. Quite a few are semi-professionals who entertain at children's parties, after-dinner shows and so on. The rest are amateurs who practise their magic just as a hobby.

Edwin told me that he had originated over 500 of the tricks on offer, and when I asked for an example of how an idea had come to him that he had been able to put into practice he quoted an instance during a lecture to the Magical Society in Manchester, when he suggested the possibility of extending magic painting beyond the conventional painting book on which it mysteriously appears. Why restrict it to a book, he suggested? Why not colour a house with magic painting?

Back in Bideford he made a white model house, worked a little magic on that and hey presto – the house became coloured. Like all good tricks the big surprise comes at the end when a rabbit appears inside!

To make tricks like this economical the Supreme Magic Company has to sell a quantity of each one. What makes each unique to individual magicians is their presentation. That's what gives each performance its personal stamp.

At one time, when dove magic was very much in demand, the company used to supply doves too. These were white Java doves which, Edwin said, don't require a lot of training. They have to get used to being handled and have to grow accustomed to noise, but as long as the magician has the right sort of doves that is about all the conditioning they need.

Nine miles round the coast on the A39 is BARNSTAPLE, the home of Royal Barum Ware that takes its name directly from the Roman name for the town *Barumensis*. Although there is no written evidence to confirm the local understanding that the town was granted its first charter by King Athelstan as long ago as the year 930, the town is without doubt one of the oldest in Britain.

The present name is Saxon, meaning 'a fortified market town', which as far as the market is concerned still holds true. Every Tuesday and Friday a market is held in the old Panier Market, with its twenty arched doorways facing out to Butchers' Row. Quite a large proportion of the stalls still sell farm produce from the surrounding area, making the market an important occasion for people from the area to get together.

Across the narrow street from the Panier Market are rows and rows of little shops, all white. We counted seven butchers' shops, but each had about three windows, so there were really about thirty windows all displaying meat. To be perverse, we went to talk to Steve Taylor, one of the two regular *fishmongers*, and he sketched in the street's history for us. Originally, he told us, the little shops were used as stables to accommodate the horses that were brought to the market. As time went on they became little lock-up shutter shops, taken over largely by butchers – a good thirty at one time.

On the slab was something I had never seen before. It looked rather like Bombay duck and was, in fact, a form of dried fish, although its name – Toe Rag – might not lead you to think so. 'It's a salt cod,' said Steve, adding, 'if you could get a little closer to it you could probably smell that it's like a pair of old socks.'! Soaked in water and fried with butter, it's delicious – so he assured me. It can also last a long time. After hanging in the shed for a couple of years he reckoned it tasted better than ever.

Tea fish is another local delicacy, eaten at tea time by many families in the area during Lent. At one time it used to be hung outside the shops and a few of the local dogs used to take quite a fancy to it, so the bottom piece of fish was never eaten!

Queen Anne's Walk is another old part of Barnstaple connected with trade. In the middle of the seventeenth century the old Walk, or Merchants' Exchange, was covered in and a mushroom-shaped stone was erected where, according to local hearsay, business transactions were carried out. The placing of hands and money on the top of the stone was traditionally taken as a symbol of good faith and integrity.

On the way to Queen Anne's Walk we passed under Barnstaple's famous Long Bridge with its sixteen arches spanning the river Taw. Stan Trent, a mine of information on local history, told me that the first three arches are still called the Maiden Arches, said to be named after two elderly ladies who worked as seamstresses in Maiden Street, which still exists today. Tradition holds that they used the profits they made from their sewing to build the first arches of the original wooden bridge.

I had noticed that someone had also built a chapel at the north end of the bridge: the St Nicholas Chapel, Stan told me. That was built by the de Tracy family, seemingly to ease their guilty conscience over the fact that one of their family had belonged to the group of four knights that murdered St Thomas à Becket.

Among Barnstaple's other famous names are John Gay, who wrote *The Beggar's Opera*; Henry Williamson, the author of *Tarka The Otter*; and of course the explorer Sir Francis Chichester, who was born in the village of Shirwell, just outside the town.

Moving on up Cross Street from Queen Anne's Walk, you come to the Guildhall which every September (the Wednesday nearest the 17th, to be precise) is the centre of Barnstaple's famous fair, which dates back to 1274 when it began as a horse fair. On the first day the town's dignitaries and their guests sit in the Guildhall in great ceremony and drink the toast to Barnstaple Fair in a secret brew of spiced ale passed down from each chief beadle to his successor. The proclamation that opens the fair is first read in the Guildhall by the town clerk, after which the 'Hand of Friendship', a large white glove garlanded with flowers and set on a long pole, is pushed out of the top window to greet all the people who are visiting the town. The official party then parades around the town where the proclamation is again read at the South Gate and Queen Anne's Walk.

I suppose when most people think of the picturesque North Devon village of LYNMOUTH, up around the coast from Barnstaple, they recall the terrible flood disaster of August 1952 which claimed the lives of over thirty people. After days of monsoon-like rain the swollen waters of the rivers East and West Lynn converged on the stricken village in a wall of water forty feet high, sweeping aside many buildings in the centre and carrying the helpless victims far out into the Bristol Channel.

When we were there on a glorious September day it was hard to picture that appalling tragedy. In fact, apart from the now tranquil sound of the two rivers, the only noise of rushing water in Lynmouth that day came from the unique cliff railway which carries freight and up to forty passengers 475 feet up and down the steep valley wall.

As Bob Jones, the engineer in charge, explained to me, this railway was designed by his grandfather to work on an ingeniously simple use of the counterbalance principle. Both the cars, connected by a cable that runs up and down the 900-foot rails, have huge tanks capable of holding two and a half tons of water, which are always filled when the cars are at the top. To set them moving the two drivers release their brakes. If nothing happens the one at the bottom discharges water until his car is lighter than the one at the top, and away they roll up through the glorious cliff scenery that makes Lynmouth a favourite holiday destination for thousands of visitors each year.

5 The cliff railway
   at Lynmouth.

WELLINGTON in Somerset is probably best known for its associations with the Duke of Wellington, victor of the Battle of Waterloo, in spite of the fact that he only visited the town once. He was still in France when he was ennobled and wrote to his brother asking him to pick somewhere in the West Country that resembled the family name of Wellesley. Apparently the brother studied a map and settled on Wellington, with the result that today the Duke's obelisk stands on Black Down to commemorate the fact.

If the Iron Duke's association with Wellington was somewhat accidental the town can still point with pride to quite a history. Egerton Bennett started the forerunner of the modern mail-order catalogues here, developing it to the point where by the 1860s he held some thirty Royal Warrants of Appointment, and through a catalogue printed in five languages sold clothes and blankets to every crowned head in Europe.

I also learned that the aerosol spray was developed in Wellington and that the *City of Truro*, the first train to run at one hundred miles an hour, had achieved this distinction between Wellington and Whiteball Tunnel – at night, so as not to frighten the local populace, by all accounts. And where did the puttees worn during the Boer and Great Wars come from? Yes, from Wellington, made by Fox's, who still export cloths all over the world; they were the only firm that could make the shade of khaki to meet with official approval.

I love chrysanthemums and my visit to Wellington was made complete when I went to the Frank Rowe Nurseries on the outskirts of the town. They are run today by Frank's sons Philip, Brian, Derek and Stewart, and all four greeted me and acted as my guide through the various greenhouses that cover five of their nine acres.

Frank Rowe had started the business in 1927 when he had bought part of his father's farm. He had begun as a general market gardener and then specialised more and more until for the last twenty-five years Rowe Nurseries have grown nothing but chrysanthemums – 400 different varieties of them. They are busy with cut flowers from October until Christmas, but the main part of their business is not with the flowers themselves but the production of cuttings and plants which they sell only to other growers. They produce something like 15,000,000 cuttings and plants every year.

Several of the greenhouses were strung with rows and rows of electric light bulbs. 'That,' said the brothers, 'is so we can fool the chrysanthemums and make them flower when we want them to flower. We've got to make them think it's autumn at any time of the year and then they will form their flower buds. We put the lights on at night to prevent the plants forming buds until they've made sufficient growth.'

'There is no fixed temperature for chrysanthemums,' said Brian.

'For spray varieties a night temperature of 14 or 15 degrees centigrade will make sure the buds initiate. We're experimenting all the time with spray varieties, trying to pick out a few that will be commercially viable in seven or eight years' time.' They create the spray by removing the centre bud and allowing all the side shoots to develop to produce four or five or even up to thirty flowers on a single stem. 'The chrysanthemum was brought to Europe from the Far East, probably from Northern China 300 years ago. It's China's national flower,' said Philip. 'The most popular colours sold today are whites and yellows, but I like the reds and bronzes as much as any.'

Around the Blackdown Hills to the south of Wellington, still close to the Devon–Somerset border, is the town of CHARD. Two tiny streams run down Chard High Street, one on either side. One, I was told, turns south and finds its way eventually into the English Channel. The other turns north and heads for the Bristol Channel.

Chard's rural setting belies its spirit of commercial and industrial enterprise. Hanging from the ceiling in the small museum in the High Street was the model of an 'aeroplane'. Len Hoskins, the curator, explained that in 1845 a chap called John Stringfellow was experimenting with powered flight and devised a machine made of cotton fabric and wood, and powered by a light steam engine. He built this on a wire and the plane actually flew along the wire, off the end and then crashed into a wall. 'As far as we know,' said Len Hoskins, 'this was the first powered flight ever made anywhere in the world. What's more, Stringfellow's experiments were with fixed wings, whereas all his competitors were trying flapping wings.'

The first powered flight is not the only first that Chard claims. In the 1860s a man called Gillingham made the first artificial limb, and during the Boer War and the Great War Chard boasted the premier factory in the world for artificial limbs. It is also proud to be the birthplace of Margaret Bonfield, the daughter of a laceworker, who in 1929 became the first woman ever to sit in the Cabinet.

Chard is close to the borders of Devon. However, it describes itself as an industrial town and one of the things it makes is pantographs. A pantograph is an instrument for copying drawings or plans, shaped rather like a parallelogram. However, a visit to the factory of Brecknoll Willis at the bottom of the town provided another definition. They are one of only two firms in the world making pantographs, and they export 85 per cent of all they make. Ken McQueen explained to me that the firm had started in 1894 at about the time of the start of electric tram cars. The poles that connected the tram car to the overhead wires were paralleglogram-shaped, people called them pantographs, and the name stuck. However, it was not, I was told, until recently that the *Oxford English Dictionary* carried this second definition of the word.

Four hundred years ago Nummer Mill was making flour. It is still working today and is still a water mill, but its products are very different. Jim Young took me on a tour. Up ladders we went, through narrow doorways, across creaking floorboards – the danger of a bumped head ever-present. It was altogether a most unusual factory. About twelve people are employed here by two famous firms, Coates and Simpsons. For 250 years Coates have been making their brushes and nail brushes in the traditional way using satinwood, ebonies, laurelwood and bone and ivory. Simpsons joined them at Chard in 1940, evacuees from the London Blitz. They make shaving brushes that sell for anything from £5 to £350 (these are made of bone and ivory). They find their customers in the world's most famous stores. They favour badger hair, which is fine, soft and very durable, but they also use hog bristles from the wild boars of Germany and Poland. All the work is done by hand and I watched fascinated as skilled fingers gathered up the bristles, arranged them neatly and trimmed them for shape. The head of the brush, the knot, is fixed into the handle with a cement. 'We dip the knot,' said Jim Young, 'into some adhesive, drain off the excess, pour some adhesive into the handle, place the knot into the handles and leave it to set overnight.' It sounded simple, but the skills are acquired over many years.

Making the hair brushes was just as skilful, although they use a tougher bristle from the wild boars of India and China. I watched as one man patiently drilled holes in the wood that would take the bristles, the lines of holes slightly curved to match the shape. The bristles are held in place by brass wire, the assembly is done not in the factory but by out-workers – work which takes thirty five to forty minutes for every brush.

Nestling at the foot of the Blackdown Hills on the banks of the river Isle, the market town of ILMINSTER is another happy blend of deep-rooted history and forward-looking initiative.

In his house overlooking the town George Maher, the retired headmaster of the sixteenth-century boys' grammar school, gave me a roll-call of some of Ilminster's famous sons and daughters. There were the brothers Thring, the elder of whom became headmaster of Uppingham and was second only to Arnold of Rugby among Victorian public-school masters. In 1846 his younger brother, still studying at Cambridge, wrote a book called *The Simple Game*, in which he laid down a code of football rules that was adopted for the most part by the Football Association when it was established in 1863.

Oxford has perhaps even closer academic and sporting ties with Ilminster. Nicholas and Dorothy Wadham, founders of Wadham College, Oxford, lived a few miles from the town and at one time Nicholas was a governor of the gammar school. So it was only appropriate that Sue Brown, a former pupil of Ilminster's girls' grammar school, was selected to be Oxford's first woman Boat Race cox in 1981, since she was also a member of the Wadhams' own college.

Other old pupils distinguished themselves further from home. In 1857 the Victoria Cross was awarded in the Crimea to Ilminster's Major Elton on the first day that that decoration was ever won, and Field Marshal Lord Harding made his name in Cyprus in the mid-1950s, dealing with the crisis there.

Jordan's, about a mile and a half outside the town, was the home of John Hanning Speke, one of the band of Victorian explorers who went in search of the source of the Nile. According to his own account at least, he was the man to find it. Dillington House, about the same distance away down the Langport road, which today is a college for adult education, was, according to Peter Epps, its managing director, 'the Chequers' of the American War of Independence. Lord North, George III's Prime Minister at the time, conducted his share of the campaign from there, which considering the three days it took for messages to reach London, not to mention the army on the other side of the Atlantic, coupled with his lordship's rather ponderous approach to the war, might account for our loss of those particular colonies.

All the same, America still loomed large over Ilminster two

centuries later. At the time of our visit Minster Stone, manufacturers of fine stone fireplaces and garden ornaments, had three container-loads of their garden-ware on the high seas bound for Boston, where they were destined to grace a hotel patio on the sixteenth floor. Meanwhile, orbiting hundreds of miles above was a piece of laser equipment measuring the sun's rays that had been designed and made by Gooch and Howskill, one of Britain's most advanced high-technology companies, but still based in Ilminster's lovely old market square where it had started in an attic forty years ago! And nearer home the Ilminster Majorettes, providing a more lighthearted American influence, under the guiding hand of Mrs Joy Dalley, have established themselves as one of the principal majorette groups in the country, notably with their baton-twirling expertise. I know it would have completely flummoxed me if I'd tried anything more adventurous than a gentle two-finger twirl.

6   The Ilminster Majorettes with some of their trophies.

However, I was able to put my fingers to better use under the genial instruction of George Walsh, then British snuff champion and runner-up in the world. Of the 460 snuffs manufactured from the finest of fine tobacco in the UK, which can include anything, it seems, from strawberry and raspberry essences to menthol, his favourite has the splendid name Crumbs of Comfort, of which he was wont to take up to 150 pinches a day. But what is the correct way of taking snuff?

'Tap the box,' George explained. 'Open it up. Take a pinch between your forefinger and your thumb. Tap it on the side of the box. Put it to your nose and sniff. That is, after you've passed it all round to your friends.'

That I could grasp, but I was intrigued to know how you compete at snuff-taking. What are the rules? What makes a champion? In a nutshell, it is a matter of taking fifty pinches of different snuffs as quickly and as cleanly as you can (twenty-five if you're a lady). Each competitor moves down a long table where twenty-five servers with tiny spoons put a pinch of snuff on the back of your hand for you to sniff one after the other. Time-keepers and judges are on hand to supervise and disqualify anyone who coughs, sneezes, or blows the snuff off his hand.

When George won the championship he managed to do this in sixty seconds! What's more, he didn't incur a single penalty point for having any snuff left on his hand or around his nose. Judging by the very mild snuff he let me try, I have a feeling my performance might not have been quite so dignified.

TAUNTON, the county town of Somerset, was the setting for the Bloody Assizes held by Judge Jeffreys following Monmouth's rebellion in 1685. Somerset folk paid dearly for their support of the ill-starred duke. In three days Judge Jeffreys tried 526 people and hanged at least 193. Their punishment didn't stop at hanging, for they were drawn and quartered, and their remains were used to decorate the market places and trees throughout the country for a decade afterwards.

In North Street I visited the British Telecom Museum – not the only one of its kind in the country but the first, having opened thirty years ago. Among the exhibits was a telephone with Chinese characters instead of numbers. I asked how they had come by that and Peter Povey, who was acting as my guide, answered it, 'It was in a batch sent to Yeovil, but they didn't speak Chinese in Yeovil.'

My next question was about an instrument that I thought looked rather like a toadstool. 'That's called a butterstamp telephone,'

said Peter, 'named after the stamps once used for marking butter.'
It was one of the first commercial telephones, and a pretty primitive instrument at that. To speak, you held it to your mouth and
shouted, and when you wanted to listen to the reply you held
the same piece up to your ear. There was no bell to summon the
person you were calling to the phone, so to attract their attention you had to tap the earpiece/mouthpiece with a pencil.

I was also shown an early switchboard which had been in use
at the turn of the century and was capable of carrying about fifty
lines. 'That would have been more than enough in those days for
Taunton,' said Peter.

His knowledge of telephones seemed inexhaustible. He told
me that the first telephone in Britain had been installed in
Plymouth because Alexander Graham Bell, inventor of the
instrument, had come to this country for his honeymoon and
first stepped ashore there. I have always regretted that I didn't
ask where the second phone was, but I did learn that Bell
used wires alongside the railway lines, the railways' telegraph
circuits, and in this way he was able to communicate over a
distance of fourteen miles.

Taunton stands in the heart of Somerset cider country, where
plentiful supplies are ensured each season in the annual wassail
ceremony which takes place during the twelve days of Christmas.
Its object is to encourage a good crop of apples, which in practice
combines with a jolly good party as well. Pride of place goes to
the Wassail Queen, attended by her escorts or handmaidens.
There's also the all-important Pailbearer, charged with carrying
a pail of mulled cider.

Once the celebrants are suitably cheered and primed in the
marquee where the refreshments are provided, the Wassail
Queen is borne into the orchard to the tree chosen to be
wassailed. There she takes a pitchfork with a piece of toast on
it, dips this into the mulled cider and puts it into the boughs
of the tree. The toast encourages good spirits, which come in
the form of robins. Some of the mulled cider is then poured
into a two-handled wassail mug which is emptied around
the root of the tree to encourage good growth. Men with
muzzle-loaded guns step forward next and fire shots into the
tree to get rid of any evil spirits. Then it's three hearty cheers
and a rousing chorus of the Wassail song:

Old apple tree we wassail thee
And hoping thou will bear
Hat fulls, cap fulls, three bushel bag fulls
And a little heap under the stairs.

A tree, a thorn tree to be precise, lies at the heart of one of the many legends surrounding GLASTONBURY twenty-two miles north-east of Taunton up the A361. It was here that Joseph of Arimathea apparently settled after fleeing Palestine with a few faithful followers after the crucifixion of Our Lord. Resting on a hill nearby he stuck his staff, cut from a thorn tree, into the ground and this is supposed to have burst forth into leaf and blossom, which Joseph took as a sign that he should stay to found an abbey.

Leaving aside Joseph's involvement, the ruins of the abbey confirm that Glastonbury Abbey was an enormous establishment covering a total of forty acres during its heyday. The abbey itself was almost 600 feet from end to end, and the massive tower of which only the impressive archway still stands was over 200 feet tall.

7 Glastonbury Abbey.

In answer to my question as to why such a huge abbey should have been built here, Leslie Ashby, custodian of the abbey, suggested that it was 'without doubt the first Christian sanctuary in the country and that presumably does give it a place of prominence'. By way of confirmation he added, 'At the Council of Basel, it is interesting that British bishops were granted precedence over the bishops of both France and Spain, because Christianity came to England before it reached either of those countries.'

The other legend associated with Joseph of Arimathea is that of the Holy Grail, the chalice or bowl used by Jesus Christ at the Last Supper on the eve of his crucifixion. Joseph brought this to Glastonbury too, by all accounts, though Geoffrey Ashe, the author and authority on Glastonbury and its fascinating history, told me that in his opinion the legend of the Holy Grail was more likely to be a symbolic arrival of Christian values in this part of Somerset rather than the physical presence of the grail itself.

Whatever its origin, the legend of the Holy Grail formed one of the key elements in the wider legends surrounding King Arthur, so it wasn't all that surprising to come across a sign in the abbey grounds announcing the site of King Arthur's tomb, where in the year 1191 the bodies of King Arthur and his Queen were said to have been found and removed in the presence of King Edward and Queen Eleanor. Over the site a very fine black marble tomb was said to have been erected. This, of course, has long since disappeared, although during excavations small fragments of black marble were found, indicating that that part of the story may quite well have been true. (The identity of the two bodies found there has still to be solved – if it ever can be.)

Returning to the thorn, I wondered if there was still any evidence of it in the abbey. 'I suppose what you could call the great-great-grandson of the original thorn has been here a very long time,' said Leslie Ashby. 'It's a curious tree. It's like a hawthorn but it blooms twice a year, not necessarily at exactly the same time, but it does bloom in May and then again in November or December.

'It is not a native of this country,' he added mysteriously. 'I have been told that it is a native of the Near East, which is curious.'

Curious indeed, and one of the several reasons to visit Glastonbury if you ever have the chance.

The South

8 Selborne, Hampshire.

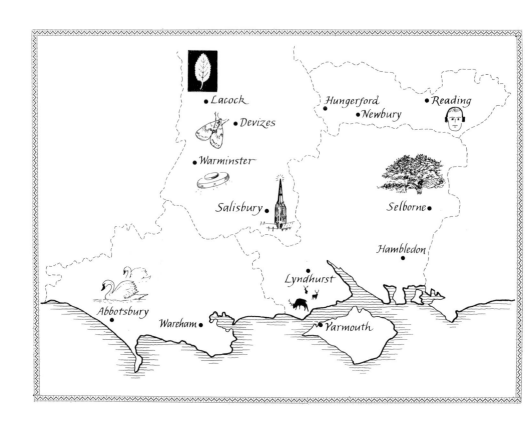

Lacock

Hungerford
•Newbury

•Reading

•Devizes

•Warminster

Selborne•

Salisbury•

Hambledon

Lyndhurst

Abbotsbury

Wareham•

•Yarmouth

The county of Wiltshire has mainly wartime memories for me, because we were stationed at Warminster for about two years, learning to handle our tanks on Salisbury Plain. On one exercise my scout car drove into a ditch, I was flung forward and my not inconsiderable nose hit a particularly hard bit of the armour on the car. Result – a messy nose, and in spite of some clever stitching I still have a large scar today.

My headquarters was in a garage and one day we were all issued with berets. These are not the most becoming of headgear and I quickly realised that I would look fairly comical with it on. So I paraded my forty or so fitters and storemen and told them that I was going to put it on my head. I told them that they could then laugh for two minutes. After that, if I caught anyone laughing at me they would be put in close arrest. It worked! They had a tremendous laugh but got it out of their system. It was my best bit of leadership in the whole war.

Personally, I always find Wiltshire rather an eerie place, with Stonehenge, the earthworks of Avebury and the cold wildness of Salisbury Plain. If I were asked which is my favourite county I would have to plump for Dorset. First of all, it offers so much sheer beauty with its peaceful and unspoilt countryside, still free from the roar of modern motorways. It has such variety – the rolling fertile hills, the lush valleys with the narrow winding lanes, the small valleys and hamlets, the thatched cottages built of Purbeck stone and the quaint names like Piddletrentide, Affpuddle and Puddletown. Then there are the cliffs round the Isle of Purbeck – matching those of Cornwall for size and grandeur.

I first went to Dorset in 1923 when we lived there for two

years, first at Upwey near Weymouth, and then at Moreton near Dorchester. Upwey has a famous wishing-well at the end of the long village street and I had many boyhood wishes, most of which have luckily come true. Moreton was where T. E. Lawrence lived, and where he was buried after his motor-bike accident. It was here that a kind neighbour called Colonel Parks bet my sister half-a-crown that I would one day keep wicket for England. I'm afraid my sister has never been paid – she's still living in hope!

I remember being told about Thomas Hardy and his stories of the Dorset countryside and people, and visiting the famous Abbotsbury swans. And, of course, as a boy I was particularly interested in the Cerne Abbas Giant – the figure of a naked man cut into the chalk hillside, displaying his manliness for all to see.

I also saw much of Dorset during the war. I joined the Grenadier Guards at Shaftesbury – at that time the only town in England without a railway station. We were later stationed in a girls' school at Parkstone. I hasten to add that it had been evacuated, but there were still notices on the dormitory walls where the Guardsmen slept: 'Please ring the bell if you need a mistress during the night.'

After the war in the fifties we began to go on holiday with our children to Swanage. We had a small cottage in the quarry village of Acton, a great place for fossils – especially dinosaur footsteps imprinted in large slaps of Purbeck stone. For the last fifteen years we have had a house on the cliffs at Swanage, and have a fine view of the bay and the monument in honour of King Alfred's victory over the Danes in Swanage Bay in AD 877. A really delightful place to spend a quiet holiday.

Across the water is the Isle of Wight, with Queen Victoria's Osborne House and Sandown and Shanklin, where Arthur Askey and Tommy Trinder started their careers in concert parties on the pier. The other half-mile-long pier at Ryde used to have the best collection of vulgar seaside postcards. To save embarrassment to the buyer each card was numbered and he just had to ask for a number without revealing the nature of his choice. These have now disappeared.

My first visit to Hampshire was in 1924, when we went with our tutor in the side-car of his motor-cycle to see Hampshire play Notts at Dean Park in Bournemouth, which in those days was in Hampshire, not Dorset. I remember the bald-headed, red-faced

Arthur Carr, white handkerchief knotted round his neck, hitting the Hampshire bowling past his rival captain, the portly Lionel Tennyson, standing at mid-off. About eight years later I went to Portsmouth to play cricket against the United Services. During a hilarious evening we were shown over the royal yacht and I was allowed to sit on the special lavatory seat reserved for Queen Mary. It was made of a sort of chamois leather beautifully soft and warm to the skin.

Whilst at Oxford we used to travel to Winchester every year to play cricket against the College, and also against the Greenjackets at St Cross, so that I got to know and love this beautiful city. I have visited it many times since, and once on *Down Your Way* claimed the Wayfarers' Dole of bread and ale at Britain's oldest charity, the Hospital of St Cross, the right of any visitor or traveller.

Since the war I have visited and passed through Hampshire many times. With the coming of the M3 it has lost some of its peace and charm, but it still has some delightful villages tucked away in the Test Valley, and its fishing and shooting rivals the best in Britain. It is a county of large and prosperous farms, and still produces the finest strawberries.

As a county, too, it is steeped in the history of cricket. Hambledon was the cradle of English cricket, and the Bat and Ball Inn still stands there on Broadhalfpenny Down, where in the mid-eighteenth century the village of Hambledon beat All-England. Hambledon today is well known for its wine and mineral waters. Another link with cricket can be found at West Meon, where Thomas Lord, who created Lord's Cricket Ground, is buried.

Berkshire is now rightly called Royal with Windsor Castle, Windsor Great Park and Ascot. It is dominated by the river Thames and provides a contrast of towns, industrial Reading, leisure town Maidenhead, Newbury and its racing and Hungerford with its antique shops and fishing on the river Kennet.

In the years before the war I used to visit a house near Hungerford owned by some rich friends of mine. They were quite keen on their wine and were often a bit the worse for wear. One day their butler came swaying in with the vegetables, which he proceeded to drop in one of the guests' lap. 'Pinnock,' said my host. 'You are drunk.'

'Yes, sir, I am,' he replied. 'And it's about my turn!'

In spite of my earlier comment on the rather eerie feeling Wiltshire always gives me, the lovely little village of LACOCK that lies mid-way between Chippenham and Melksham is full of happy memories – it was here that Tony Smith and I recorded our first programme together. The village buildings represent every architectural period from the thirteenth century onwards. It is spotlessly clean and tidy, and as far as I remember there wasn't a single television aerial to be seen.

Lacock is perhaps most famous for its ancient abbey, built just after 1232 for the order of Augustinian Abbesses. It lasted as an abbey proper for just over three centuries until its dissolution in 1539. Lacock was actually the last nunnery to be dissolved in England, for the simple reason that no fault could be found with the ladies living and working there at the time. From the reign of Queen Elizabeth I the abbey remained in the Talbot family until 1944, when the house, the village and the principal farm were bequeathed to the National Trust.

9 *Down Your Way* in Lacock – with the people I talked to in making that programme.

Outside the gates to the abbey is a most spectacular medieval barn that houses the Fox Talbot Museum, a photographic museum created by the National Trust in honour of William Henry Fox Talbot.

Bob Lassam, the museum's curator, confirmed that the negative – positive process of photography was certainly invented by Fox Talbot, the then owner of the abbey, when he first photographed its famous oriel window in 1839 using this method. Fox Talbot's interest in photography stemmed from an earlier interest in drawing, I learned. Like many amateur artists at the time he made use of an instrument called a *camera lucida*, which was developed later into the *camera obscura*. Both of these reproduced the image of a scene which the artist could then trace. What Fox Talbot wanted to find was a way of making the image permanent.

'He was a scientist,' Bob Lassam explained, 'and he knew that silver salts are sensitive to light. So he started making experiments by coating paper with common salt and drying it, and then silver nitrate and drying it. He put this in a frame with a leaf and tried to get an image. He didn't have very much success at first, but then he realised that his solutions were wrong. By modifying these he got his first images as photogenic drawings.'

In August 1835 he took his famous 'photograph' of the oriel window at Lacock, which is really the first negative ever produced. Bob reckoned the exposure would have been from four to five hours, and the camera Fox Talbot used was a small wooden one made by the carpenter in the village. Copies of these cameras, which his mother called mouse-trap cameras, are in the museum, and when an experiment was conducted with one of them not long before our visit it still took two and a half hours to take the picture.

If photography was an unusual pastime when William Henry Fox Talbot was alive, I wonder how many people today breed foreign moths and butterflies for a hobby? We found someone who did in DEVIZES. His name was Arthur Cleverley and he told me that he had been fascinated by moths and butterflies since his boyhood. His grandfather, who worked as a professional gardener, kindled his imagination with descriptions of the butterflies and moths he had seen. The young Arthur was also deeply influenced by Gene Stratton Porter's novel *A Girl of the Limberlost*, which tells the story of a young American girl who pays her way through college by collecting and selling moths. In about 1938, he told me, he saw an advertisement in *Boy's Own* from someone selling foreign moths and he was able to buy a North American moth, which is mentioned by Gene Stratton Porter in her book.

Since seeing that first moth emerge from its chrysalis Arthur has bred many thousands more from eggs he gets from fellow breeders all over the world. So I asked him to explain the various stages a moth goes through.

'From the egg stage the caterpillar starts to feed, because it's usually pretty ravenous,' he said. 'As they grow they shed their skin approximately five or six times. The skin doesn't grow with them, so as the caterpillar grows the skin splits and it emerges in a new skin. In the case of silk moths, they spin a cocoon when they're fully fed and form a chrysalis inside. A lot of these over-winter as chrysalises, the moth emerging in May or June.'

In the greenhouse where he keeps his moths there were trays containing cocoons, some of which looked like little sausages and others, like the one I picked up, looked rather like large nuts wrapped round with leaves. The chrysalis inside this one rattled when I shook it. Arthur told me that it had come to him as an egg from Iowa State University.

'At the emerging time you can hear the moth actually scratching inside the cocoon,' he continued. 'Then it breaks its way through one end. The moth will fight its way out, taking approximately a quarter of an hour to struggle free. Once it's out it will find somewhere to climb up on, and directly it starts to climb up it starts to fan its wings backwards and forwards until they are fully expanded. But it must not be touched at all while this is going on. If it's touched its wings will crumple and they'll never expand again.'

Can it fly at that stage? I wondered.

'Not until its wings have dried and hardened,' said Arthur.

What astonished me was hearing that most moths live for about a fortnight during which they breed, lay their eggs and then die without eating or drinking anything.

For a dozen years DEVIZES was the home town for 9 Ordnance Battalion of the Royal Army Ordnance Corps which was based a couple of miles outside the town. From the commanding officer I heard that the battalion consisted of various elements of supply: food, petroleum, stores and, as he described them, 'un-usual little funnies like the bakery and bath unit'.

The mobile bakery intrigued me because nothing like that existed during my army days. Apparently it is the only field bakery in the British army and consists of two containers which can be put on trailers and hold all the equipment needed to produce enough bread to feed a small town. There are ovens, dough machines and mixers in there that, when operated by three shifts of eight men working twenty-four hours a day, can produce thousands of loaves of what, I was assured, is first-class bread. The unit was deployed during the Falklands War and produced enough bread to feed the entire force of several thousand through-out the campaign.

I well remember that when I was in the army washing consisted of little more than making do with a basin out in the open, so I wanted to hear about the bath unit too. It sounded a superb piece of kit, capable of providing hot showers for up to 200 bathers an hour all housed under canvas. Ten chaps can shower at the same time, after which they go into an area where there is a hot-air dryer that blows you dry very quickly whichever country you are in. As we were speaking, one of the battalion's two companies was using this shower unit in the snows of Norway, where they had rigged it up in a couple of hours, broken the ice in a nearby stream to feed in the supply pipe, turned on the boiler and got down to business. It sounded a great improvement on army life in my day!

During the war I spent part of my time stationed in WAR-MINSTER while we trained on Salisbury Plain, all 92,000 acres of it. In the middle of the war the little village of Imber in the centre of the plain was just being evacuated, so that troops could be trained to fight in built-up areas. When *Down Your Way* went to visit the Warminster Garrison I learned from the commanding officer that by the end of the war the village resembled any other in north-west Europe over which a battle had been fought.

'The church still stands,' Lt-Col. Peter Houghton assured me. 'and remains consecrated. Indeed a service, or two services, are still held there on the first Saturday in September of every year.'

Nowadays Warminster is famous for its many sightings of UFOs and in *Down Your Way* I interviewed Arthur Shuttlewood, a retired local journalist who is the author of a good many books on UFOs. He told me that the first sighting he knew of as a journalist was made on Christmas Eve 1964. Since then hundreds have been noted. More than mildly curious about what was sighted, I asked him to elaborate on what he and others have actually seen.

'Various things,' he began, 'but mainly unidentified flying objects that normally come above us at blistering speed, making no sound whatever. The only sound we've heard is after there has been a landing of a craft, and there have been several witnessed landings on the ground. When we've rushed up to the craft it's just "whooshed" away, very much like the sound of a vacuum being expelled.'

Among the collection of photographs he showed me I picked out a couple: one that looked like the shape of an egg, the other like a Mexican's hat. The 'egg' one had been taken by a local photographer, Arthur said, in the presence of police officers and other 'responsible' people. The picture of the 'Mexican' UFO was taken in 1965 – the first photo of the 'Warminster Thing', as it has become known.

It seemed incredible that Arthur had been able, not to mention brave enough, to approach these mysterious objects, but he reckoned he had been within ten feet of one. 'It dwarfed me as I stood there watching it,' he said. 'It could have been forty to fifty feet across and it hovered above me.'

I asked if he had ever seen any of the occupants of these craft.

'We haven't actually seen them get out,' he admitted, 'but we've had many weird things happening. Giant figures have been seen walking alongside them. They're translucent shining figures, diaphanous even. There's no definite structure to them. Yet they're huge, huge creatures.'

One of Arthur Shuttlewood's colleagues had the courage to approach one of these 'men from outer space' and walked right through it!

When I turned to the possible reason why Warminster should be visited by UFOs far more than anywhere else in the country, Arthur suggested that they may have been coming to the area for millions of years – possibly before mankind appeared on earth. He reckoned that they may have guided early man to Warminster and Salisbury Plain, which quite possibly has a sacred significance for the visitors from outer space, just as it appears to have had for the builders of Stonehenge and the stone circles at Avebury.

Just near Warminster is Longleat House. When we visited it for *Down Your Way* we were amazed to find that Lord Bath had set aside a complete room full of Hitler memorabilia, to counterpoint his extensive collection of Churchilliana housed at one end of the Great Library (there's also a rather poignant room with items collected from the brief reign of Edward VIII).

The most surprising part of this for me was the collection of Hitler's own paintings, which were really good watercolours. I had always thought he was just a house painter, which shows how good our wartime propaganda must have been. But the pictures at Longleat show that he was obviously a very accomplished artist in his own right. On the desk was a nice bottle of hock which had been retrieved from his bunker, as had the charred remains of a napkin with Hitler's intitials in the corner. The collection also includes a rather frightening set of maps of England, all marked out with the German invasion plans and strategy to be put into place once this country had been invaded.

Twenty-one miles down the A36 from Warminster is SALIS-BURY, famous for its cathedral spire, which is the tallest and most beautiful in Great Britain. I don't think I shall ever forget the interview I did with Roy Spring, the Clerk of the Works, to give him his full medieval title. He was the most recent in a succession that stretches back to 1218, and among his duties he described to me the process of inspecting the top of the spire and maintaining the special aircraft-warning sign right on the top, 404 feet above the ground. The memory of it still turns my stomach.

The climb to the top begins with a series of staircases up to the roof and into the base of the tower. 'Then to the base of the spire, in the interior of which remains the original scaffolding from which they built it,' he said. 'There are ten ladders put in about 1740, up which one goes. At the top of the tenth one there is a little platform, and then there is a small door in the north wall of the spire, which one opens very carefully. Outside is a 360-foot drop to the floor.' (I was audibly groaning by this stage.)

'You put a leg over the sill,' Roy continued,' and reach for an iron rung underneath. You put a hand out and reach over the top for another one. And then you gently ease the body through the opening. The rungs are placed alternately either side of one angle of the spire. Climbing up the iron rungs, you get to the cap-stone, which of course projects outwards, so you have to lean back a little bit to reach for one over the top and pull yourself over.

'What I like to do is to stand on top of the aircraft-warning light and hold on to the rod of the cross. There's nowhere to sit, and if you stand on the aircraft-warning light it's more comfortable than the cap-stone, because that has a sloping edge. From there the view is marvellous – providing the wind's not blowing!'

10 Roy Spring climbing the spire of Salisbury Cathedral.

And what about the wind, I wondered, scarcely daring to enquire.

'There are times when one wouldn't go up,' Roy said, 'but I have been up when there's a very high wind blowing and it can get very frightening [which has to be an understatement if ever there was one]. If the wind is gusting, one minute it's blowing you against the spire and the next minute it's trying to tear you away. Then the spire starts to move, probably six inches either side of centre.' The view from the top was splendid, he assured me, and I was more than happy to take his word for it.

The other interview which I specially remember from Salisbury was when we visited the Common Cold Unit, where for years they have been trying to find a cure for our colds. They were doing this by inviting volunteers to stay at the unit, and then deliberately trying to give them the cold germ. Unfortunately, the experiments hadn't been terribly successful. The snag for us, though, was that the man in charge, whom we interviewed, had such a bad cold that he could hardly speak!

Salisbury was the Melchester of Thomas Hardy's novels, the Wessex of whose books lies largely in the neighbouring county of Dorset. One would be hard put to find a more English setting than the lovely village of ABBOTSBURY, ten miles west of Weymouth, which was appropriately chosen as the location for many of the scenes in the film version of Hardy's first great novel, *Far From the Madding Crowd*.

You might be forgiven for thinking, as I did, that the Hardy whose statue stands on Black Down, a few miles inland of Abbotsbury, is the novelist. I was wrong, however. This Hardy was in fact Nelson's flag captain at the Battle of Trafalgar, Sir Thomas Masterman Hardy, who was born in the nearby village of Portisham.

Apart from a few traces near the Abbotsbury church, there is almost nothing left of the monastery around which the village developed. In spite of this, elements of its life and influence are still evident today. The only intact building that remains is the magnificent tithe barn, measuring 275 feet by 35 feet, which is said to be the largest in England.

Down by the shoreline, however, the monks have left behind the swannery they helped to establish. Twenty minutes from the village and across a couple of fields, you come to the edge of the Fleet, the long, narrow salt-water lagoon that lies sheltered behind the seventy-foot high ridge of Chesil Bank, and Abbotsbury's famous colony of mute swans, reckoned to be the oldest of its type in the world.

No one knows for certain when the breeding of swans began

here, but at some stage in their stay the monks must have developed a taste for young swan, and thereafter it graced their tables on feast days until the monastery was dissolved by Henry VIII. Today anything from 400 to 1000 swans will gather on the Fleet to feed on the common grass rack and nest among the reeds on the level shoreline. (The reeds, incidentally, provide much of the thatching material used in Dorset.) And in the breeding season visitors can watch the cygnets being hatched in the nests without disturbing the parent birds.

Swans are not the only birds of interest on the Fleet. The ringing station situated near the swannery is an important centre for the ringing of wild duck like teal, mallard and pintail, and the collection of information which goes towards the study of their migratory patterns.

If young swan is no longer part of the Abbotsbury diet, one hangover (and 'hangover' may be the word in some cases) from the monastery kitchen is 'fermiti', a potent local dish and one of the few intoxicants you can get drunk on from eating. We were introduced to this by John Wood, a local farmer, who explained how fermiti is made. You start with wheat, which is soaked in water for two days. When this first stage is completed, currants, raisins and sultanas are added and the whole lot is cooked slowly until the wheat breaks and the mixture ferments. The final ingredient is cornflour, which thickens the brew until it is the consistency of a good rice pudding. Once this is done, it's ready to serve. Traditionally, fermiti was only eaten on Good Friday, although John remembered the time when it used to be made in five-gallon buckets to be sold liberally round the village.

Rising above the village are terraced hillsides – 'lynchets' to give them their official name, 'lawns' their local one – which provided at least some level ground for agriculture. Overlooking Abbotsbury from one of these hilltops is St Catherine's Chapel, a small place of worship built entirely of stone, roof and all, without a single piece of wood anywhere in its entire structure. Since the fourteenth century, when it was erected, this has been a popular destination for would-be brides, who traditionally go to ask the saint for a little help in finding a husband. Placing knees and fingers in specially hollowed holes in the large stone blocks, they recite:

St Catherine, St Catherine, lend me thine aid
And pray that I may not die an old maid.
A husband, St Catherine,
A good one, St Catherine,
But arn' a one [anyone] is better that narn' a one [none
   at all].

'Did it work?' I asked. Monty Cribb, the Chairman of the Parish
Council who told me about it, was in no doubt. 'It must have
done,' he said, beaming, 'judging by the size of the families they
used to have here in those days.'

For all its Englishness, though, the visitor has only to go a
little way out of Abbotsbury to find the exotic splendours of
its sub-tropical gardens. These were first laid out early in the
eighteenth century by Elizabeth, the first Countess of Ilchester,
and have been extended throughout their history to the point
where they include among the principal plants nearly 1000 different rhododendrons; 650 varieties of camellias; a wonderful collection of olearias, myrtles and escalonias; and many of the larger
trees, including twenty-three oaks out of the forty originally
planted.

From the East come Chinese palm trees with trunks wrapped
in what can eventually become coconut matting, while from the
other side of the world comes the giant rhubarb tree from Brazil,
with leaves that can sometimes shelter eight or nine people. Each
year this grows a tall spiked flower, like the flower on a normal
rhubarb plant, but growing to a height of four feet.

Abbotsbury has another botanical claim to fame which makes
an annual appearance on 13 May, Garland Day, when the children
of the village carry garlands of flowers from house to house,
collecting small change to pay for their annual day out. For over
thirty years the custom has been kept alive by Mrs Nell Arnold,
who told me that it dates far back into pagan times, to an era
when Abbotsbury's people used to decorate their fishing boats
with flowers to persuade their gods to bless the sea.

There are still fishing boats at Abbotsbury, and Mrs Arnold's
son was one of those who used the technique of seine fishing,
where a large net is rowed out from the beach in a wide
semi-circle, reaching about 400 yards from shore at its furthest
point, before coming back to the beach again. There it is pulled

11 Garland Day at Abbotsbury.

in, bringing with it a catch, mostly of mackerel, if all goes to plan.

The *Down Your Way* visit to Bovington Camp near WAREHAM was doubly nostalgic for me; not only had I trained there during the war, but outside the Tank Museum is a Sherman tank like the ones I served in. This was a good old tank. It was tough and could go along at about eighteen miles an hour as far as I remember.

At the end of the war appeared the Centurion, a marvellous tank which came along just a bit too late really to help in the victory. One of them forms the museum's most spectacular exhibit. This has been sectioned from front to back, so that you can walk right through the middle of it and get a very good idea of how claustrophobic a tank can be.

There are over 150 tanks, tracked vehicles and armoured cars on display at Bovington, from the earliest Mark I that went into action for the first time on the Somme in September 1916, right up to the tanks used by the army today. Incredible as it sounds, it was the Royal Navy which designed the world's first tank, and before the name 'tank' had been coined the new vehicles were known as 'land ships'. This explains why those early ones bear the initials HMLS, which stand for His Majesty's Land Ship.

The reason why the name 'tank' was chosen is rather amusing. When work started on building the first ones, the factory workers were told that they were making water carriers. Sir Albert Stern, who was the chairman of what was to become the Tank Corps, decided that since he would be the chairman of a committee called the WC Committee he would be looking for another name. So he changed it to tank.

These tanks from the Great War must have been frightful to travel in, as the two still in running order at the museum prove – 'like Hades on the move' as the museum's curator described them. In action they took a crew of eight, four of whom were required to drive the earlier models. Moving at walking speed at the very best, they were designed to crush wire, climb parapets and cross trenches, and in their first appearances on the Western Front they achieved spectacular successes.

Across the water, on the north-west corner of the Isle of Wight, lies YARMOUTH, the southern terminus of the car ferry from Lymington and for many visitors their landfall on the 'friendly isle'.

Short as the distance by sea may be, the island does have a certain mystery for many from the mainland, judging from some of the questions put to Wilf Eccleston, the information officer we spoke to, and his staff. He is often asked for directions to the duty-free shop by people convinced that the island is on a par with the Channel Isles. Another favourite question from visitors is directions for driving round the Needles lighthouse and rocks in their cars. He has had another man comment that Henry VIII's choice of location for his castle, right next to the ferry terminal, seemed rather strange, and the one which made me chuckle most was the question as to whether or not visitors were allowed to feed the dinosaurs in the dinosaur park at Black Gang Chine!

One name I hadn't reckoned on finding on the Isle of Wight was the Dutch surname Postma, but I'm very glad that I did have the chance of meeting Andries Postma, who lives near Yarmouth, because he is the only maker of coin watches that I have ever come across.

In the nineteenth century it became possible to make ex-tremely flat watches, and it was a challenge for a watch-maker to test his expertise with one of these. Normally a watch case would be made according to the size of the clock or movement; in the case of the coin watch the coin itself determined the size of the case and a movement had to be made to fit into that very small space.

Taking up that challenge after he had attained his master's degree, Andries Postma set about making a modern coin watch that was really practical, could be used every day and was shock proof. He succeeded in his quest and today his coin watches are sold all over the world, using valuable old coins from a number of countries. He told me that the smallest coins with which he has worked are a gold sovereign and a Victorian shilling. No matter which coin he chooses to use, however, each watch has to be designed individually, first beginning with a scale drawing many times larger than the finished watch.

In layman's terms the coin is split down the middle and then brought back together again when the watch is completed, with no visible joint. Inside is a carefully designed bedding, where the high-quality swiss movement is kept in place as a tiny, flat parcel. The glass is set parallel with the face of the watch, so that it is barely visible, and looking at it you would think that you could actually touch the hands.

Over the Solent from Yarmouth lies the New Forest, with its capital and administrative centre at LYNDHURST. The forest covers some 97,000 acres, two-thirds of which is owned by the Crown and managed by the Forestry Commission on its behalf. The rest belongs to the various manors donated by the Crown during the centuries since the forest was established after the Norman Conquest. About 35,000 acres of the forest is open space covered by heather, gorse and bogs, the rest is given over to trees: Douglas fir, larches, spruces, western red cedars, as well as great areas of oak.

I learned from George Cross, a former Chief Forester, that four types of Commoners' rights exist within the New Forest: the right of pannage, which allows the commoners to turn pigs out into the forest to feed on beech nuts and acorns; the rights of 'turbary', which permit a small number of people to dig peat turfs; the provision of 'estovers' of wood, which are made by the Crown to certain properties, whose owners have the right to fetch stacks of timber and take them home completely free of charge; and the right to graze cattle and horses.

Four distinct species of deer live in the New Forest, and hunting, the chase and falconry were the very pursuits that brought the New Forest into existence. To find out about venison and the best way to prepare it we went to the premises of John Strange, the well-known butcher in Lyndhurst whose firm has a contract with the Forestry Commission and consequently specialises in venison and venison products. Outside the shop they were advertising venison sausages made according to a recipe that has been handed down through the family for over 150 years. Pâté, faggots and the venison itself were also appetisingly on display.

From John's wife, Desirée, I got a few tips on cooking venison, which she pointed out is a denser meat than beef, pork or lamb. As it has no fat, it is usually best to marinate venison, I was told. Her favourite way of cooking a haunch, for example, is to make a flour paste out of flour, red wine and herbs, and then spread this over the haunch. Once it is completely covered it goes into a very hot oven for ten minutes, after which the heat is reduced to a low temperature at which the meat is allowed to cook for five or six hours. Once cooked, the haunch comes out of the oven. The flour skin is peeled off and the succulent meat is served with a full-bodied red wine.

Another advantage of the absence of fat in venison is that it is good value for money, as well as being an ideal meat for people who are watching their weight.

Lyndhurst is also the headquarters of the ancient Verderers' Court, which dates back well into the fourteenth century. The verderers are the judicial officers of the royal forests. They are ten in all: one appointed by the Queen, four by public bodies like the Forestry Commission and the Countryside Commission and five elected by the commoners. The verderers sit in public once every two months in the splendid Verderers' Hall in the village. There they are concerned with the amenity of the forest, in which they co-operate closely with the Forestry Commission to provide facilities for everyone who uses the forest.

Four adjusters carry out the Court's work, and it is their job to look after the animals on the 70,000 acres of forest and common land on which they roam. Each adjuster has a horse as well as a car with a cattle trailer or horse trailer. This is also fitted with a two-way radio which keeps the adjusters in touch with the police, who, if they hear of an accident to a pony or a cow, can get on the radio to one of the adjusters who can be on the spot in a few minutes.

There are probably several thousand people who are entitled to grazing rights, although the actual number who turn animals on to the New Forest amounts to fewer than 400. Commoners have an inalienable right to ride the New Forest in search of their animals, whereas the general public ride there by courtesy of the Forestry Commission. The celebrated New Forest pony has now been established as a distinct breed, and there is a stud book that prevents adulteration from other breeds. Their welfare is carefully watched over as well. As there is obviously considerably more for them to eat in the summer than during the winter months, the verderers and their adjusters have the powers to tell owners to remove their ponies from the forest if they fall below a certain standard of health.

To mark the occasion of my 500th *Down Your Way* we accepted a kind invitation to visit the old village of HAMBLEDON, thirty miles north of Portsmouth. Between 1750 and the 1790s Hambledon became the leading cricket club in England. Not only did they lay down many of the original laws but also beat a good many All-England teams. In their early days they played up on Broadhalfpenny Down, about two miles from the village, where the old Bat and Ball Inn served as the pavilion and headquarters of the club. Here we started the programme, just across the road from the pub, which was doing a roaring trade that day. For one of the few occasions on *Down Your Way* I was batting on a familiar pitch, so to speak, and my interview with the then captain of Hambledon Cricket Club, Colin Barrett, was more an exchange of happy cricketing history.

I was delighted to hear that the modern club still has a strong family feeling about it. Colin's son was in the side, his wife made the teas and his mum scored. It was also good to hear that the majority of the players were under thirty years old, which ensured continuity for the future.

It was much the same two centuries ago, when Hambledon enjoyed its golden years of success. Richard Nyren, the landlord of the Bat and Ball back in the mid-eighteenth century, really got things started and it was his son John who recorded the great Hambledon players in his book, *The Cricketers of My Time*. Broadhalfpenny Down proving to be rather windy, the club moved to Windmill Down, though Colin admitted that that too could be a bit breezy. Today the club plays at Brooks Lane, which has been its home for the last hundred years.

12 The Bat and Ball on Broadhalfpenny Down.
The monument in the foreground commemorates the prowess
of the Hambledon cricket team 200 years ago.

What seems so extraordinary today is the money involved in cricket two hundred years ago. They used to play for 500 or 1000 guineas. There was betting, too, and the players were each paid two or three guineas a game. One of the club's record books covering the twenty years from 1772 until 1792 shows that Hambledon played for a total sum of £21,000, and came up on top at the end of that period by about £12,000 – a staggering amount of money in those days. I remember being told that Hambledon played against the All-England side fifty-one times and beat them on twenty-nine of those occasions.

Seeing the monument opposite the pub reminds one too that many of the laws of cricket made by Hambledon Cricket Club are still the same today. They got the width of the bat right at four and a quarter inches. The weight of the ball is the same. And of course Hambledon introduced the third stump after a chap called Lumpy Stevens bowled to the celebrated John Small and the ball went between his two stumps without removing the bail.

There were marvellous characters playing for Hambledon at that time. Thomas Brett was the fastest and straightest bowler of his day – and it was of course all underarm bowling then. Tom Sueter was a terrific singer, though Colin said they have to wait for the Welsh touring sides before they have singsongs like the ones he used to lead. There was the wicketkeeper, George Lear, who always had a long-stop, although it was said that nothing ever got past him. But then the wicketkeepers didn't play with gloves in the days when he was behind the stumps – nor did the batsmen, if it comes to that. Silver Billy, or Billy Beldham to give him his full name, was probably Hambledon's most famous batsman. And David Harris, who was the club's leading bowler for the last twenty years of its pre-eminence, must have made life very uncomfortable for many a nervous batsman facing him. It was said of him that 'Fair qualities of his heart shone through his honest face. The finest fast bowler, he would grind batsmen's fingers to the bat.'

One mustn't forget the spectators either, among them the Duke of Dorset who used to pace up and down, knocking the heads off the daisies with his stick when he was anxious. There are still plenty of daisies on the chalk to remind one of the hours he must have spent walking up and down in the out-field.

At the same time as Hambledon Cricket Club was enjoying its heyday, the naturalist Revd Gilbert White was recording the flora and fauna in and around his native village of SELBORNE, fifteen miles to the north-east. It was here that he wrote his famous book, *The Natural History and Antiquities of Selborne*, which was published in 1789. As I learned from Dr June Chatfield, the curator of the Gilbert White Museum housed in Wakes, his old home on the village street, this book was based on the naturalist's lifetime of observations.

Gilbert White was primarily a zoologist with a particular interest in hibernation, though like many men of his day his interests and knowledge were spread over a wide field of study and research. He kept very meticulous notes on natural history and was particularly interested in making first-hand observations rather than relying on other people's work. More than forty years of careful field work and note-taking lay behind his book, which has become established as a classic of English literature.

His garden calendar offers a vast amount of information on the lay-out of his garden, so much so that the present garden has been retained as an eighteenth-century garden very similar to the one he would have known.

The celebrated naturalist died four years after the publication of his great work and was buried in Selborne churchyard on the north side of the church, which apparently was rather unfashionable in those days. He has a very simple gravestone, as he directed, which just has his initials and the date of his death. His grave is not to be confused with the tombstone in front of the altar which commemorates his grandfather, who was also called Gilbert White and was vicar of Selborne. This was a position that his grandson never held, for Gilbert White junior had been educated at Oriel College, Oxford, while the benefice of Selborne was a gift of Magdalen College.

Outside the old twelfth-century church of St Mary's stands a huge yew tree which is recorded as being 1300 years old and has probably been standing a good deal longer than that. In the side of the church there is a little door through which the devil was evicted once a year, and inside I noticed a case containing an enormous dog collar which looked as if it would have been a good fit on a horse. Apparently this was worn by an equally enormous Great Dane which belonged to a former incumbent of Selborne, who fell out with his parishioners and used to have to walk through the village with this dog to protect him. It seemed that the villagers objected to paying the tithes due to him and expressed their feelings a little too vehemently for his liking.

The other curious feature of St Mary's is the clock in the tower. It has only got one hand and that only shows the quarter hours. If you don't happen to know what hour you are in, you have to wait for the next one to be struck. Time can't have meant a lot to the people of Selborne when this was installed.

The end of the eighteenth century and the early years of the nineteenth were times of great canal-building, and over the downs to the north the Kennet and Avon Canal was dug to form a link between Bristol and Reading, where it joined the river Thames to provide a continuous waterway right across the south of England. The canal was dug in the first quarter of the last century, though the last boat to pass along its entire length struggled through in the early 1950s. In recent years the British Waterways Board have undertaken major restoration work, ably assisted by the Kennet and Avon Canal Trust, an organisation of volunteers' who help keep the restored section of the canal in tip-top condition.

In particular certain members of the Trust are appointed lock managers, to maintain locks when they become operational once again. On our visit to NEWBURY we went to Newbury Lock to meet John Gould, the lock manager, to find out how the restoration work was progressing.

By that stage the canal was workable from the Thames at Reading halfway to Newbury. There was then a section that was awaiting restoration. From two miles below Newbury to Crofton pumping station, fifteen miles further west, it was again navigable.

A little beyond Crofton the canal reaches its highest point, where it is 450 feet above sea level. From here it is workable as far as Devizes, where a flight of twenty-nine locks drops the canal 250 feet over a distance of two and a half miles. Work was still being undertaken on these five years ago, but on the final stretch between Devizes and Bath, where the canal joins the Avon, boats were once again chugging along at the statutory four miles an hour.

Newbury Lock can accommodate sixty-ton boats measuring seventy feet long and fourteen feet six wide, with a draught of up to four feet. With dimensions like these I wondered how on earth they managed to get such big vessels towed by horses through tiny Newbury Bridge, which lies just beyond the lock. There is no tow-path under the bridge and a sign above reads: 'The captain of any vessel allowing horses to haul across the street will be fined' – not an unreasonable request when you consider that until recently the bridge carried the main A4 London to Bath road!

'In order to get a good speed on the boat before she went through the bridge,' John said, 'the horse on the end of, say, two hundred feet of hauling line would get that boat moving as fast as it could until the towing mast of the boat was right up close to the bridge. By that time the horse, two hundred feet ahead, had gone round the corner and right across the street. That's why the sign was put up.'

Rope marks in the wall show where the towing lines were slipped at the very last minute as the bows of the boat shot into the tunnel. With the boat having to start from the lock only eighty yards away, it must have been a tremendous effort for the horse to build up enough speed. I'm not surprised that boat captains were tempted to let their horses pull across the Bath Road until the very last minute.

If you go to Newbury Lock, look for the large white wooden arrow about two feet long which hangs on the wall of the lock cottage. This was used in times of strong current to float the hauling line downstream through the tunnel to the waiting boat, so that it could be pulled through by the horse which had been led over the other side.

We couldn't go to Newbury without visiting its famous race-course, especially as *Down Your Way* had been there thirty-five years before. Richard Dimbleby had been the presenter for that programme and I was delighted to be able to interview the very manager and secretary he had spoken to, Frank Osgood, who joined his uncle just after the war and whose son is ensuring the family's close connections with the course into a third generation.

Although Newbury racecourse is comparatively young, the first race being run here in September 1905, it has had an interesting history. As we discovered at Lambourn, transporting horses by rail was a difficult business and there was an obvious need for

13 Newbury racecourse as it looked in 1947 after wartime service.

14 The first post-war race meeting at Newbury in April 1949, following
two years of reinstatement.

a racecourse to serve the needs of the stables at Lambourn itself
and in the surrounding countryside.

Looking at the beautiful green turf, it is hard to envisage it
covered with thirty-five miles of railway track, harder still to
imagine a mile of the course concreted over. This is exactly what
happened, however, after the American army took it over in 1941
as a supply depot for their landings in North Africa.

After the war Frank Osgood and his uncle worked on it for
eighteen months, restoring the course in small parcels. 'We had
literally to scrape off all the gravel that they'd laid down for the
railways lines,' he told me. 'We had to take up the concrete road
too, and we brought in more soil and laid over 750,000 turfs.'

I'm sure Newbury must rank as one of the very few racecourses
that has its own railway station, thanks to the arrangement between the donor of the land and the Great Western Railway, to
whom he gave land at the same time to build the station. His one
stipulation was that the railway should provide an excursion
train from London to every day's racing at Newbury. To this day
there is still a very good service running on race day to the course
which takes only fifty minutes from Paddington.

Eight miles west of Newbury along the river Kennet is the town
of HUNGERFORD which celebrates its colourful Hocktide cere-

mony every year on the second Tuesday after Easter. The celebration of the Hocktide stems from traditions established in
Hungerford around the year 1350, when John of Gaunt, who had
obviously been well received on a recent visit, granted a number of
Commons rights to the houses then standing in the town. In all
there were said to be ninety-nine. Some of the present number are
made up by original houses that have survived from the fourteenth
century, others stand on the sites of those that received John of
Gaunt's grant of hunting rights on the common and fishing rights
in the river Kennet.

From the middle of the sixteenth century the Commoners have
appointed a Constable of the Town and Manor to take charge of
their affairs. He is assisted by a group of Trustees, a Bailiff who
collected quit-rents, and a Portreeve who collected rents from the
various fairs which used to visit the town in days gone by. There
are two Ale-tasters (or Testers) who used a most unusual method
of testing the beer brewed in the Commons houses. First they
poured a small quantity of beer on to an oak seat, and then they
sat on it in a pair of special moleskin breeches for a specified
period before standing up and examining whether or not the beer
stuck to their trousers. I should think it must be some relief to
the present-day Ale-tasters that this particular tradition has been
done away with, now that breweries are responsible for their own
quality control. There are also Overseers of the Common, Water
Bailiffs and Keepers of the Keys of the Common Coffer.

On Hocktide Day the Commoners gather for their Hocktide
Court, at which the officers are elected and the rules concerning
the common rights are read and revised when necessary.

Before the Court is convened two other officers, the Tuttimen
or Tithemen are sent out by the Constable from the Town Hall to
visit all the ninety-nine Commons houses to collect the tithes. At
each house they are given money (in the old days it used to be a
penny). They are usually given some sustenance to send them
happily on their way and the ladies of the house frequently
receive a kiss.

By tradition the two Tuttimen each carry a pole decorated with
a lovely nosegay. Right at the top is an orange sitting on a spike
in a little copper cup. Next to that is a ring of laurel leaves. Then
comes a ring of polyanthus, preferably red ones to represent John
of Gaunt's red rose of Lancaster. A ring of blue anemones

represents the town colours of Hungerford. These are comple-
mented by ten or twelve bunches of daffodils.

After the Court has sat and after the Tuttimen return from their
visit to the ninety-nine houses with the Commons rights there is
a formal luncheon attended by a distinguished guest. Then comes
the Shoeing of the Colts. Anyone who hasn't attended the lunch
before is literally shod by the official blacksmith, who takes the
colt's foot between his knees and hammers a horse nail into the
heel of the shoe.

Children used to be given a half-holiday on Hocktide day when
they scrambled for pennies in front of the Town Hall and the
houses visited by the Tuttimen.

READING, the capital town of Royal Berkshire, is seventeen
miles east of Newbury at the confluence of the Kennet and the
Thames. It is a town made famous by beer, bulbs and biscuits
and has often been called the most typical and representative of
all English towns. Its history is admirably displayed on the town's
crest. At the top sits a mitre, symbol of Reading's famous abbey.
Two lyres are shown, recording the fact that monks from Reading
are believed to have been the first to record music on paper. A
couple of rams indicate the fine wool industry that once thrived
in the town. The right-hand one shows the two rivers that flow
through the town. The other ram bears a portcullis symbolising
the fact that Parliament sat at Reading at one time.

The bulb and seed business and the biscuit-making have left
Reading now. Even the huge Courage brewery stands just outside
the town boundary. There is plenty of light industry and micro-
electronics to take their place, and there is also a home-from-home
for *Down Your Way*, the BBC Monitoring Service across the
Thames at Caversham.

Here the staff monitor broadcasts from some forty to fifty countries in thirty languages. We were visiting at the end of 1984,
when their energies were being directed to Western and Eastern
Europe, the Soviet Union, North Africa, Iran and Afghanistan, as
well as the English-language broadcasts of other countries further
afield like Argentina, Canada and Australia. There is also an
exchange agreement with the service's American counterpart,
and between them they manage to cover the whole world.

About half the monitors are native speakers, and the rest are
British language graduates. Working an eight-hour day, each

one listens to half a dozen bulletins covering news broadcasts, current-affairs magazine programmes, features of political and economic interest, documentaries and programmes on international affairs. From time to time there are major events from certain countries, like the May Day speeches from the Soviet Union.

Each monitor records his or her own bulletin and makes notes as it is being broadcast. Then this is taken away to be transcribed. If the item is of sufficient importance a few sentences are typed up and taken at once to the news room for immediate transmission to the BBC and government departments like the Foreign Office, Cabinet Office and Ministry of Defence, and to anyone else who subscribes to the service. Otherwise the monitor will produce a transcript at greater length which then goes to the newsroom and the editorial department. In addition the Monitoring Service produces a summary of world broadcasts six days a week, covering four principal areas of its work, with a separate economic section.

I asked whether this centre was ever the only one to gather certain items of news.

'That's really what makes our work so exciting,' answered Linda Eberst, the Assistant Controller Coverage, who showed us round. 'A recent example I can give you would be after 13 December 1981 when martial law was declared in Poland. Correspondents were unable to get their material out of the country and yet we listening in Caversham were able to provide a service to everybody covering exactly what was happening in Poland.'

Listening isn't all they do now. In recent years they have started watching Moscow television, which, as Mrs Ebert admitted, does add another dimension to their work.

Amongst all this sophisticated technology I was amused to see a very comfortable cardboard box in one corner of the Listening Room occupied by a very contented-looking black cat. What was his story?

'He was a stray we found wandering in the grounds a few years ago,' I was told. 'He was immediately adopted by the staff here and his name is SAM, which, stands for Senior Assistant Mice.

The South-East

15 Oasthouses near Kemsing, Kent.

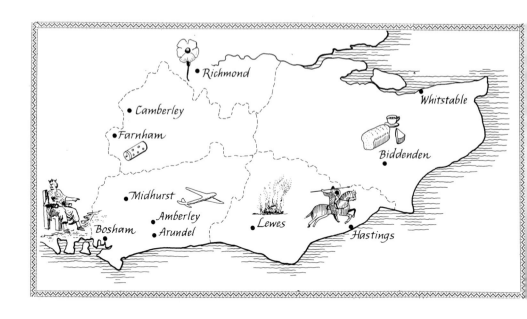

I largely associate Surrey with men in bowler hats, carrying rolled-up umbrellas, rushing up to London in the mornings and dashing back again in the evening – in other words, commuters from this vast commuterland with its large mansions adjoining some of the best golf courses in Great Britain. There are not so many bowler hats these days – it is the fashion to be hatless – but, as we have found in *Down Your Way*, Surrey does tend to depopulate itself during the day, so perhaps there is not quite so much community life as in other counties further away from London.

My first realisation that Surrey existed was when I was given my first bat in 1921 – a 'Force' signed by J. B. Hobbs of Surrey and England. And of course the Oval has played a big part in my life ever since – by means of the radio to start with, listening to Patsy Hendren describing the regaining of the Ashes in 1926. In those days he had to be rushed back to Savoy Hill by taxi and I still remember his words: 'The Oval crowd were real glad, and all was merry and bright.'

Camberley has wartime memories for me. I went to the Royal Military College at Sandhurst as an officer cadet in October 1939. Most of us were in our late twenties, many worked in the City and we all had cars. They were kept in a garage in Camberley and on the first Saturday morning were driven up to the College for us to go off in them for the weekend. This practice was soon stopped because they had all been parked on the parade ground, and when we came back from a route march there was no space left for us to parade.

I have several friends in the Cranleigh–Guildford area and have the honour to be an Honorary Life Member of the Shamley Green Cricket Club. This is a charming village between the two towns, and the village plays cricket on a green in the centre. It has one snag. There is a right-of-way across the pitch. They still talk of the day when Gubby Allen, ex-England captain and fast bowler, was playing for someone's eleven against the village. He took his usual fast run-up to the wicket but had to stop suddenly before delivering the ball. A formidable-looking lady was pushing a pram, containing a baby and her shopping, right across the pitch. No one, not even an ex-England captain, was going to interfere with her right-of-way!

I first became acquainted with Sussex in 1921 when I went to a preparatory school at Eastbourne called Temple Grove. The school has moved to Uckfield and the old buildings are now the HQ of the Dental Records Office or something like that. Anyway, if you have false teeth details of them are kept in the old school chapel. The school had some strange characters as masters. There was Bill Fitch, who smelt of moth balls; Bill Wigg, who kept his glasses in a Three Nun tobacco tin; and the headmaster, who was nicknamed Bug. He lost an eye after being hit by a racquet when playing squash. Someone who didn't know this met him once and told a friend afterwards: 'I've just discovered that Mr Waterfield has a glass eye. It looks so real you can't really tell.' 'How did you find out, then?' asked his friend. 'Oh,' he replied, 'it just came out in the conversation.'

Sussex is nowadays rather overbuilt and seemingly full of airports and motorways. But I always think of the downs and chalk cliffs, and of the Grand Hotel, Eastbourne, where my parents took me out to lunch and tea from school and we listened to Albert Sandler and his Orchestra, who used to broadcast from the domed lounge in the hotel which the BBC said had perfect accoustics. Twenty-five years later my wife Pauline and I spent the first week of our honeymoon at the same hotel.

Kent is one of my favourite counties because of its great connection with cricket. It has some lovely county grounds: the Mote at Maidstone; the Neville Ground at Tunbridge Wells, with its rhododendrons; and, of course, the St Lawrence Ground at Canterbury, with stands named after great players of the past like Frank Woolley and Leslie Ames. Every August the Canterbury Week – *not* Festival – is a delightful occasion, with marquees for the various Kent clubs and picnics from the backs of cars parked round the ground. There used to be a band, but a visiting player – I believe from Essex – complained that it interfered with the play. There is also the famous lime tree *on* the field of play. It was at Canterbury that they are said to have had a streaker who rushed past two old ladies sitting in deckchairs. They say that one of them had a stroke and that the other one couldn't reach him!

The northern part of Kent is overcrowded and commercialised, but further south in the 'Garden of England' there can be few more beautiful parts of the country, with its orchards, hopfields and oasthouses. Especially in the spring with the apple and cherry blossoms enriching the colourful countryside. I once picked cherries there – that delicious brown and white Napoleon species which are very difficult to find these days. Picking has become too expensive and they haven't yet designed a machine to do the job properly. But the hop fields still attract hundreds of pickers every year, many from the East End of London, on what to them is their summer holiday.

The coast is, of course, famous for the white chalk cliffs of Dover – such a welcome sight to the returning traveller. And up in the north-east tip of the Isle of Thanet are holiday resorts such as Margate, Broadstairs and Ramsgate. We used to broadcast a lot of seaside concert parties from Margate in the early fifties, especially the open-air entertainment at the Oval, an open oval amphitheatre with a bandstand as a stage. It was here that after – or even during – a performance the artists used to go round collecting money from the audience in their deckchairs – 'bottling', it was called. I was thrilled once when I told Cecil Johnson's Concert Party a joke, which they put into one of their cross-talk acts. I remember it got a good laugh on a warm sunny evening. Here it is:

'I was walking along the beach the other day and I saw a girl slowly drifting out to sea. I rescued her.'

'What did you do?'

'Oh, I threw her a cake of soap.'

'A cake of soap? Whatever for?'

'To wash her back, of course.'

Happy days.

One of my most amusing broadcasts came from New Romney

station on the Hythe and Dymchurch Railway. It was re-opening for the summer season and the local Mayor in his robes and chain of office was to go on the first journey. They placed him in one of the small open carriages right at the back of the train. A large crowd on the platform waited for the guard's whistle, and I was busy at the microphone describing the scene. The great moment came, the guard blew his whistle, the engine gave a toot and off went the train, with the Mayor waving regally to the crowd. Alas, they had forgotten to hitch his carriage to the rest of the train. It quickly drew away from the station, leaving the Mayor stationary at the platform, still waving vigorously goodbye. The laughter from the crowd on the platform nearly sent our transmitters off the air.

Until *Down Your Way* went to RICHMOND I hadn't realised that the poppies we buy for Remembrance Day are made there at the Royal British Legion Poppy Factory. It was very impressive – I had never seen so many poppies. Bill Mutimer, who guided us through the works, said that a certain number are also made in the Lady Haig Factory in Scotland, but the Richmond works is the main supplier for this country, and indeed many European countries as well.

With production figures approaching 50,000,000 a year, the workforce of about 120 is kept well occupied.

I also saw a marvellous display of wreaths that had been made in the factory, and over 70,000 of these are produced in a year, though not all of them are used on Remembrance Day. Many organisations have their own special services on various days throughout the year, and they want their particular wreaths for those occasions.

Bill seemed the ideal person to answer a question I had often mulled over. When was the symbol of the poppy adopted?

His answer was pretty precise – 3 May 1915. This fell during the second Battle of Ypres, the battle in which poison gas was used for the first time, incidentally, and it was the day on which a Canadian doctor, Colonel John McRae wrote a poem in the dug-out which served as his field dressing-station. That poem has since become known as 'Born of fire and blood', and Bill reminded me of its closing words:

> If ye break faith with us who die
> We shall not sleep, though poppies grow
> In Flanders fields.

That poem was subsequently published in *Punch*, where it deeply impressed an American lady by the name of Moina Michael who wrote a reply which ended:

> Fear not that ye have died for nought,
> We've learned the lesson that ye taught,
> In Flanders fields.

This in turn inspired a French lady by the name of Mme Guerin to start having poppies made in France, so that they could be sold to raise money for people returning from the devastated areas.

The British Legion was being formed at this time, and the organisers decided that they needed something for an emblem both to commemorate the dead of the war and to act as a fund-raising emblem. So they bought poppies from France for their first Poppy Day appeal in 1921.

However, the British Legion soon decided that they needed a source of supply in the domestic artificial-flower industry and were approached by Major George Howson, MC, who set up the original poppy factory. He started off in premises in the Old Kent Road in June 1922, and Bill told me with evident pride that there were still three men working at Richmond who had started out in those first premises almost sixty years before.

I was among some of the first recruits to undergo training at Sandhurst when it became an OCTU (Officer Cadet Training Unit) during the war, and when we visited what is now the Royal Military Academy, Sandhurst, during a programme from CAMBERLEY I reminded the adjutant that drill played a very important part in our training. Did it still?

'I'm the adjutant and I'm responsible for drill, so I must say that I think it plays a vital part,' he answered. 'It's really the basis of everything we do. It teaches a young man self-discipline. It teaches him to react to orders. It teaches him how to hold himself – bearing, turn-out and how to behave as an officer.'

I remember life there being pretty tough; we were always being chased around and didn't seem to have much time to think. That still applies, apparently, especially during the first five weeks when training is very tough indeed. 'It goes on for long hours,' I was told. 'They're up very late and they have to get up very early in the morning. There's not a lot of time to sit down, I'm afraid. The whole aim of our course is to develop, improve and teach leadership in all our officers. This is the thing we consider to be absolutely vital.'

In my day there used to be one passing-out parade a year, but today the Sovereign's Parade, as it is known, is held three times a year, with the salute being taken by either the Queen herself, another member of the Royal Family, a minister or a very senior officer in the army.

The unique element of the Sovereign's Parade which I asked to have explained comes right at the end, when the adjutant rides a white horse up the steps into the magnificent colonnaded Old Building, where we were talking.

'That was started back in the 1920s by the then adjutant who later became General Browning, famous in the airborne division,' his successor told me. 'His old groom came to visit me the other day and he told me that the Captain, as he liked to call him, was a very smart officer who took great care of his uniform. At the end of the parade one day it suddenly came on to rain and, instead of going off in the normal way, he thought the quickest way was to go up the steps and under cover, which is exactly what he did and it's been done ever since.

'We've always used a white horse. This particular one has been doing it for several years. He's good at it and knows he's going to get a lump of sugar when we get inside; if I'm lucky I get something rather stronger.'

I found out the origin of another piece of twentieth-century military history during our visit to FARNHAM, the most westerly of the towns in Surrey. Bill Ewbank Smith, the author of three books about Farnham, proved to be a source of intriguing information.

Among several interesting footnotes to history he told me that the two-minute silence observed at Remembrance Day services originated in Farnham. This was the brainchild of an estate agent by the name of Alfred Agar, who found himself organising a fête to raise funds for the army in May 1916. In the course of thinking about a suitable symbol for the fête he hit on the idea of a two-minute silence. Following the fête, the idea was sent to the government, who accepted it as a symbol of world peace. It has been observed on Remembrance Day ever since.

Delving into one of Bill's books I came across an interesting gobbet of motoring history. John Henry Knight, who was a member of a wealthy farming family in the neighbourhood, was reputed to have built the first car in England in 1895. As a result of driving this on the public highway he was summonsed by the police for failing to have a man walking in front carrying a red flag. This was the legal requirement for a locomotive in those days, but Knight argued in court that his was a different type of vehicle and therefore not subject to the legislation. Bill said that the case made legal history and was the first legislative reference to motorcars.

When the railway arrived in the 1840s the local authority was informed that the track would cross the main road south of Farnham by means of a level-crossing. When the line was laid, however, the gates were hung so that they were closed against the road for most of the time and not against the railway line. There was so little road traffic at the time that this seemed the most sensible course of action. Once the road traffic increased, of course, the position of the gates had to be reversed.

Probably Farnham's most famous son was the radical Parliamentarian William Cobbett, who lies buried in the churchyard. Asked to name his two greatest achievements, Bill picked out Cobbett's book *Rural Rides* and *Hansard*, which he initiated.

While we were there we went to visit one of the most original museums I have ever come across. For one thing it was a portable museum, and the other extraordinary fact was that the 'curator' had spent a total of five pounds on collecting her 2000 exhibits. That was how it came to be known as the Museum on a Shoestring.

This is in fact a working-class museum that Jean Parratt, a local journalist and lecturer, dreamed up in the early 1970s. It consists of all sorts of fascinating bits and pieces from bygone days, organised in a series of suitcases that she takes with her to give her various talks. All the exhibits were collected from demolition sites or house clearances, where people had found interesting old bottles, old newspapers – anything that had come to light.

One of the items Jean showed me was a tube with small holes

in it, about the length of half a pencil with a screw in the bottom
to open it up. She asked me if I had any idea what it was. I hadn't
a clue.

'Well, it's a holiday souvenir,' she explained. 'If you look in
the top you'll see six views of Hastings. But the main part of it is
very useful indeed. If you suffer with fleas biting you at night, all
you've got to do is to take this to bed with you. Before you go to
bed, you unscrew the end, put a nice thin piece of fresh meat
inside, screw up the end and put it underneath your pillow.

16 Jean Parratt displaying some of the exhibits
in her Museum on a Shoestring.

'At night it's much easier for the fleas to crawl in through these
holes to suck the blood from the meat than it is to pierce your
skin. They swell up with the blood so they can't get out of the
tube, and in the morning all you have to do is go to a fire, unscrew
the end, pull out the meat with the fleas still attached to it, drop
it on the fire and you'll be rid of them. If any of them linger
around in the daytime all you have to do is put a piece of tape

through the ring in the top, put another piece of meat inside, hang it inside your clothing and the fleas go in that way.'

I found it almost unbelievable that this was really used by people, but Jean assured me that it was quite common until the end of the Great War.

Nineteen miles south of Farnham is the lovely old Sussex town of MIDHURST, where I had the opportunity to find out about a game I had seen in pictures but never actually seen being played. The game was stoolball, one that is particularly associated with Sussex, and no one was better qualified to tell me about it than the President of the Midhurst Stoolball Club, Mrs Gladys Werry.

Stoolball, she informed me, is supposed to be the forerunner of cricket and probably evolved in the Haywards Heath area in the fifteenth century. Today it is principally a women's game, though the occasional men's team does compete. (Teams, by the way, consist of eleven players a side).

17 Stoolball at Midhurst.

Stoolball is played with a bat which has a conventional cricket-bat handle. It is about half the size of a tennis racket, with a solid wooden face that is slightly rounded at the back. The ball is white, made of cotton and paper and covered with kid leather; it's about half the size of a cricket ball.

The wickets in stoolball are quite different from those in cricket. A stoolball wicket consists of a pole with a piece of wood measuring one foot square on the top; together they have a total height of four feet eight inches. As you might expect, the bowler has to try and hit this, bowling underarm from a distance of ten yards. There are eight balls to an over.

The pitch in stoolball is sixteen yards long, with a batsman at either end. Runs are scored just as they are in cricket. You can be out in the same way too, with the exception of being stumped; in stoolball that is one peril a batsman needn't worry about.

I was told that in days gone by ladies used to wear long skirts to play stoolball and it wasn't unknown for them to cheat a little by holding out their frocks to catch the ball. In consequence, one of the rules of stoolball which again differs from the laws of cricket is that you have to make a clean catch in your hands; you can't knock the ball on to someone else, for example.

On a small peninsula between two creeks four miles west of Chichester stands the delightful little town of BOSHAM, which is a popular centre for artists and yachtsmen today, but has a history that takes it right back to the Roman occupation. I was indebted to Angela Bromley-Martin, a local historian, who gave me a fascinating description of Bosham down the centuries.

Bosham is only two miles from the Roman palace at Fishbourne from which the Romans mounted their campaigns in the West Country, and there is a great deal of archeological evidence to show that the Romans were in Bosham too. It lies in a very well protected little area at the top of Chichester harbour, from where it would have been possible, if a tower had been built, to watch over any shipping entering the harbour and thereby gain at least four hours' warning of any sea raids.

Bosham has been continually settled since Roman times, and in the early eleventh century its Saxon church was built during the reign of King Canute. It may even have been built to his orders.

What is certain is that the chancel of Bosham church is depicted on the Bayeux Tapestry in Normandy. As Angela Bromley-Martin told me, in 1064 Harold (who as King Harold was killed two years later at the Battle of Hastings) set out from Bosham in his longboats to visit Normandy. On the Bayeux Tapestry he is shown attending a service of blessing in the church and a feast in the manor house before setting out on his voyage.

King Canute had close connections with Bosham as well; in fact Bosham is one of the half dozen places along the south coast of England where it is claimed that he sat in his chair and ordered the tide to turn back.

18 Bosham harbour with the church where Harold received his blessing before sailing to Normandy.

'He had his capital at Winchester', Angela told me. 'Bosham is only a day's ride from Winchester, and it is thought that he had a manor house here and used Bosham rather as the Queen uses Sandringham.'

I asked her how the story about Canute and the tide started.

'I have a theory,' she replied, 'and some people may dispute this, that the Saxon word for "chair" is in fact *char*, and *char* means a dyke. It's very easy for the words *char* and "chair" to get muddled over the centuries and I think that Canute built a dyke across the harbour to Chidham, which is the village on the other side of the creek here. I don't think this could have been a terribly good dyke and it broke down, which is said to be the reason why he didn't manage to keep the tide back.'

'It's also interesting that some 700 or 800 years after Canute somebody did build a dyke across the harbour, the remains of which can still be seen and it's always known as "mud wall". That stood for about thirty years and all the land north of it was reclaimed for farming, but after thirty years there was a tremendous gale which broke the whole thing down.

'It's interesting to know also that there are about half a dozen other places along the south coast which claim the same distinction of Canute sitting on his chair, and they're all places where it would have been very sensible to have built a dyke.'

When we went to AMBERLEY, some fifteen miles to the northwest of Bosham, I interviewed someone who literally had no trouble in keeping his head above water. At seven feet two inches Ian Spofforth was certainly the tallest man I have ever seen, and by his own estimate was probably the fourth tallest man in the country.

Like an awful lot of other people, I fear, I had to admit to being inquisitive about how he coped with everyday matters like beds, doorways and clothes. In each case the answer was that he approached them with commendable common sense and a complete lack of fuss.

'If a bed has no footboard, it's no problem,' he told me. 'I just stick out. And if it has a footboard you merely put a further mattress on top to raise it over the level of the footboard.'

Doors didn't present a problem, he said, because his eyes were always on the look-out for low lintels, unlike someone of, say, six feet five, who suddenly came across a six-foot-three doorway. To my surprise everything he was wearing was off the peg, too, supplied by shops that specialise in clothing for taller people.

Although Ian had played basketball while he was in the army, he said that he hadn't particularly enjoyed it, even though his height enabled him to jump and push the ball down into the net rather than having to throw it up. However, he was an international fencer, representing Great Britain in the world championships between 1958 and 1963. There were two other international fencers who were around six feet six at the same time, but he managed to beat both of them 'because,' as he readily admitted, 'although they were probably technically much better fencers, they really couldn't take the trouble to fence what they described as "uphill", having fenced "downhill" all their lives.'

Ian's stature won him a place in the film of *Chitty Chitty Bang Bang*, where they wanted a tall person to dance a sort of mocked-up waltz. But I knew he was also famous for having walked across the river Thames.

'I stayed within my depth the whole way,' he said, 'but once the water got up to my neck I wasn't really walking. I was just making way with my hands. But I could always stop and put my hands in the air to show that I could stand. This was on the old Roman ford between St Thomas's Hospital and Westminster.'

On 27 June 1909 Amberley was the setting for a remarkable event when a glider was launched off the top of Amberley mount, which stands at a height of 500 feet overlooking the village; it soared out over the valley, returned over the launch site and made a safe landing. Apparently that was the first manned flight ever to take place in a glider in this country and almost certainly in Europe as well.

My immediate question was: 'Why in Amberley of all places?'

The reason seems to have been that there was a great flight enthusiast by the name of José Weiss living in Amberley at the turn of the century. He made a number of gliders but the really successful one was the one they made in Houghton village hall, which is close to Amberley. This was constructed in the course of a few weeks out of bamboo and canvas tied on with tarred string. When it was ready it was hauled up on to the top of Amberley mount.

Although Weiss had designed the glider, his wife wouldn't let him fly it and the pilot's lot fell to Gordon England, who became celebrated as a racing driver at Brooklands, where he raced Austin Sevens of all things. He soared out over the village, banked and flew over the launch point at a height of about forty feet and landed very gently close to the Amberley–Storrington road.

The whole flight may have lasted no longer than fifty-eight seconds, but it was the first time that anything like it had ever been accomplished in England, and it wasn't until 1911 that the Wright brothers exceeded that flight at Kitty Hawk in the USA.

A few miles to the south of Amberley is the town of ARUNDEL, famous for its castle, which is the ancestral home of the Dukes of Norfolk, and its Roman Catholic cathedral. Arundel also has several museums, and the one we chose to visit was Potter's Museum of Curiosities (which has since moved to Cornwall).

The curiosities turned out to be an extraordinary assortment of stuffed animals which had been gathered together by a taxidermist named Potter, who started his collection at the age of seven in 1842. Mr Potter assembled his stuffed animals into a series of tableaux. The first we looked at showed Cock Robin's Funeral, in which there were ninety-eight different species of birds. I heard from the curator that it took seven years to complete that one display.

A rather less gloomy subject was the Kitten's Wedding, which showed twenty kittens dressed immaculately in their wedding finery, all of which had been made by Potter's daughters. The kittens, the curator was quick to point out, were not despatched simply to go into Potter's glass case. He was well known in the neighbourhood and local gamekeepers and farmers were always leaving dead animals with him to be used in his work.

Twenty squirrels comprised the members of a gentlemen's club depicted in the case called the Upper Ten, in which they were displayed smoking cigars, playing cards, and drinking champagne. Down below was the contrasting scene of the Lower Five, which was quite obviously a working man's public house frequented by water rats.

To my way of thinking one of the best scenes was the Rabbit School, with slates and exercise books, the teacher and the blackboard, and a staggering amount of detail – not to mention the forty-eight rabbits that Potter used.

Each year on the feast day of Corpus Christi a floral carpet is laid in the aisle of Arundel's Roman Catholic cathedral. The first was laid in 1877 at the suggestion of Henry, 15th Duke of Norfolk. I heard from the three ladies responsible for the work that the carpet takes a day to prepare and a day to lay. I saw a picture of one they had prepared a few years earlier and I was struck by the symmetry they were able to maintain in their design.

With a carpet that measures ninety-seven feet from one end to the other the number of flowers used runs into tens of thousands – two thousand roses alone were used in the border of the carpet I was looking at.

LEWES, the county town of East Sussex which lies thirty-six miles east along the A27 from Arundel, enjoys a rather more robust form of celebration each year on 5 November – Bonfire Night. Like a lot of people, I had heard about this although I had never actually seen it myself; so I was pleased to be shown a video-recording of it when *Down Your Way* went to Lewes, and to have a chance to chat to the secretary of the Bonfire Council.

There seems to have been some form of bonfire celebration in Lewes on 5 November ever since the Gunpowder Plot of 1605. The celebrations really came into their own in the 1800s, and today there are five separate bonfires around the town on the night of 5 November, except when the anniversary falls on a Sunday; when this happens the bonfires are lit on the previous evening.

19 Bonfire Night in Lewes.

On the video I saw the Bonfire Boys, as they are called, parading through the streets in their striped Guernseys which have traditionally been worn since 1846, when the various Bonfire Societies came into being. In those days the celebrations were fairly boisterous affairs and everyone wore matching tops as a form of disguise.

In addition to the bonfires there are processions going through the town with lighted torches, fancy dress, bands and tableaux – each of which is organised by one of the Bonfire Societies. The first processions begin at about five-thirty in the evening and they last right through the night until after midnight. In the middle of the evening, at about half-past seven, four of the five societies join together to form the Grand Procession which parades right through Lewes High Street, and this can take an hour to pass by.

One of the most striking features are the torches – 25,000 of them in all. Made of tow and hessian, dipped in paraffin, these provide very dramatic lighting for the evening's festivities. The bonfires look very impressive too, standing up to thirty or forty feet high.

Each year there is a firework tableau displaying some well known event from national history. The one I saw depicted Guy Fawkes in the cellars of the Houses of Parliament. Eight separate firework sequences were employed in this, going off at timed intervals and lasting ten minutes in all. It was very impressive and must have used thousands of fireworks.

Throughout its history Lewes has occupied a strategic position on the south coast, none more so than after the Norman conquest when it acted as one of the possible escape routes back to Normandy until the invaders had got a firm grip on the country. Duke William and his army landed near HASTINGS, of course, thirty miles further east along the coast.

Although I could claim to know the year in which he landed and the Battle of Hastings was fought, that was about the sum of my knowledge until I went to the old court room in the Town Hall, where a panoramic display of the battle is laid out, with all the troops as they fought on that day. My first question to local historian Barry Funnel was: 'Which day was it?'

'The battle took place on 14 October 1066,' he answered, 'and it was all over within the day. It took place on the high land about five miles to the north of the town, on what is known as Senlac Hill. Today that is the site of the present town of Battle; indeed Battle Abbey was built on the site of the battle.'

How many had taken part in it, I wondered?

'Opinions differ,' Barry said, 'but modern historians tend to think that Harold had about 10,000 troops in all – not all first-line troops; many of them were the equivalent of "Dad's Army". While the Normans had about twice that number, including cavalry. Their invasion fleet consisted of something like 700 flat-bottomed barges, and we know from the Bayeux Tapestry that horses were brought over in them.'

After landing somewhere on the coast between Pevensey and Hastings, William marched to the town, where he set up his headquarters to prepare for the eventual march on London. It is likely that he was in Hastings for some little time before the battle took place. On the battle plan laid out in the old court room William's forces are shown down in the valley, facing Harold's up on the hill.

'Harold had marched rapidly from the north,' Barry continued, 'where he had been engaged in battle with Viking invaders. Obviously he arrived somewhat tired and weary, but he selected a very advantageous point to defend.'

At the start of the battle the Saxons were able to defend stoutly against the attacks made by the Norman cavalry. In the first six hours of the battle, in fact, the Saxons inflicted considerable losses on the Normans. It was later on in the day, when the Normans appeared to be retreating, that the Saxons broke ranks, started to chase them and were counter-attacked in what became the end of the battle.

What about the story of poor Harold getting the arrow in his eye?

Barry told me that he wasn't killed by this, as the legend tells it. Apparently he drew the arrow from his head himself and continued to fight on with his troops. In the end he was killed by being struck down in hand-to-hand combat.

In 1966 the 900th anniversary of the Battle of Hastings was commemorated in a magnificent embroidery in the court room which shows all the stages of English history in twenty-seven beautifully worked panels, each nine feet long. It took the ladies of the Royal School of Needlework in London just over a year to complete.

The final panel shows Sir Winston Churchill giving a victory salute on the White Cliffs of Dover, but a little further back I spotted something that interested me – the first television broadcast.

'This is something which few people appreciate,' Barry told me. 'Television was actually invented in Hastings by John Logie Baird in 1924, and the very first outdoor pictures ever seen on a television screen were of people walking backwards and forwards in front of the door of this town hall.'

Over the years I had been asked to be a member of a great many clubs, but no invitation gave me more pleasure than when I was asked to become a member of Hastings's famous Winkle Club. This came into being in the early 1900s when the fishermen of Hastings, poor as they were, wanted to do something to help the poor children of the district over the Christmas period. They hit on the idea of forming a club, and while they were discussing what sort of emblem they should have, along came someone with a bucket of winkles. That gave them their inspiration. The winkle became their symbol; it had to be carried by every member, who had to produce it whenever he was challenged to 'winkle up' by a fellow member. If he didn't have a winkle on him he had to pay a fine, and that is the money that goes to charity. I've certainly been caught often enough for not having my winkle with me!

Since its beginning the club has gained a lot of very famous members. In 1927 it took on a national aspect when the then Prince of Wales went to Hastings to open the White Rock Pavilion and was made a member. The national press gave this quite a spread and from then on everybody wanted to join.

The Duke of Edinburgh was made a member in 1966, but had a little difficulty in finding his gold winkle after the lunch at which he had been presented with it. On the way out from lunch he saw the secretary and president of the club and started fumbling for his winkle. Seeing his predicament, the secretary rushed up, gave him an ordinary one and said, 'Here you are, sir. Here's one for week-days.' So I feel that I'm in distinguished company in the Winkle Club.

The lovely village of BIDDENDEN, which is situated in the Weald of Kent, twenty miles to the north of Hastings, has the oldest charity in England, dating back to 1134. This was the year in which the celebrated Biddenden maids died. They were a pair of Siamese twins who left the income from their small farm to be used to help the poor of the parish. For the last eight and a half centuries this has been distributed on Easter Monday. Today it takes the form of a loaf of bread, a pound of cheese and a packet of tea which are handed out to the old-age pensioners of the parish at the old workhouse.

The two maids are also recalled in the biscuit made of flour and water which bears their imprint and is given to visitors to Biddenden.

WHITSTABLE on the north Kent coast is a town which claims eight world firsts. The first divers in the world went to work in Whitstable in May 1826 when they were engaged to dive on the wreck of the *Royal George*. Among the things they brought up were guns which were cast to form the bronze capital on Nelson's column in Trafalgar Square.

On 3 May 1830 the world's first steam-drawn passenger train went into service at Whitstable a few months before the Liverpool-to-Manchester line was opened. In connection with the railway, the first passenger tickets were also issued in Whitstable and the line also had the first steam locomotive with forward-looking cylinders. And Whitstable harbour was the first in the world to be served by a railway.

The first steam-boat to sail to Australia set out from Whitstable as well. She was the eighty-one-ton vessel *William IV*, which was skippered by a Whitstable man.

The town also claims the world's first sea cadets, founded by Henry Barton in 1854.

And in 1920 Whitstable had the distinction of building the first council houses in the world, which I found remarkable.

Whitstable is also the home of pudding-pan pies, a local dish originating from an old Kentish recipe; it is made of ground rice with a pastry cover with currants and nutmeg on the top. In Whitstable the fishermen's wives cooked their pies in dishes that their husbands had brought from the wreck of a Roman ship which had foundered just off the town at what is known as the Pudding Pan Rock. So the dishes became known as pudding pans and they gave their name to the Lenten pies made in the town.

While finding out about these I also discovered the origins of another time-honoured Kentish custom surrounding the Hooden Horse, a type of hobby horse made of a horse's head on a pole with a long cloak behind it. The one I saw in Whitstable had sea shells down its nose, little bits of holly between its ears and a jaw that worked with a sort of clicking noise.

The Hooden Horse, I gathered, is the central figure in an ancient

Kentish custom that used to be performed by farmworkers on
21 December each year. They would visit houses, singing and
collecting money for their Christmas feast. The Hooden Horse
was usually accompanied by several characters: the rider, a man
who would lead it with a whip, another man dressed as a woman
and known as Molly (she used to walk behind the horse with a
besom broom), and last but most importantly the one who collected the money for the feast.

The Hooden Horse was taken up by the East Kent Morris
Dancers who not only use it at Christmas time but also during
the celebrations that come after the hop-picking is over.

While we were in Whitstable we heard of another long-
established custom in Kent which still has an enthusiastic following; this is the game of bat-and-trap, which we saw demonstrated
behind a pub called the Jolly Sailor at the end of Joy Lane. At the
back of the inn is a lovely pitch of smooth lawn, twenty-one yards

20 Ray Price, landlord of the Jolly Sailor,
showing me the rudiments of bat-and-trap.

long by four and a half yards wide. At one end are a couple of posts rather like goal posts, and at the other is a concrete area on which stands the trap where the ball was placed at the start of play. The ball is a hard rubber one, heavier than a cricket ball at seven and a half ounces and measuring two and a quarter inches in diameter. The bat used to hit this is wooden and oval, with maximum dimensions of eight inches in length and five inches in width. Around it is a band of steel that protects the edge from its constant knocks against the spoon of the trap, for the trap is balanced rather like a see-saw. With the ball in place the other end of the trap is raised, and when this is struck with the edge of the bat the ball is catapaulted into the air for the batsman to hit between the posts at the other end of the pitch.

There are eight players to a side in bat-and-trap, and while one side bats the other lines up behind the posts to field the balls hit by the batsmen. While the batsman aims to hit the ball between the posts, the fielders try to throw it underarm back up the pitch to strike a small flap five and a quarter inches square and marked by a black spot two and a quarter inches in diameter. If they do manage to hit the flap the batsman is out. If they don't he scores one run. The batsman can also be caught out, which is very unusual, or can play himself out by hitting the ball outside the lines marking the sides of the pitch, or by failing to hit it between the posts, of course.

A batsman in bat-and-trap is allowed to knock the ball up three times before hitting it to get his eye in, but he must hit it on the third time. A good score is reckoned to be eighty or ninety runs per leg and the players have three legs each, though I must say it looked as if a very keen eye was needed to return the ball to hit the little trap.

London

21 The City of London.

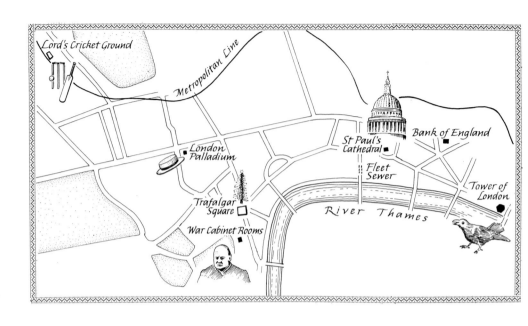

Bud Flanagan used to sing 'Maybe it's because I'm a Londoner', and I suppose that is what I am. Although born and brought up in Hertfordshire, I have lived in London all my working life. My theatre visits started at matinées on my way back to Eton, my first being *Rookery Nook* at the Aldwych with Ralph Lynn and Tom Walls. These Ben Travers farces used to run for about a year, and from 1927 onwards I used to pay a yearly visit to see such shows as *Thark, Cup of Kindness* and *Plunder*. As a change I went to see *The Ghost Train*, which gives you some idea of my theatrical tastes. When at Oxford in the early thirties I began my flirtation with the music hall, and the Palladium, Holborn Empire and Chelsea Palace were regulars on my list.

I first came to live in London in 1934, when I joined the family coffee business in the City. I was the guest of a godfather in an enormous house in Queen's Gate, with butler, footman, house-maids, cooks and goodness knows what. The butler was a great character called Target. He was mad on racing, and as he handed round the dishes would whisper tips for the next day into my ear.

I soon began to appreciate the other attractions of London. We were very near to Hyde Park and I found it a delightfully peaceful place, with the Serpentine, horses cantering round Rotten Row, and the distant hum of the traffic in the distance. I soon discovered Speaker's Corner at Marble Arch, where on Sundays we would go and listen to soap-box speakers, and also join in the heckling. The main character was Charlie, who talked about nothing in particular but loved all the back-chat. I always remember one heckler shouting at him: 'Charlie, if a cat has kittens on a pillow, are they caterpillars?' Nothing daunted, Charlie would switch his subject to cats.

London is lucky to have the vast open spaces of its parks; if you look down from an aeroplane it is amazing how much space there is. They all differ in character. St James's Park with its lake and birdlife is perhaps the most beautiful, and Regent's Park with the Zoo, the open-air theatre and numerous football and cricket pitches certainly the most active. There is even golf and tennis, boating on the lake, music at the bandstand, and herons nesting high up in the trees.

I soon explored the City and all its famous institutions and landmarks – the Guildhall, the Mansion House, the Tower of London and the Monument. At the top there is a superb view of the Thames and all its famous bridges, especially Tower Bridge, London Bridge and Waterloo Bridge. In those days there was a maze of busy docks, and markets like Billingsgate (fish) and Smithfields (meat). Fifty years later the skyscrapers have taken over the skyline, but down below the narrow alleys and streets such as Lombard, Cheapside and Moorgate all remain much the same.

I have never been very keen on museums, but Queen's Gate was in South Kensington so I was well placed to visit many of them, like the Victoria and Albert, Science Museum and so on.

I also began to enjoy the nightlife, especially the entertainments where there was a cabaret or a band. For about five shillings I would have scrambled eggs and a glass or two of lager in the balcony of the Café de Paris and watch the world-famous entertainers perform. Harry Richman, Noël Coward, Florence Desmond, Sophie Tucker (with Ted Shapiro at the piano), Douglas Byng – the list is endless. At the Monseigneur were Roy Fox and Lew Stone, whilst at the hotels were the bands of Ambrose and Harry Roy at the Mayfair, Jack Jackson at the Dorchester, Sidney Lipton at the Grosvenor House and Carol Gibbons at the Savoy. London in the thirties was certainly a gay place, if one dare use the word, but there were no gambling clubs and no striptease or nude shows, except at the Windmill, where the girls posed in the nude but were not allowed to move even a flicker. Believe it or not, I used to go there to see a very funny comedian called John Tilley, who did an uproarious act as a scout-master. But of course I lived in hope of one of the beautiful statuesque girls moving – but they never did.

After three years I moved to South Eaton Place to share digs with a schoolfriend, William Douglas-Home. The digs were kept by a lovely couple called Mr and Mrs Crisp. He was a retired butler and she had been a cook in all the big London houses. When he started as a kitchen boy he had to work in a basement with iron bars on the window. He was looking out one day when two lady passers-by peered down and saw his face staring through the bars. 'Poor man,' said one of them, 'and so young too.' We used to have small dinner parties and he sometimes dressed up as a flunkey with powdered wig and knee breeches, much to the amazement of our guests. On one occasion when he was serving the vegetables we asked our guests: 'Do any of you know of a good butler? We are thinking of making certain changes here.' He then dropped the dish as if overcome with shock, and hurriedly left the room in tears.

Yes, London was great fun, and as soon as I got out of the army in 1945 I came back to live there again, starting with a room just off Baker Street – in order to be near Lord's. When I married my wife Pauline in 1948 we started off in a small flat whilst she looked for a house. My one stipulation was that it should be in St John's Wood, to be near my beloved cricket. She was immediately successful and we have been there ever since. We started about a hundred yards from Lords, and after nineteen years moved to half a mile away. Sixteen years later we moved to our present house, three-quarters of a mile from Lord's and appropriately called Boundary Road.

St John's Wood is a perfect place to live. All the streets are tree-lined and if, like us, you are lucky enough to have a house and not a flat you will also enjoy a garden. Sitting in our garden, you wouldn't believe that Piccadilly was only three miles away, and that you can be on the M1 in ten minutes and at London Airport, door to door, in thirty. It still has a village atmosphere. Neighbours know each other, everyone seems pleased to see you, you can wear any old clothes and find little pockets of shops tucked away between the posh rows of houses. It has changed a lot since we first came, with tall blocks of flats and large private hospitals. But Lord's, except for some new stands, stays tradition-ally much the same, and in contrast don't forget that the Beatles made all their hit records at the Abbey Road Studios. In fact Paul McCartney lived just opposite us in our first house in Cavendish Avenue. It was a fortress-like place, and I never saw him. But I did meet his butler exercising the dog, and he told me that the Beatle lived a night-time life in order to avoid the crowds which collected outside his gate. He used to get up at 11 p.m. and walk around St John's Wood during the night. A strange existence.

With my job at the BBC, I have had to travel a tremendous lot both in this country and abroad. I have worked most weekends and bank holidays and, when the cricket correspondent was at the beck and call of the newsroom, had to dash in and do odd pieces about cricket for the news or sports programmes. So I have never commuted. It would have been impossible to do so.

I have always been about ten minutes away from my job and I have never regretted it. My wife sometimes pines for the country, but our lovely garden which she has created makes a very good substitute. St John's Wood is a good place in which to live. When I'm not working I walk in the parks, go to the theatre or weed, clip or mow in the garden. And of course when the sun shines I just pop up the road to Lord's and watch cricket. I am happy to call myself a Londoner.

London was the setting for some memorable broadcasts of *Down Your Way*.

For programme number 1500 we returned to Lambeth, where the very first had come from in December 1946. To mark the occasion we asked the Sun Life Stanshawe Band to play a brand-new arrangement of our signature tune 'Horse Guards, Whitehall', by Haydn Wood. I started them off with the baton and for the first time ever I think listeners heard the theme tune right through.

One of the people Stewart Macpherson interviewed on that first programme was the broadcaster Monty Modlyn, whom it was my great pleasure to interview again 1500 *Down Your Way*s later.

Monty and I talked about life in Lambeth, but the theme for that special programme was a boat journey down the river Thames from Lambeth Bridge to Tower Bridge. Our guide and skipper for this was PC John Woodhouse of the River Police, who proved to be a mine of fascinating information about the river. Almost as soon as we had got underway he started telling me about Lambeth Palace and mentioned casually that Admiral William Bligh is buried in the graveyard there; he is perhaps more famous for an earlier stage of his career, when as Captain Bligh he was master of the *Bounty* when the celebrated mutiny took place.

22 Conducting the Sun Life Stanshawe Band in a new arrangement of the signature tune to mark the 1500th *Down Your Way*.

From the river you notice a great many details about London's buildings and bridges which somehow get overlooked from the bank. For instance, as we passed the Palace of Westminster John drew my attention to a set of carvings just above the ground-floor windows. These are the coats of arms of every reigning sovereign from William the Conqueror to Queen Victoria, in whose reign the Palace of Westminster was built.

As we approached Westminster Bridge I asked John the signifi-cance of the truss of hay that one sees hanging from London's bridges every now and then.

'It goes back to medieval times,' he said, 'when hay barges were brought in from the west of London down the river Thames to feed the thousands of horses that were used in London itself. Very often as they went underneath the bridges with their very high loads, some of the hay would be caught on the rough underside of the bridge. It's become known now that that's a mark to look for when perhaps there's limited headroom going through a bridge.'

Just the other side of Westminster Bridge we spotted a couple of barges carrying household refuse to be used for land-filling further down river. 'Over a million tons of household refuse is transported by river every year,' John added.

Passing Cleopatra's needle on the Embankment, he told me the story of this obelisk's rather dicey passage from the banks of the Nile to the banks of the Thames, after the people of Egypt had presented it to this country well over a hundred years ago. 'It was placed in a tube, as one would place a cigar in a tube,' John began. 'Then it was rolled down the beach and towed through the Mediterranean and up through the Bay of Biscay on its way to London. Unfortunately the tug towing it got into a bit of heavy weather. The line parted and Cleopatra's needle and its tube floated off into the distance.

'The tug returned to England, where the crew said that they were very sorry but they'd lost the needle. They were promptly told to go back and find it. Of course they did find it, towed it back and it was erected on the Embankment where it has stood for over a century.'

As we approached Blackfriars Bridge John pointed out the interesting carving on it. Just above each of the buttresses is what appears to be a pulpit, apparently to record the old Blackfriar's monastery which used to stand on the north shore. Another interesting feature of Blackfriars Bridge is the collection of birds carved on the piers. Both sea birds and inland birds represent the range of wildlife found on the Thames between its source in the Cotswolds and the point where it flows into the sea.

We left the river at Tower Bridge and climbed up into the control cabin to find out about the history and working of this most stately of London's bridges. It took eight years to build and was completed in 1894. Since then any vessel with a mast of thirty-one feet or more has a right to demand the bridge to be opened. Nowadays they have to give twenty-four hours' notice, though the bridge must open for them at any hour of the day or night.

It takes two and a half minutes from the moment when the traffic lights turn to red for the bridge to open fully and provide vessels passing through with a clearance of 140 feet.

I remembered that on one occasion a bus had actually jumped across the bridge while it was opening and asked the bridge-master how that had happened.

'Nobody was very proud about it,' he admitted, 'but corners were being cut and there were errors on both sides. Gates and so on which should have been shut weren't shut. And various interlocking devices were not in fact in operation then. This of course has all been tightened up since then – but the fact remains that a bus-driver thought he could beat the lights, as it were, and he ended up jumping a three-foot gap. I think he broke all his springs.'

Not that Tower Bridge was intended primarily for road traffic when it was built. Apart from the ferries, there were no crossing points below London Bridge and the aim of the new bridge was to provide a means for people to cross the river as London grew and developed on both banks. In its early days 90 per cent of the bridge's traffic was pedestrian, which is the reason why the high-level walkways and the design of Tower Bridge evolved as it did.

Down by the river just upstream of Tower Bridge is Traitor's Gate, the entrance through which many prisoners were taken into custody in what is officially called Her Majesty's Royal Palace and Fortress of the Tower of London.

One's first impression of the Tower is that there are an awful lot of towers in it – twenty in fact, together with two bastions. Tower Green was the site of numerous executions, including those of three Queens of England. The last person beheaded there and the last to lose his head by the axe in England was Lord Lovat, who was executed in 1747, and the axe used on that occasion is on display today.

As for prisoners, the last notable one in modern history to be held in the Tower was Rudolf Hess, who spent four days in the Resident Governor's house in 1941.

The Tower of London is manned by thirty-seven Yeoman Warders, or Beefeaters to give them the commonly used nickname

which they share with the Queen's Bodyguard of the Yeoman of
the Guard. At those times any fit man of good physique could
buy a Yeoman Wardership for the most insubstantial sum of £309.
If he lived long enough to retire he could sell the appointment
thereby regaining his £309. But if he died in office the money was
forfeited to the Crown. This gave rise to the ancient toast which
is still offered to every recruit Yeoman Warder: 'May you never
die a Yeoman Warder.'

23 The White Tower
    in the Tower of
    London.

In actual fact the Duke of Wellington changed all of this in 1826
when he was appointed Constable of the Tower of London. He
made an order that none but deserving, gallant and meritorious
discharged sergeants of the army should be appointed Warders
of the Tower. By and large that form of recruitment has stood
ever since.

Of all the duties performed by the Yeoman Warders the Ceremony of the Keys is probably the most famous, and I asked the

Chief Yeoman Warder to take me through this because I had an inkling that there was something rather special about it.

'The Ceremony of the Keys is the ceremonial way of locking up the Tower of London for the night and it's been going on now for some 700 years,' he began.

'At precisely eight minutes to ten I emerge from the Byward Tower carrying a candle-lit lantern and the Queen's Keys. I march up Water Lane and join an escort of the Keys which is furnished by the main guard [usually part of the Household Division]. I hand over the lantern to a member of that escort known as the lantern carrier and then under the orders of the sergeant of the escort we march from there to the West Gate, where I lock the gates. During the time that the gates are being locked the escort turn in and present arms.'

This procedure is repeated at the Middle Tower and again at the Byward Tower. Then the Keys and escort make their way back through the darkness until challenged by a sentry demanding, 'Halt, who goes there?'

'The Keys,' answers the Yeoman Warder.

'Whose Keys?'

'Queen Elizabeth's Keys.'

'Pass, Queen Elizabeth's Keys, and all's well,' comes the reply.

After that the Keys and escort march under the Bloody Tower towards the main guard, which by that time has turned out under the officer of the guard.

'Now, at a suitable distance from the guard,' said the Chief Yeoman Warder, 'the escort are halted. The officer of the guard then orders the escort and guard to present arms as compliment to the Queen's Keys. I then take two paces forward, remove my Tudor bonnet and in a loud voice shout, "God preserve Queen Elizabeth," to which the guard and escort reply "Amen".

'Then a drummer, standing to the rear of the guard, sounds "The Last Post" on his bugle, and unless something has gone very much awry the first note from that bugle will coincide with the first stroke of ten on the barrack clock.'

I thought that timing was incredible, but I gather that it is very rare for them to be more than two or three seconds out.

The Tower of London would quite literally not be the Tower of London if it weren't for its ravens, and one of the Yeoman Warders is charged with the important duties of Yeoman Ravenmaster to ensure that they remain in good health and, most importantly, remain at the Tower. According to legend, if ever the ravens leave the Tower of London a great disaster will befall England, the royal palace nearby will fall down and that will be the end of our royalty.

There were eight ravens in residence when we visited, all with their wings clipped just enough to prevent them from flying too far and disappearing over the walls. During the war I gather that the numbers dropped as low as two, which must have caused considerable worry, but they managed to build up the complement before disaster struck and they are thriving now – not as a 'flock', apparently, but as an 'unkindness' of ravens, to use their appropriate collective title.

The ravens do pretty well, as far as I could judge. They get a ration of meat every day and then supplement this with whatever they can scrounge or pinch off the visitors. The oldest of them lived until he was forty-four, but the average life-span is twenty-five to thirty years.

They are all listed by name beside their cage – most of the names being male, I noticed, although several of the birds are in fact females. It seems that their donors didn't know what sex they were and some poor females like George have been landed with names that aren't entirely appropriate.

In the run-up to the wedding of the Prince of Wales and Lady Diana Spencer *Down Your Way* went to another of London's famous landmarks, St Paul's Cathedral, where the royal couple were to be married a few days after the programme was broadcast.

It was in the crypt of St Paul's, where we opened the programme, that the Bible was read in English for the first time, an act of faith that led to the reader's subsequent death in Newgate prison. But the cathedral has always held a prominent position in the life of London and the nation.

I asked the Dean how he regarded the cathedral, and his answer was that it is very much a people's church. William Morris called it 'God's railway station', and it does seem to attract worshippers of many different denominations from all over the world. The Dean was particularly pleased, therefore, that it had been chosen for the forthcoming wedding, because it is such an open church both architecturally and spiritually.

The Dean had to admit, however, that St Paul's was slightly

out of practice when it came to royal weddings as the last one held there took place in 1501. They were all slightly surprised that the cathedral had been chosen, though, as he reminded me, the old saying about 'robbing Peter to pay Paul' meant taking something from Westminster Abbey to give it to St Paul's.

During the Napoleonic Wars St Paul's became something of a *salon de refusés*, to quote the Dean, when Westminster Abbey decided that it probably had enough generals buried there. So St Paul's has some splendid people buried beneath its floors. The Duke of Wellington is there, and so is Admiral Nelson.

'Nelson is fascinating,' said the Dean. 'His body was brought back from Trafalgar in the mast of the French flagship which he had defeated. When he came to England the British Civil Service, as it were, searched around and found that they'd still got the beautiful marble tomb made for Wolsey, who hadn't been allowed to use it because of his row with the King. So that was brought from Windsor and Nelson is buried under Wolsey's monument.'

24 Nelson's tomb in St Paul's Cathedral.

Sir Christopher Wren, the architect of St Paul's, has a very plain tombstone with an inscription that simply reads: 'If you want to see my monument, look around you.'

Wren of course came on the scene following the Great Fire of London in 1666 which caused such terrible damage to the great medieval cathedral that had stood on the site. The church authorities' first thought was to see how much of the old building they could preserve. Wren wasn't terribly keen on this idea, from all accounts, and stayed in Oxford until the Dean of St Paul's wrote to say that the old building couldn't be saved and would he design an entirely new building.

Wren started work in 1675 and building continued until 1723, when he gave up the surveyorship a few years before his death at the age of ninety-one. Unlike the architects of many great cathedrals, he lived to see his great work completed and was actually hoisted to the top of the cross with his son to watch him perform the 'topping out' ceremony that marked the end of the building work.

I had heard that the cathedral moves rather like a ship, and the Surveyor to the Fabric confirmed that it is built on clay – part London clay and part potter's earth. This moves according to the amount of moisture in it, so the masonry will crack and move. Temperature affects the fabric too. Some of the great cracks and settlements which date from Wren's time, several more than an inch across, open and close. If these were filled solid, I was told, there might be a risk that subsequent movement could push out the end wall of the transept. So these contractions and expansions are monitored daily by electronic instruments which measure their movements to one-thousandth of an inch.

The Old Lady of Threadneedle Street, or the Bank of England as she prefers to be known, is only a few streets to the east of St Paul's Cathedral, and it was in the vaults beneath the bank that we opened one of the most unusual of all the *Down Your Way* programmes I presented – the one which explored what goes on underneath London. In spite of living in London for more than fifty years, I had no idea of what happened beneath the city's 616 square miles.

Accompanied by the chief manager of the Foreign Exchange division of the Bank of England, I went to look in amazement at the gold bars housed in this particular vault. There were approximately 5000 piled around us, each of which was worth just over £100,000 – and this was just one of several similar vaults. Quite rightly, I wasn't told how many there are in all.

It amused me to hear the vault described as containing the bank's 'petty cash'. The gold belongs mainly to central banks abroad, along with members of the London market, and it stays in the bank until the customers ask for it to be moved out of the building or into other storage facilities. London, I learned, holds a sizeable proportion of the world's gold, but the largest official reserves are those in the United States of America, where one-third of the world's official gold reserves are housed.

The bars I saw and tried to pick up were pretty heavy, each weighing about twenty-eight pounds. To be acceptable for international debt repayment in London they have to comprise 995 parts gold out of 1000, the remaining amount consisting of some residual element like copper, silver or platinum.

From the rarefied vaults of the Bank of England we moved to the somewhat earthier realms of London's sewers at a point where

25 Flushers at work in one of London's main sewers.

one of them passes under the pavement opposite Blackfriars Bridge. This was the Fleet Sewer I was told, which carries sewage all the way down from Hampstead. Although there was a fairly acrid smell down there, it wasn't unpleasant, thanks largely to the amount of water used for washing and cleaning which dilutes the raw sewage on its way down from north London.

I was very impressed by the safety precautions taken by the team of Flushers who guided us down there. They were careful to report their position as soon as they got out of their van, and before anyone went down below ground they tested the atmosphere to check for dangerous or explosive gases.

The Flushers carry out routine maintenance in the sewers, maintain constant inspections of their condition, clear any blockages that occur and provide safety cover for any contractors working in the system. And there are a lot of sewers to be managed. Between them north and south London have 150 miles of trunk sewers – and that figure doesn't take into account the smaller sewers that come under the responsibility of the local authorities.

We couldn't go under London without going on the Underground, and we travelled with the curator of the London Transport Museum along part of the very first underground line, opened in 1863. This ran from Paddington along what is now the Metropolitan Line to Farringdon in the City, using locomotives operated by a modified form of steam engine. From that initial length of underground railway – the world's first, in fact – the network has grown to something in the region of 260 miles of line.

Building a new line these days is a little more difficult than it was back in the middle of the last century because of the greatly increased number of public services – gas, telephone, water mains, etc – laid beneath the surface. Most modern tube lines are about eighty feet deep and most are dug by boring machines, although a certain amount of the excavation is still done by hand-held machine tools.

Travelling down from St John's Wood to Baker Street sometimes feels as if we are travelling at 100 mph, although I was told that the speed between normal stops seldom rises above 40 mph.

As it turned out, we weren't the only people fascinated by what lies beneath the streets of London. In the only interview in the programme above ground, we interviewed Ellis Hillman, who had made a detailed study of the subject. Among his surprising discoveries, or non-discoveries as it transpired, was the lost Crystal Palace Pneumatic Railway which was known to have run under Crystal Palace park, but the precise location of which was still unknown.

There is also the Post Office railway, opened in 1927, which carries large numbers of parcels beneath the capital and on which I once travelled as a parcel myself.

He told me a very interesting story too about the original tramway tunnels at Holborn Kingsway. At the turn of the century there was a proposal to extend the whole tramway system, which was quite well advanced by that stage, into a complete network of tramway tunnels. Had those proposals gone forward in the early LCC days, Ellis suggested, 'It is conceivable that the tube system we know today would have been totally different'.

On a slightly morbid subject he also told me that London has six square miles of cemeteries!

We ended that programme beneath London in a place where history was made during the war. These were the Cabinet War Rooms near Horseguards Parade. There we met Sir John Colville, who during the war was assistant private secretary to Sir Winston Churchill and his principal private secretary after the war.

In spite of great efforts taken to construct these rooms, Sir John said that it was discovered that they would not have been able to withstand a hit by a very heavy armour-piercing bomb. It was therefore decided to add a further layer of concrete above, which Sir John said led to a disastrous incident for Sir Winston. 'Churchill, being by inclination a builder, thought he knew all about it,' he explained. 'And I remember on one occasion he got so angry that he leapt over a girder and landed plumb in a pool of liquid cement.'

During the periods of heavy bombing during the war the Cabinet Rooms were used a good deal for meetings of the Cabinet, the defence committee and the chiefs of staff. 'In the evenings we used to assemble in a small room where they now sell souvenirs,' Sir John said, 'and used that as a mess. We lived off tinned soup, sardines, tinned sausages and an occasional glass of beer if we were lucky. There would congregate the three chiefs of staff, Attlee, Ernest Bevin – all sorts of people. And one learnt a great deal of what was going on in the war in those nightly sessions down there.'

We interviewed Sir John in the room that had served as Sir Winston's bedroom, where he composed several of his famous speeches, including the beautiful tribute he paid to Neville Chamberlain after his death in November 1940.

Moving up Whitehall to Trafalgar Square, we conducted a series of pretty chilly interviews for a Christmas *Down Your Way* one year. From the Norwegian ambassador (whom I have to admit was interviewed in the warmth of his embassy) we heard the origins of the huge Christmas tree which the people of Oslo have given to the people of London every year for more than forty years.

He told me that even under German occupation the Norwegian resistance movement managed to send a Christmas tree each year to King Haakon while he was leading his government in exile in London. This, and the feeling among many Norwegians at the end of the war that they wanted to express their thanks to the Londoners who had looked after them so generously, led to the sending of the tree, which has been erected in Trafalgar Square every year since 1947.

Like millions of tourists I heard from London's senior tourist guide that the square was laid out in the last century to commemorate Nelson's great victory in 1805 at the battle of Trafalgar. Nelson's column was erected a little later towards the middle of the nineteenth century, and Landseer's four lions came a few years after him.

Quite a number of statues are dotted about Trafalgar Square in addition to Nelson, high on top of his column. There are a couple of generals who made their names in India: Napier and Havelock. In front of the National Gallery stands James II, dressed rather incongruously in a Roman toga. George Washington is in the square, too, and so is George IV, seated on horseback but without any stirrups for some reason. Across the road on a traffic island is the mounted figure of Charles I, looking down Whitehall to the site of his execution. This is actually a very old statue that was hidden during the time of the Commonwealth and only brought into the open again after the Restoration of Charles II. His statue also marks the spot where the old Charing Cross once stood, and where all distances to and from London are measured; until that interview I had always thought they were taken from Hyde Park Corner.

We also met Norman Cook, who was responsible for the maintenance of all the statues and monuments in the area. From him I learned that Nelson's column is 170 feet 6 inches high, with Nelson himself standing 17 feet high. The statue is carved in Portland stone, the column is made from granite and the Corinthian capital that surrounds the base of the statue is made of bronze.

Knowing that Nelson was given a clean from time to time I wondered how on earth people got up there to do it. Norman said that the cleaning was done every two years by the firm of steeplejacks which had been doing it on and off since 1906. They get up to the top using ten-foot ladders which they tie around the column until they reach the statue. Once there they remove in the region of three hundredweight of pigeon's muck from around the capital.

It is not easy to see from the ground which way Nelson is looking, but Norman told me that he is looking towards the Admiralty building and beyond that to his fleet of ships that are on the top of the lamp-posts all along the Mall – something else about Trafalgar Square that I never knew.

On the other side of Soho stands the London Palladium, which was one of my favourite haunts as a young man. As befits the world's most famous theatre, it is splendidly appointed and the number-one star dressing-room, where I interviewed Louis Benjamin, the managing director, was absolutely magnificent. This was built specially for Yul Brynner when he played the King of Siam in the run of *The King and I* and, as Louis Benjamin said, 'If you're going to live in a theatre for fifteen, sixteen months, he believed – and we endorsed it – that you should have some comfort.' So they built him a sitting-room, a dressing-room, a bathroom, everything you could imagine.

Louis has been associated with the Palladium since the age of fourteen and has seen most of the great stars who have appeared on its famous stage. I wondered if he had any recollections of the celebrated time when Danny Kaye had come over after the war?

'Yes,' he said, 'I had the good fortune to be here as second assistant manager. That was just a sensational situation of a show opening to a minor advance booking and the following morning the queues were round the block.

'There were two episodes in which I was involved slightly. The news went out so quickly that everyone who doesn't normally come to this theatre was coming – including Winston Churchill. He arrived a little late, and being a polite gentleman he decided to wait on the side of the stairs until the act that was on finished. This particular act was a very old comedian who wasn't going awfully well; everyone wanted Danny Kaye. When he finished there was mediocre applause. Then Churchill walked in and the whole house stood up and cheered – and the comedian came on again and took another bow!

'I believe also that Princess Margaret came to see the show and went back home to tell her family how wonderful it was. A secret request came with the message that the King and Queen wanted to come with the two princesses, but they wanted to sit in the stalls and not in the Royal Box.

'We tried to allocate four seats in the front-row gangway but these were already sold. So it fell to me as assistant manager to stop the original owner and offer him seats a couple of rows further back. But the man said that he would only move for the King of England, and as I wasn't allowed to say who it was I had to say to him, "Look, if you'll please sit where we put you and you're not satisfied with who comes in we'll refund your money completely at the end of the show." '

For my 600th *Down Your Way* the BBC were kind enough to allow me to invite listeners down *my* way to St John's Wood, and when 133 programmes later I came to do my very last *Down Your Way* we went to Lord's cricket ground, which seemed an appropriate end to my 'innings'.

I made my first visit to Lord's in 1927 to be coached and in 1930 saw my very first Test match there. Since the war I had commentated on just over fifty Test matches from the ground. So it's very much a second home for me. Up on the scoreboard they had kindly put 733 for 1, last player 733.

Just at the back of the Pavilion at Lord's is the library which houses the MCC's marvellous collection of books. There is also the Memorial Gallery, which is open to the public, incidentally. Up on the first floor I interviewed the curator, Stephen Green, while all around us were pictures, memorabilia, treasures, the story of the cricket bat, plates, a lovely bronze figure of Alec Bedser bowling, caps from all the counties and the countries, ties from every cricket club, and pictures of all the grounds, all of which he looked after so lovingly.

I asked him to pick out a couple of the 10,000 or so books and pamphlets the MCC has in its collection, and he produced a very old and frail-looking one dating from 1712 which had the alarming title *The Sabbath-breakers: or the Youngman's Dreadful Warning Piece.*

His other book was the first copy of Wisden's *Cricketing Almanack* from 1864. Nowadays they have great difficulty in fitting all the cricketing facts and figures into an enormous volume, but this first edition really did have to be spun out a bit with details of the Boat Race, the Derby, the St Leger – everything under the sun.

Looking at the pictures, Stephen picked out one of his favourites which shows Lord's as it was in its centenary year, 1887. This depicts a completely imaginary match taking place between England and Australia. All the players in the picture were real enough, but they never actually played against each other as two teams. There is a wonderful panoramic view of the ground with the old pavilion, which was taken down shortly afterwards. Everyone who was anyone in Victorian society was included in the picture too. The Prince and Princess of Wales are shown walking along in the out field while the game was in progress, which might have been stretching artistic licence just a little. All Prince Edward's girlfriends are shown in the front row as well, including the actress Lily Langtry, who is painted turning away as he strides past with Princess Alexandra.

Stephen reckoned that perhaps the finest painting in the MCC's collection is a complicated one of a gentleman from Amsterdam holding a narrow cricket bat, by a Swiss artist who painted in the French school. So the picture has a Dutchman playing an English game in Italy painted by a Swiss artist of the French school, which we agreed might explain some of the very odd details included in it.

Among the great collection of cricket bats is the famous one used by Len Hutton when he scored his 364 against Australia in 1938. This has a nice cartoon by Tom Webster on the back showing the Australian wicket-keeper with a beard as long as Moses at the end of the thirteen hours and twenty minutes he was at the crease.

There is something of a tradition of long service at Lord's. Talking to the secretary, Colonel John Stephenson, I heard about one member of staff who was still cheerfully working away in the club office at the age of ninety-one.

26 Recording my last *Down Your Way* among the cricketing treasures at Lord's. The painting showing Lord's in 1887 is in the background.

My last interview at Lord's and my last on *Down Your Way* was with Denis Compton who started his career as a young professional at Lord's selling scorecards, bowling at the members and pulling the heavy roller out in the middle. He vividly recalled his first appearance at Lord's when he walked through the Nursery Gates in 1933 to become one of the MCC ground staff. In that capacity he used to sweep the ground, as well as selling match cards and pushing the roller, of course.

I remember sitting up in the stand watching Denis playing for Middlesex in 1936 when he made eight-seven against Northants. That was his second game for Middlesex, he said.

'My first was against Sussex at Whitsuntide when I came in and batted as number eleven, as I was playing as a bowler. I had a partnership of about thirty with Gubby Allen and I was given out LBW. Gubby turned to the umpire, who was a famous character called Bill Bestwick and said, "That boy wasn't out, Bill. You're a damned old cheat."

'And he said, "I know he wasn't out but I was dying for a wee and it's quarter past six." '

Denis told me another lovely story about facing the great Harold Larwood. 'He was off a short run then,' he said, 'but it was the fastest thing I've ever experienced. I'll never forget – he bowled me a short ball which I somehow hooked for four and he ran down the wicket, shook me by the hand and said, "A wonderful shot, son" – which was very nice.'

Denis chose Frank Sinatra singing 'My Way' as his piece of music, which was a fitting way to sum up his outstanding career – and all in all it didn't seem out of place to play me into the Pavilion, so to speak.

East Anglia

27 The river Bure, Norfolk.

When I was a boy my grandfather lived in the village of Harlow in Essex in a house called Terlings. What a change he would notice now, with the flourishing new town and the old house now the Council Offices. Incidentally, we used to call it Tarlings, but they now pronounce it as it is spelt.

My grandfather had worked in Brazil with our family coffee business and when he came home brought with him a black Brazilian manservant called Otter. I remember him well waiting at table with white gloves. One day the local otter hunt turned up at Terlings because someone had pulled their legs and told them that there was an otter up at the big house. They got quite a surprise when Otter opened the front door and asked them what he could do for them.

When working in the City we would make occasional visits to the Essex seaside towns like Clacton and Southend. One very hot night we motored down after work to Southend, walked along the pier, got a breath of fresh air and drove back again. Although the roads were not so good there was far less traffic and the journey took no longer than it does today.

After joining the BBC we broadcast many seaside shows from the end of the piers and enjoyed the local joke: 'It's obvious. It sticks out a mile.' 'What does?' 'Southend Pier.' Actually, this is wrong as its real length is, I believe, a mile and a quarter. In the fifties and sixties we used to broadcast county matches on the old Home Service – half-an-hour in the morning, and half-an-hour in the afternoon. This was a magnificent 'school' for the likes of Rex Alston, John Arlott and myself. There would just be the commentator and a scorer, which meant one had to keep going for half-an-hour by oneself. Nowadays, alas, there are no such broadcasts, so the poor would-be commentator has nowhere to learn his trade, except possibly on local radio covering Refuge Assurance games on Sundays, or in that admirable medium, hospital radio.

Essex was fun to visit. The county side has always been a cheerful team who enjoy their cricket and used to play on a mixture of grounds – Clacton, Southend, Westcliff, Brentwood, Romford, Colchester, Ilford, Leyton and Chelmsford – though I bet I have left one out! They had a travelling circus with a mobile scoreboard on wheels, and tents and chairs were all carried around and set up at the various grounds. It wasn't very economical but it enabled the whole county to see their team.

Essex is another of those counties near London which has become urbanised and commercialised, but it still has thousands of acres of profitable farmland, and some of the most beautiful villages in England. To my way of thinking it is a perfect mix.

Unfortunately I went to the 'other' place, so know little about Cambridge or Cambridgeshire. My principal recollections are a college ball in the early thirties, a speech to the University Cricket Society and commentary on cricket at Fenners. In fact at a Sunday match there in the late fifties or early sixties we tried out the action replay for the very first time on TV at a cricket match. That always makes me think of the Irishman who made a brilliant catch at second slip but missed it on the action replay! There have also been visits to Newmarket Races, though I have a feeling that Newmarket was then in Suffolk. When watching races there my admiration for the skill of the racing commentators increases even more. The horses come head-on at them, stretched across the course, or sometimes in two bunches one on the stand side, one on the other, which makes the job even more difficult. There are sometimes about thirty two-year-olds whom the commentator may never have seen before. He has to learn the colours and name of the owner, the name of the horse, the jockey and the trainer – and believe me they *do* have to learn the hard way, sweating away over colours in their hotel bedrooms. It must be *the* most difficult course in the world on which to commentate, compared with the circular courses in America and Australia.

I always think that one is entering a different world in East Anglia. 'Very flat, Norfolk,' said Noël Coward in *Private Lives*.

And he was dead right. But I always found Norfolk a dramatic place with its fens, marshes and constant fight against floods and the incursion of the sea. The roads are straight and often narrow, with a canal running alongside. There are vast stretches of farmland, providing the best in sugar beet, vegetables and cereals. The pace of life – especially in the quiet pretty villages – is much slower than elsewhere in England. And when you want beauty you only have to go to Norwich or for a sail on the Broads.

It is the same in Suffolk – large open farmlands with little protection from wind and rain, except in the many attractive little villages. The East Anglian people are friendly, but there is still that feeling of being a stranger.

We were made especially welcome during the war, however, when our 5th Guards Armoured Brigade was stationed near the battle area of Thetford – in later years the scene of much of the filming for *Dad's Army*.

I remember well a visit of inspection from General Sir Bernard Paget, who was in command of the Home Forces at the time. He was immaculately dressed in breeches and highly polished shiny top-boots with spurs – very much the general with lots of medals and red tabs. He clambered with difficulty up on to one of our high Sherman tanks, and then, not surprisingly, he slipped and slid all down the face of the tank, ruining his boots and damaging his smart khaki tunic. Tank crews may have looked rather scruffy, but there *was* a reason for it.

My whole life was re-shaped as a result of our camping in some woods near Thetford. Two BBC war correspondents, Stewart Macpherson and Wynford Vaughan-Thomas, were attached to our brigade to brush up on their war-reporting techniques. They came to supper in our mess in the wood, and we had a hilarious time. I got to know them then, but didn't see them until after the war when I happened to run into them again. That was pure luck, but because of it they persuaded me to do a microphone test for the BBC Outside Broadcasts Department. I had had no idea of joining the BBC up until then, but I was looking for a job and thought I might as well have a go. After I had interviewed passers-by in Oxford Street, the BBC said it wasn't very good but at least I kept talking and didn't dry up. So I got the job and haven't stopped talking since – all thanks to Norfolk!

Anyone who travels regularly on the Central Line on the London Underground will recognise the name Ongar – it's the last station at the eastern end of that line. Fewer, I suspect, would imagine that one of the country's architectural gems lies barely a couple of miles from the station in the small hamlet of GREENSTED. There are only a few houses here. There are no shops. But Greensted has a church that is unmatched anywhere else. It's the oldest wooden-walled church in the world.

Carbon dating has shown that it goes back to 845, when Saxon craftsmen used the split boughs of an oak tree to construct this simple church measuring thirty feet in length by ten feet wide. Although the thatched roof has been replaced, the oak walls have stood the test of time for 1100 years and are now so hard that it is practically impossible to drive a nail into the timber.

When it was first built Greensted Church had no windows. What little natural light there was filtered in through small holes. Rush torches provided artificial light, as several scorch marks testify, and the smell inside from the mutton fat in which the torches were dipped must have been indescribable.

Up in the wall of the west end is a stained-glass window showing the head of St Edmund, the only piece of original stained glass in the church. The remainder of the glass that surrounded it was stolen and somehow ended up in Australia, from where it was sent back to Greensted on a sailing ship which unfortunately sank during the voyage, taking the glass with it to the bottom.

I hadn't realised that St Edmund was the first patron saint of England. As a boy king in this part of the country, Edmund was martyred by the Danes in 870. By 1013, when the fighting with the Danes had subsided, it was decided to find the martyr a final resting place in the town that we now know as Bury St Edmunds, and on the way there his body rested in Greensted Church.

The name Greensted means 'a clearing in the wood', and evidence from beneath the floor of the church suggests that there may originally have been a Druid shrine on the site.

For all its age, however, the church is very much an active, functional building. Every Sunday a service is held at half-past ten perpetuating nearly twelve centuries of Christian worship.

If you drive twenty miles eastwards from Greensted along the A414 through Chelmsford, you reach the estuary of the river Blackwater at MALDON. Now, think of Maldon and you think of salt – crystal sea salt. Down at the water's edge the Maldon Crystal Salt Company has developed an industrial practice that is certainly unique in this country and probably in the rest of the world as well.

28 The salt store at Maldon.

The tidal rise here is something like twenty feet, and every fortnight the spring tides bring even higher tides surging into the estuary. The water flows over acres and acres of saltings, or salt marshes, which have become impregnated with salt over hundreds of thousands of years. Water flowing over them absorbs this salt, raising its own salt concentration. When the tide reaches its highest point the company opens its reservoir sluices, allowing the water to flow in until the tide turns and they close them again. This traps enough water to keep them busy until the next spring tide a fortnight later.

From the reservoir the water is pumped through into filter beds, large underground concrete tanks where it is circulated constantly by pumps until it achieves almost total clarity.

Once it is clear enough to be used, the water is pumped into evaporating tanks where the temperature is slowly raised to boiling point, at which stage the salt begins to crystallise on the surface of the water. After twenty hours the whole batch will have formed into little pyramid-shaped crystals, quite different in appearance from the runny salt we are used to using from other sources.

Maldon Crystal Salt is a totally natural product, and I'm assured by those who know about these things that its taste is immediately distinguishable. It has a soft, mellow taste as opposed to the harder, sharper taste of most table salt.

The climate in this part of Essex, dry and comparatively sunny as it is in relation to the rest of the country, suits the growing of seeds, as I discovered standing beside something called an 'odd crop' field belonging to John King and Sons of COGGESHALL.

On the way there we had passed fields of wheat and barley; the firm's basic income comes from selling cereal and pulse seeds. The 'odd crop' field is where they try out experimental seeds for a variety of different plants. The first thing about it that struck me was the polythene that was then covering large areas of the ground. Tests have shown that this helps trap the early spring warmth, giving the seeds a good start to their growing season. The shoots push their way through holes in the polythene and continue to grow strong and vigorously. I saw two crops of maize – one growing through polythene, the other standing normally in the field – and the polythene crop must have been a good eighteen inches taller than the other.

It's clever stuff, this polythene. Not only does it give the seeds a head start, but it is also self-destructive, or photo-degradable to give it its technical name. This means that it actually breaks down into tiny pieces under the effect of sunlight. By harvest time they reckoned it would have been well on the way to disappearing.

Elsewhere in the field a crop of lentils was growing. I also saw a crop of sunflowers looking like a Van Gogh painting in the distance. With 20,000 tons imported into the UK every year to make sunflower oil for margarine, it would obviously help our balance of payments if even a small proportion of that demand could be met by home-grown plants. So at John King's they were plugging away at developing a sunflower that would grow in this climate.

They had one peculiar crop, fenugreek, which stands for 'Greek hay', which grows rather like a garden pea and produces pods. It has two quite unrelated uses: providing a flavouring for curry powders is one, while in the pharmaceutical trade certain parts of the steroid drug are extracted from fenugreek.

Something very dear to the firm's heart is the idea of developing an indigenous 'baked-bean' crop. That may not sound too crucial to the layman, but when you consider that we import 80,000 tons of baked beans a year, the saving that could be made from growing our own takes on a great deal of significance. The 'baked-bean' strain that I saw under trial had been developed at Cambridge University, though to find suitable climatic conditions it was actually being grown south of Paris, where the climate is closer to that of the Great Lakes region of North America where most of the imported beans are grown. The first harvesting had gone well, I was told, and they hoped it would gradually become possible to develop a bean that would grow successfully in the UK.

29 Dr Colin Leakey examining a 'baked bean' crop
grown by John King and Sons at Coggeshall.

On the road into Coggeshall from Braintree we passed a sign for the Isinglass Factory, G. P. Swinborne and Co., which attracted me because this I knew constituted another gap in my general knowledge. It turned out that isinglass consists of the air bladder of certain species of fish mainly caught in tropical waters, with the best isinglass of all coming from the sturgeon. Its use is nothing whatsoever to do with fish: processed isinglass is used to clear both beer and wine. And as it has been used for this purpose since ancient times, I was anxious to discover how anyone had found out that it had this remarkable property.

The logical explanation seems to be that back in those times it was common for travellers to carry their wine in animal skins. Seafarers sometimes found animal skins hard to come by and resorted to using fish bladders instead. In the course of a voyage it was found that the acid in the wine worked on the walls of the bladder with the result that the wine became brilliantly clear instead of remaining murky.

Picking up one of the fish bladders that had arrived at the factory, it looked like a large potato crisp or that Indian delicacy Bombay Duck. After being sorted according to size and having a thorough wash in clean water, the bladders go into tubs containing hydrogen peroxide to be purified.

From here they are transferred to a second set of tubs containing a solution of tartaric acid which breaks down their fibrous structure over a period of twenty hours or more, by which time they will have become completely dissolved.

All that remains is for the isinglass to be packed in barrels to be despatched to the brewers. And with only two firms in the country specialising in this unusual trade, their wares are sent all over the world.

Twenty minutes eastwards along the A120 brings you to the oldest town in England, Camulodunum, as it was called in the first century BC, or COLCHESTER as it is known today. This was the principal settlement of late Iron Age Britain and it seems likely that the Romans may have intended it to be the principal town of the new province of Britannia. Around the year AD 55 the temple of Claudius, the major temple of the province, was built on the site now occupied by the Norman castle, and visitors can still go into the Roman vaults under the castle.

When the Normans arrived the temple had fallen into ruin but, realising its strategic significance (anyone invading England from the east coast has to pass through Colchester to reach London), William the Conqueror cleared the Roman site down to ground level and began building his castle, which has the largest surviving Norman keep in the country. The plan of Colchester Castle and the plan of the White Tower in London are very similar, but the White Tower is only half the size of Colchester. Experts think that Colchester may have been the original experiment from which the White Tower was developed. Just to add to its interest, it is largely built of materials used to construct the Roman town, so the bricks were already a thousand years old when the Norman masons began using them to build the present castle. With a history like this it is easy to understand how Colchester has been an important garrison town for the last two thousand years.

History and tradition sit very happily in a town as old as this, and perhaps its most celebrated annual event is the Oyster Feast which is held towards the end of October. I was very kindly invited one year, though I declined because I don't eat oysters, but the Oyster Feast regularly plays host to people in public life, far more distinguished than the likes of me. Members of the royal family, sporting and showbusiness celebrities and eminent politicians are regular guests.

These days oysters form a small optional part of the feast, though there are plenty available for those who like them; 2000 oysters are ordered at every feast, but as over half of the 300 guests usually don't eat oysters there are a good dozen available for those who do.

In September each year the opening of the oyster fishery takes place when the mayor and councillors go by boat to Pyefleet Creek, home of the best oysters in the British Isles, I am reliably informed – they are native oysters and the water in the creek makes them fatter than most others.

Once there the mayor dons his robes of office and the fishery is officially declared open. The loyal toast is drunk in gin followed by ginger bread. The mayor then makes the first dredge of the season from a fishing smack, after which the whole party goes ashore on Peewit Island in Pyefleet Creek, where the old fishery used to be. There they tuck into a seafood lunch and have another jolly good feast, I imagine.

Colchester stages another annual banquet with a name that immediately appealed to me, the Thieves' Dinner. This is held by the Colchester Association for the Protection of Property, an association that has been in existence for over 200 years and claims to be the oldest in the country. As its name suggests, this was founded to further law and order in the town at a time when no regular police force was in existence. Local businessmen and tradespeople banded together to protect their property and instigate prosecutions against anyone caught stealing from or otherwise causing damage to it.

The first prosecution listed in the beautifully kept minute book cites the case of one Solomon Carter, who stole a pair of sheets and was publicly whipped for this offence. The last one was at the end of the last century; the police having taken care of things since then.

Today the membership has reached beyond the tradesmen of Colchester to include members of the professions, the police force and the services. With their guests, there are normally over 250 present at the Thieves' Dinner, held on a Wednesday in February with a menu that traditionally consists of smoked mackerel and steak and kidney pudding. The dinner is also the occasion when new members are elected; proposers have to put forward their names by means of a pun based on their name and occupation – an occasion for a good deal of amusement.

Ten miles through the little winding lanes north of Braintree is the village of TOPPESFIELD where Ted Wilson and his son Chris opened a Museum of the Working Horse back in 1973. Here they have collected old ploughs, farm implements and horse-drawn vehicles of every description. There are also working displays of horse-related skills like farriery, blacksmithing, harness-making and wheel-making.

The sight of a saw pit got us on to the subject of wheel-making, for it was here that the wheelwrights would have sawn their logs into planks two, three and four inches thick before stacking them and leaving them to dry for seven years. It was arduous work in this saw pit, and dirty too if you happened to be the 'bottom dog' – the man standing in the pit underneath the log pulling the saw down. He had to wear a broad-brimmed hat to keep the sawdust out of his eyes. The 'top dog' (and this is the origin of the expression) had a slightly easier time of it, standing on top of the log pulling the saw up. But either way it must have been hard work sawing through a thick tree trunk.

'Three different types of timber are used in building a wooden wheel,' Ted Wilson told me when I asked him to describe how it was done. 'We use witch elm for the hub, oak for the spokes and ash for the sections of the rim called the felloes. Each felloe has two spokes, so there are always an equal number of spokes in a wooden wheel.

'When we make the iron tyre, we measure the circumference of the wheel and then cut our iron tyre to length, but we always cut it off short. By using a three-rollered mangle we can turn the iron into a perfect circle. To join it we use a forge fire. The ends are heated and hammered until they fuse together. You get a very good and strong weld in this way.

'But, bearing in mind that we always make the tyres too small, it always confuses people how we get the tyres on. Well, we clamp the wheel down on to a tyring platform. Then we heat the tyre up to a good red heat. There's someone standing by with lots of cans of water and a big tank to replenish them from. And when it's ready you get the tyre in position and quickly hammer it down. Now you've got to be very quick indeed with the water because there's red-hot iron on tinder-dry wood. The quenching down is quite a spectacular operation because you've got all the steam going up so you can hardly see the wheelwrights. And as soon as the iron starts to cool it contracts and all the joints tighten up nice and firm.

'The tyre would stay on the wheel for a considerable amount of time, but we always drill a hole to coincide with the centre of each felloe, through which we put an iron pin. This is because an iron tyre will always stretch when it's been running on the road for a time, and with no nails, screws or glues used in the building of a wooden wheel the whole assembly is held together by the iron tyre that's shrunk on. If the tyre stretched and the pins hadn't been put in, it could fall off.'

Inside the workshops there are marvellous examples of horse collars being made, but I couldn't make head or tail of one that seemed to be being made with bells attached to it. These were team bells, Ted explained, peculiar to Kent and Sussex because of the narrow lanes in those two counties. Meeting another wagon head-on could prove to be a bit tricky on many of these, especially if each vehicle was drawn by four horses. The four bells in each box are tuned to play a different chord, and it was said that drivers could tell whose horses were approaching by the sound they heard ringing towards them.

PETERBOROUGH, the country's fastest-growing city and the only city to be designated a new town, is nineteen miles north of Huntingdon. Peterborough's centre-piece is undoubtedly its magnificent cathedral, largely Norman in construction but with quite the most imposing west front of any cathedral that I have seen, which dates from the thirteenth century.

Catherine of Aragon and Mary Queen of Scots were both buried here. Catherine is still here in a tomb which was restored in 1895 by means of an appeal made to every little girl in the country named Catherine to donate one penny towards the work. Mary Queen of Scots only spent twenty-five years in Peterborough Cathedral before her son, James I, asked for her to be moved to Westminster Abbey.

Among the reasons why Peterborough is growing so rapidly is the number of businesses moving to the town. One of the biggest employers we visited has its world headquarters here – and in the case of the world's largest travel agent, Thomas Cook Limited, 'world headquarters' is no exaggeration. I was immediately impressed by their spanking new building, fronted as it is by a marvellous-looking cricket ground.

The original Thomas Cook has a number of notable firsts to his name. He instigated the world's first package tour, a train ride from Leicester to Loughborough complete with cream tea and temperance lecture (he was a great temperance worker) all for one shilling.

At the time when Jules Verne was publishing *Around the World in Eighty Days* Cook was leading a party on a world tour. He took 220 days over this and charged his clients at the rate of a guinea a day!

In 1874 Cook organised and issued a 'circular note' which in fact was the world's first traveller's cheque.

Unusual holidays and travel plans became something of a speciality of the firm's, too. I saw a picture of a group of Indian maharajas who were being taking by Cooks on a tour at the instigation of the British government, keen that Indian princes should gain a wider perspective of English culture. In fact, in the firm's old headquarters in Berkeley Street there used to be an Indian Princes' Department with the sole responsibility of looking after them and their retinue of servants.

Probably Thomas Cook's most famous exploit came about in

Egypt during the crisis that blew up in Sudan when General Gordon became besieged in Khartoum. The British government were at a bit of a loss as to what to do. Cook, on the other hand, had acquired an amazing knowledge of the steamer traffic on the Nile, so they asked if he would organise the expeditionary force to go to Gordon's aid. Unfortunately, they asked him too late, and the relieving force arrived three days after the poor fellow had been killed.

Going round the huge international headquarters in Peterborough which acts as the nerve centre for 1000 offices in 143 countries around the world, the thing that caught my imagination was the computer known as the Travel Information Bank. At the press of a few buttons it seemed to tell you everything you could possibly want to know about any country in the world. I gather that this is really just a modern version of what the firm has been trying to do ever since its foundation. Central Information Services, as the section used to be known, consisted of a lot of clerks sitting round at high-top Victorian desks copying out by hand useful travel tips like the cost of taxis and the sort of clothes to wear, which were then posted off or sent to clients by messenger. Today each Thomas Cook branch has a terminal giving direct access to the hundreds and hundreds of pages of information stored in the computer.

Traditionally, Fen people have been rather isolated and their folklore carries a stamp all of its own, as I discovered when *Down Your Way* went to LITTLEPORT. In days gone by the men of the Fens didn't believe in cutting their hair, probably because they had heard the story of Samson, whose strength was in his hair. They didn't believe in washing much either – that was reckoned to weaken you! In the damp atmosphere in which they lived ague and fever were common complaints and to counter this poppy-head tea was a popular remedy, amounting as it did almost to opium.

Eels were put to a number of uses in the Fens beyond providing something tasty to eat. Every man and woman thereabouts used to wear an eel garter just above their knee to stop them getting rheumatism. Gold wedding rings were almost unheard of, so they used to get a piece of eel skin and twist this into a wedding ring instead. It was also believed that a roast onion placed in your ear would cure anything that might be wrong with it. A roasted mouse swallowed whole was also reckoned to cure whooping cough or even smallpox.

'They believed you could cure warts by rubbing the white fluffy stuff inside a broad bean over a wart to make it disappear,' said Miss Eileen Gill, a retired schoolteacher who was a marvellous repository of all these traditional remedies. 'When I was a child my mother tried that on me,' she continued, 'and strange as it may seem the wart did disappear.'

One final word of caution from her was, 'You must never, never cut your nails on Sunday. If you do you'll have the devil with you all the week.'

Superstition had a lot to do with the evolution of horse brasses, as I learned from saddler and harness-maker Bert Wright, whose family firm has been established in Littleport for three generations. 'Brasses as such were originally used to ward off the evil eye,' Bert explained, 'because as we associate goodness with light we also associate evil with darkness, and they were worn to keep evil away just as an amulet was.'

I pointed out a brass shaped like an anchor and asked if he could tell me something about that. 'When you really look at an anchor,' said Bert, 'you've got the old crescent [a device that appears in many designs of horse brass] and the Christian cross.'

Another I spotted depicted an eagle and grapes. I asked what the story behind that was.

'My father always said there was a connection,' Bert replied. 'He used to say that Germany would attack France three times, the Prussian eagle attacking the French grapes – symbols of those two countries.'

Our visit to the Jockey Club at NEWMARKET yielded the origins of a couple of common idioms in English. On the first floor stands the Stewards' Room, which acted as racing's 'supreme court of justice' until the hearing of serious disciplinary cases was transferred to London. During these hearings the Stewards sat at a handsome horse-shoe table while those brought before them stood on a strip of carpet inside the door. This gave rise to the frequently used expression 'to be on the mat'.

The Card Room, adorned by its fine Adam fireplace and gilt-framed oval mirror, contains two card tables which have given rise to another English idiom. At each corner of the tables are recessed silver candle-holders which in days gone by were used to provide light for evening card games. A player who had a run of bad luck might justly comment that 'the game had not been worth the candle' and the phrase has remained in the language long after the advent of electricity.

30 The Stewards' Room in the Jockey Club at Newmarket, showing the famous horse-shoe table and the 'mat' where miscreants stood.

In its heyday before the dissolution of the monasteries, the abbey at BURY ST EDMUNDS grew to become the most important abbey in England. The story of the abbey began in 903 when the body of King Edmund was laid to rest here in a shrine that soon became an important place of pilgrimage. The abbey is in ruins today, but an indication of its full medieval splendour can be gained from what survives of the west front. This measured 246 feet, making it sixty-six feet longer than the west front of Lincoln Cathedral.

From the excellent guide book I discovered that the abbey had over one hundred different offices and positions, including unusual appointments like Keeper of Wax, Cutter of Black Cloth,

Gold Fringe Maker, Abbot's Pond Keeper, Spoons Officer (who collected the spoons after meals) and Pot Stick (he had the job of stirring the porridge).

The guide book also told me that Parliament had been convened at Bury on four separate occasions, the last time in the fifteenth century.

Bury's motto 'Shrine of a king, cradle of the law' refers to another milestone in constitutional history. On King Edmund's Day (20 November) 1214, the twenty-five barons of England met before the high altar of St Edmund's Church and before the Archbishop of Canterbury, Cardinal Langton, swore that they would make King John ratify King Henry's charter of liberties, or else they would make war on him. The result was the signing of Magna Carta at Runnymede the following year.

I was curious to know why they had chosen Bury for such an important meeting. For reasons of secrecy, I discovered. In the winter there was only one road passable into the town, that from Newmarket. This helped to make the barons more or less immune from spies who might otherwise have forwarned King John of what was afoot.

There is a lovely little theatre in Bury St Edmunds, the Theatre Royal, which was designed by William Wilkins, who designed the National Gallery. To add to its architectural charms it enjoyed something called the King's Licence, which meant that if anyone could persuade an actor to remain on the premises the bar could stay open.

It was the pursuit of another of the arts which led us to Garner Wilson's workshop in Abbeygate. Here he practices the craft of violin-bow-making which he learned at W. Hill and Sons, the famous violin-makers in London.

There are three principal components in a violin bow: the hair, the stick and the handle with the frog that adjusts the tension of the hair. The hair Garner uses is all white horsehair, either English, Canadian, South American or French, cut to a length of thirty-one inches. A cello bow takes about 275 hairs, he said; a violin bow about 125-150. The hair arrives cleaned and drawn but otherwise untreated. Garner fixes it into a sort of ferrule at the end by the handle and this in turn is attached to the screw mechanism in the handle which ajusts the tension.

The stick is made from pernambuco, a South American wood

which has all the qualities required for a bow: strength, flexibility and lightness. Garner buys it by the log, which he cuts into planks that are eventually cut into sticks. The slight curve in the bow is achieved by heating the stick and bending it by hand against a mould.

Violin bows vary very little in their dimensions, he explained. The same is true of viola bows, but not of cello bows, which can come in different lengths.

At a production rate of two a week violin bows aren't cheap, but with exports to ten countries and a thriving home market Garner Wilson and his team don't find time hanging on their hands.

I was reminded of Garner Wilson's violin bows when *Down Your Way* went to GLEMSFORD, twelve miles to the south of Bury St Edmunds down the B1066. There the firm of Arnold and Gould follow the time-honoured trade of horsehair manufacturers or dressers. As Garner Wilson had told me, the raw horsehair, taken from tails and manes, comes from all over the world: from the UK, from France, from South America, but mainly from Mongolia.

Tail hair and mane hair are used for different purposes and the two are separated as soon as they reach the factory. Sorting into four principal colours – natural black, natural grey (which is really a brownish colour), light grey and white – takes place on arrival too. The hair is pretty dirty at this stage, so cleaning in disinfectant and water comes next, followed by a gentle dry over twenty-four hours.

The 'drawing' stage follows once the hair is completely dried and up in the drawing shop I watched a lady drawing a batch of white hair using an old-fashioned cut-throat razor. 'That's the best tool in the trade for it,' I was told by Robert Gould, managing director. 'She pulls it out a nip at a time. The hair comes out in its natural lengths. The longest comes out first.'

Part of the white material I saw was going to be used to make brushes. A good deal was destined for judges' and barristers' wigs, when further bleached and mixed. And the very longest was going to violin-bow-makers like Garner Wilson.

There were also some very nice coloured plumes for the military – though not for the poor Scots Guards, who don't have a plume. 'Scotland is very good for us because of the sporran trade,' Robert

Gould pointed out. 'A considerable quantity of white hair is used, and once in a while grey and black hair for tassels.'

Any hair which is too short for the firm's normal customers goes to the curled-hair manufacturers, where it is made into a curled-hair rope of approximately one-third horsehair, one-third cow hair and one-third hog's hair. This is spun into a rope and then sold out to various furniture manufacturers. Horsehair is also sometimes used as the interlining for suits.

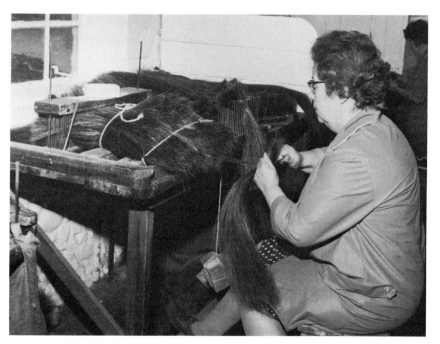

31   Drawing horsehair at Arnold and Gould's works in Glemsford.

An image of living history was conjured up for me when we went to Kentwell Hall, a lovely Tudor manor house in the Suffolk village of LONG MELFORD, to meet Patrick Phillips and hear about the 'Tudor Weeks' he organises every year. As an avowed enthusiast for the Tudor period, he had the idea of using his beautiful home as a backcloth against which to paint a living picture of life in the mid-sixteenth century.

'We're trying to encourage people to see two things, really,' he explained. 'First of all to recognise what their past is and how all modern customs and ways of living have developed. And also to show that houses such as this ... still have a very positive part to play in the life of the community.'

To achieve these ends Patrick Phillips devotes himself to re-creating Tudor life for three weeks each year, using all the features of Kentwell Hall which are so suitable for that purpose.

When we met, 250 people were scheduled to take part in this mammoth undertaking. They come from all over the country. There is a strict vetting process and ultimately they have to pass Patrick's eagle eye to satisfy the requirements. Everyone has to provide their own costume according to the very detailed costume sheets and careful scrutiny of the costume designer.

During the course of the day, from eleven to five, when school parties and members of the public come to Kentwell to see Tudor life in the flesh, all the participants conduct themselves in a fitting period manner. In the Chamber Patrick was planning to set a school room with children aged eight, nine and ten taking part under the instruction of a schoolmaster and dame. They would be taking their lessons with slate and chalk, quills and paper. Religious instruction would be forming an important part of their curriculum, writing too: a good hand was considered an important accomplishment in those days.

The food served during the day is always Tudor too, arriving in procession from the kitchens some twenty yards away, with each of the dishes being presented in turn to whoever is head of the table in the Great Hall. These dishes would all be mixed, as our forebears in the sixteenth century didn't go in for the organised courses we are used to. To provide a flavour of what might be on offer, Patrick Phillips read me a recipe for serving pigs' ears: 'Stew them in water with a cupful of wine and when they be soft hackle them in soft square pieces and do them in seasoned flour. Fry them in bacon grease with an escallop or two. Make a gravy as thick as you can with mustard, nutmeg, lemon slices and chillies and pour it over the ears.'

His description of how he fills his Tudor day sounded jolly hard work. As master of the household, Francis Clopton, as Patrick names himself after one of the family who first built Kentwell, has to deal with all the queries and decisions involved in running a large country home and estate.

He also has to keep up a constant flow of conversation with the more distinguished of his Tudor guests, covering topics of current interest in 1569 (the year he was planning to follow when we visited Long Melford). With people who might spend all day exploring the house, returning to eavesdrop on his conversation several times during their visit, there is no room for repetition. So he and his companions have to have a ready supply of conversational gambits and gossip from court, to maintain the authenticity of their discussions. Mary Queen of Scots was going to be a lively subject of interest, he told me. So were the fortunes of William Cecil, Francis Clopton's mentor, who was under some form of attack from other courtiers who thought that he was getting too powerful.

There are about thirty locations in and around the house where something is going on throughout the day. In the grounds visitors may see archers trying their skill at the butts. Some of the young gentlemen may be practising their sword-fighting with the rapier or the broadsword. Some of the rougher element may be engaging in bouts of wrestling or fighting with a quarter-staff. Others may be playing bowls; while in the delightful walled garden you may catch a glimpse of the ladies of the household besporting themselves – 'and beauteous they are to behold', I am reliably informed.

For me, as for so many other people, the county of Suffolk will always be associated with the paintings of the great landscape painter John Constable, who was born at EAST BERGHOLT mid-way between Colchester and Ipswich.

Constable was the son of a prosperous corn merchant who owned Flatford Mill and Dedham Mill, as well as a windmill on the heath at East Bergholt. So his was not the life of a penniless artist struggling in a garret. Most of his great paintings, including *The Haywain, Flatford Mill* and the *Cornfield*, were painted in London a good twenty years after he had left East Bergholt. They were painted from sketches which must have been at least twenty years old themselves, and somehow or other he managed to keep these great compositions in his head.

It is sad to think that Constable made next to no money from his painting. Throughout his life he was always desperately worried about his financial position, with seven children and an ailing wife to support. In spite of exhibiting every year at the Royal Academy, he was forty-two before he was made an Associate of the Royal Academy and was well over fifty before he was very grudgingly elected an RA proper. In his lifetime only a very few people appreciated his genius.

Flatford Mill, hardly changed from Constable's day, was one of our ports of call in East Bergholt. There I sat on a wall by a large pond, actually part of the river Stour, I think, looking at the scene that Constable captured in *The Haywain*. Across the water was the cottage in the left of the picture and somewhere in between the cart itself would have been standing. I have always wondered what it was doing in the water – not crossing a ford, that I knew.

'It's swelling the wheels, which in those days were made of wooden pieces and used to fall apart in dry weather unless they were kept damp,' explained Jim Bingley. He is the warden of the field centre now based at Flatford Mill which for thirty years has been running a great range of adult educational courses specialising in topics concerned with the countryside: botany, zoology, geography, old houses, old churches, wild flowers, bird-watching and a good many other subjects. At thirty-three pounds for a week they sounded excellent value for money and a very pleasant way of passing the time, if the weather is anything like the gorgeous spring day of our visit.

There is another historic Suffolk mill, just a little further round the coast at WOODBRIDGE at the head of the estuary of the river Deben. This remarkable old building was the last working tide mill in England. Sixty feet high and Dutch in character, it was built at the end of the eighteenth century and worked non-stop until 1957, when its massive main oak shaft finally gave way and a century and a half of milling ceased. For twenty years it stood neglected and forlorn before being saved at the eleventh hour by a trust formed by a generous benefactor who bought the mill and presented it to the town, to be preserved for posterity.

Peter Wyllie, secretary of the Friends of Woodbridge Tide Mill, kindly showed us round and explained exactly what the tide did to work the mill.

'The tide didn't in fact work it directly,' he began. 'What the tide did was to fill a pond. You must have a fall to make a waterwheel work, so the tide had to come in, fill the pond, and then the miller had to wait something from two to four hours, depending on the size of the tide and the direction and strength of the wind, before he could start working. The level of the river would have cleared the wheel by then and he could work for five or six hours until he had used the water in the pond – a big pond seven and a half acres in extent – or the next tide had reached the wheel.'

The pond no longer exists, though you can see where it was located. The tide entered through gates that opened and closed automatically with the flow of the water. Peter Wyllie told us of plans to create a small pond that would hold enough water to let a restored wheel turn for a few minutes in order to show visitors the machinery in operation. Even before that phase of the refurbishment was put into operation 6500 paying customers a year were coming to the Woodbridge Tide Mill.

32   The tidemill at Woodbridge.

In the north of the county the town of BUNGAY has become famous as a centre for growing willow for cricket bats. I was told that 70 per cent of the willow grown in England comes from East Anglia, which I could believe judging by the field near the river Waveney, where the firm of Edgar Watts grows over five hundred willows in lines that would do credit to the Guards.

Edgar Watts came to Bungay in 1912 and set up business in the first instance as a furniture dealer. A friend from Essex who knew a bit about splitting willow out to make bats started him growing his first trees, and the trade has developed from there. These are not the sort of willows one is used to seeing. They are no weeping willows, but ones grown specially for cricket-bat-making. The wood is very light and has a very long fibre; it is this fibre that provides the strength for hitting a cricket ball.

On average the trees take about fifteen years to reach sufficient maturity to make a man's bat. In view of the number that must be needed they seemed to me to be planted fairly far apart. However, Toby Watts, the managing director, pointed out that they only use the bottom seven feet six or ten feet of each tree and to keep that growing fast the trees need plenty of light and air and have to be planted with lots of space around them. To make a man's cricket bat the trunk needs to have a girth of fifty-four inches at breast height.

When the trees come into the works they are cut into two-foot-six lengths and then taken into the mill, where they are split as though cutting a cake – straight to the centre. (These split pieces are known as 'clefts'). Mallets and wooden wedges do the splitting, and from then on they are sawn normally until they end up rather like an old-fashioned haystack, as Toby described it, with a face and two edges going to a point at the back.

He showed me a couple of grains and pointed out that the crooked one wouldn't make as good a bat as the straighter grain. 'If the grain starts to run off at one edge and the ball strikes that edge, it's likely to break away,' he told me. 'So first of all you're looking for straight grain. Then you're looking for colour. Everyone likes the look of a nice white cricket bat, but as soon as a bit of colour comes in then it's down-graded. If you get slight blemishes caused by insects or knots and things like that, it's down-graded yet again.'

About thirty 'clefts' are taken from each willow tree and the firm is using trees at the rate of fifty a week. So they are potentially producing 80,000 bats a year, a lot of which are exported to India, Pakistan, Australia and New Zealand.

Just outside Bungay is the famous Otter Trust at Earsham, where I saw forty-two otters of different sizes accommodated in twenty-one pools – two otters per pool. The aim of the trust is to build up sufficient numbers of breeding otters so that they can eventually rear enough cubs to release them into the wild. For the otter is becoming very scarce almost everywhere in the UK as a result of pollution and the dredging which removes the natural cover they would normally make use of.

The smallest of the breeds are the Asian short-clawed, the manager of the trust, Nigel Palmer, informed me. The native British otter is the biggest they have at present. Otters belong to the weasel family and are very nearly its biggest members, the number one spot going to Mr Badger, the largest member of the family.

Otters are marvellous swimmers thanks to their long, powerful tails, but they run and climb pretty niftily too when they put their minds to it. At the trust they live in cages which are provided for them, but in the wild they create their own holts, which they dig out in the bank or the hollow of a tree. Sometimes they even use old drainage pipes at the edge of rivers.

In the rather more refined conditions of Kilverstone Wildlife Park near THETFORD in Norfolk, we found another of East Anglia's popular animal reserves. Here Lord and Lady Fisher have created a Latin American Zoo, a Miniature Horse Stud and Miniature Donkey Stud, according to the notice at the entrance – and when Lady Fisher showed us round I could see at once that it was certainly all of those three.

We started with feeding the monkeys, four tiny little ones snugly wrapped in what looked like hot-water-bottle covers. 'They feel the cold very much,' said Lady Fisher, 'especially the spider monkeys who don't have much fur when they're born. So I knit them little cardigans to keep them warm. The hot-water-bottle covers, as you called them, I call their sleeping bags and I wrap them in furry material, so that they can cling on to something soft and furry, which is a substitute for mother.'

She told me that these baby monkeys, one of which was only three weeks old, need feeding every two hours. Did she have to do this all through the night?

'Yes, all through the night. I have them beside my bed in a plant propagator which acts as an electric blanket underneath. I have a thermos and I mix up their milk. They squeak and wake me when it's time to be fed. When I had the first one I didn't have an alarm clock and thought I wouldn't wake up to feed it at the right times. So I rang the exchange for a call at twelve o'clock, three o'clock and six o'clock. There was a silence for a while and then the operator said. "You must be mad." I didn't like to say I was going to feed a monkey or I wouldn't have heard another word.'

Just like human babies, the little monkeys are all in nappies. 'The washing machine's going flat out,' said Lady Fisher with the airy resignation of a seasoned mum.

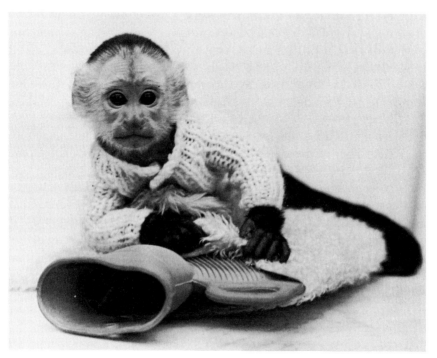

33 Cleopatra, one of Lady Fisher's spider monkeys, keeping out the cold.

Lady Fisher rears jaguars too. I saw a splendid black one prowling about the park, and later caught a glimpse of the more common spotted variety. She hand-rears them in the house until they get to a size and age when they can be moved into the park. 'And how do you know when that point has been reached?' I enquired.

'When they bite my husband,' was her matter-of-fact answer!

The miniature horses at Kilverstone are Falabellas, natives of Argentina which have been bred exclusively by the Falabella family for the last 150 years. So jealous are they of their stock that stallions are never allowed to pass out of the family's control in case another owner is tempted to begin breeding. Even President Kennedy was presented with a mare and a gelding when he received a pair as an official present.

It was an Irishman named Newton, grandfather of the celebrated Señor Falabella, who first began breeding this unique strain of horses, none of which may stand over thirty-four inches high if they are to qualify as miniature horses. Like many Irishmen, he was mad about horses and, coming across a very small but perfectly proportioned horse one day in Argentina he spotted immediately that it would probably breed very small horses too. So he kept crossing it with thoroughbreds and other full-size horses until he finally arrived at the Falabella as it is today: a charming, perfectly proportioned horse – in miniature.

Their bones are too fine to be ridden by children, but they can pull little carts quite easily and at Kilverstone they have a number of these, including a delightful miniature caravan.

'I keep saying I've only got thirty or forty miniature horses,' confessed Lady Fisher. 'But my husband says I've got sixty. He knows. He pays the bills for having their feet done.'

Eighteen miles north of Thetford, SWAFFHAM has become celebrated as the home of a medieval benefactor known as the Pedlar of Swaffham. He appears on the village sign in the market place and also on a carving in the church of St Peter and St Paul, in the history of which the Pedlar of Swaffham played a significant part.

In 1454 the church collapsed and the parson and his trusted band of church wardens, including John Chapman, a pedlar, decided to rebuild it – a task that took until 1510 to be completed. John Chapman himself paid for the whole of the north aisle, which must have amounted to quite a considerable sum with the glazing, seating and paving. Speculation soon arose as to how a man who made a living as a pedlar (chapman and pedlar being synonymous, incidentally) could possibly afford an undertaking of this scale.

The answer may lie in an old legend which says that John Chapman had a dream that if he went to London Bridge and stood there he would find something to his advantage. Off he went and, having waited two days, he was asked by a butcher why he lingered so. Chapman told him about his dream, to which the butcher replied scornfully that if he took any notice of dreams he would be in a place called Swaffham digging in a pedlar's garden and finding gold, but he wasn't as mad as all that.

John Chapman held his tongue, went home and started digging under a pear tree in his garden where, sure enough, he found a pot filled with gold. On the top was a lid with an inscription which he didn't understand. So he put it in his window and the grammar-school boys going by told him it meant: 'Under me lies a greater one than I.' John Chapman dug again and found another pot of gold, with which he paid for the north aisle of the church.

Driving around this country as much as we did, making *Down Your Way*, I don't suppose I ever stopped to think about how the thousands of road signs we all pass are actually made, and it was only when we saw a factory sign in Swaffham for IRS Signmakers, and went inside to find out what they made, that this gap in my knowledge was filled.

IRS stands for Illuminated Road Signs and in 1930, when the company was formed, it was the first to make signs with little reflecting studs that showed up at night. The modern signs they make are still reflective, but instead of having just a few beads they have literally millions of microscopic beads.

The basic sign is made of aluminium covered with a plastic sheeting. The letters and legend are placed on to the plastic. These are then vacuumed down to remove all the air before the material is cooked for eight minutes under infra-red lamps to bond it on to the aluminium. Simple as it sounds, the resulting signs are guaranteed for ten years.

As far as traffic signs are concerned, they are all made to a regulation laid down by the government. The largest sign IRS have made is a thirty-foot one on the M11. At the other end of the scale are little on/off signs on switchboards.

The South-East Midlands

34 Farmland near Beacon's Hill, Hertfordshire.

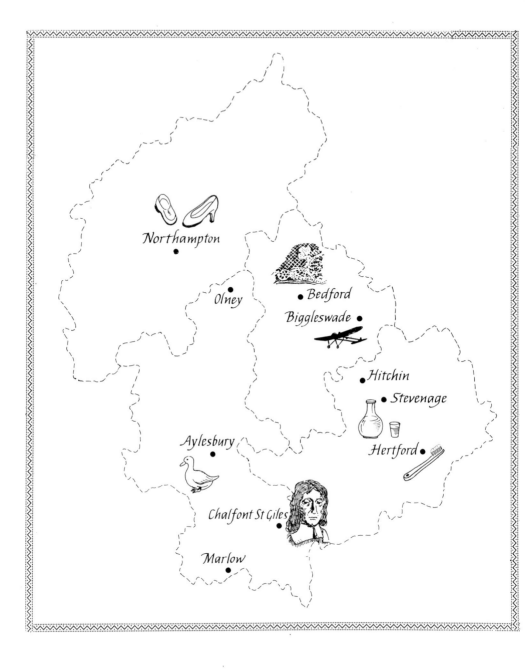

Northampton

Olney

Bedford

Biggleswade

Hitchin

Stevenage

Aylesbury

Hertford

Chalfont St Giles

Marlow

I suppose I must be classed as a Home Counties man. I was born in Little Berkhamsted in Hertfordshire, educated at Eton in Buckinghamshire, and for all my working life I have lived in London. In the thirties and forties my mother had a delightful thatched cottage in the Buckinghamshire village of Chearsley, and I spent many weekends and holidays there. She took in evacuees during the war. They came from the East End and it was a delight to see them enjoying the life of a quiet village. Laurence Olivier had a house – an old abbey – just down the road near Long Crendon, a picture village which has been used in several films. Aylesbury has grown and developed enormously, but High Wycombe is now by-passed by the M40 and seems a rather lonely sort of place. Obviously the by-pass brings more peace and quiet, but the thousands of cars which wound their way through the long valley in which the town is situated brought life and vitality.

Northamptonshire means shoes to me, and I have the brown and white correspondent shoes which I wear at Test matches made specially for me at Earls Barton. Whenever I think of the town of Northampton I remember the sad day when I visited Colin Milburn in hospital there, soon after he had lost an eye in a car accident. It was a devastating blow to him and left his cricketing future in ruins – just as it looked as if he might at last have been recognised by the selectors as a permanent opening batsman for England. And yet it was his visitors who did the crying. However badly he must have felt inside, he kept smiling and joking, just as he always did.

Bedfordshire is mostly a county I know from motoring through, but Bedford is a pleasant town with its schools and riverside walks. I also once did a broadcast in a balloon from Cardington. For some unknown reason we chose the winter to do it. We had to wait until the wind force was right – I believe about 20 mph is the maximum. We cruised along at something between 1000 and 2000 feet. Everything was very quiet except for birds, and the voices of people below, which came up clearly to us. I'm sure we should never have taken off, because it soon began to snow. It was freezing and there was little room to move in the basket as we had an engineer with our broadcasting gear and the pilot. The extra weight also made it difficult for the balloon to rise higher. The pilot began to look anxiously at some hills in the near distance, and desperately began to throw out sand bags in order to lose weight. But it made no difference, and we kept approaching the hills at the same height. So there was nothing for it but for the pilot to pull the quick-release valve to deflate the balloon. We began to sink rapidly down to earth, and I was doing my best through my chattering teeth to give a commentary. They were chattering both from fear and cold. We finally landed with a tremendous bump and were shot about twenty feet up in the air. Our gear was flung all over the place, cutting off my commentary. We hopped across the field with the wind blowing our deflated balloon along. It finally came to rest in a hedge, and we had to stand around in the snow waiting for a second party to rescue us. I have rarely been more frightened.

Hertfordshire is a surprising county. Much of it is built up and near London, but it is still possible to get lost in its narrow country lanes within thirty minutes from the centre of London. I was born in the old Rectory at Little Berkhamsted, and on a recent visit there found my and my brothers' and sisters' births in the church registry. At the start of the Great War we moved to a lovely Queen Anne house called Little Offley, about halfway between Hitchin and Luton. There we spent an uneventful war except for one bomb dropped by a zeppelin on Hitchin, which was said to have killed a chicken. I remember well the victory torchlight procession through the village and someone setting fire to the bonfire long before the procession reached it. We used to walk two miles there and two miles back to church every Sunday, and were rewarded by being given meringues for lunch – brown sticky ones. We had a pony called Raffles which used to bolt with the pony cart, and once tipped us all out when it ran up on a bank. We also had a farm, so learned all about animals. I remember once taking up to my mother's bedroom the tiny runt of a big litter of pigs, when I learnt that it was going to be killed. My action spared its life – at least until it later became a piece of bacon.

It was a lovely, unspoilt part of the country and still is.

At the lovely riverside town of MARLOW in Buckinghamshire we met Captain John Turk, Swankeeper to Her Majesty the Queen, who is responsible for the well-being of the royal swans on the Thames all year round. Captain Turk's father had been a Queen's Swankeeper and suggested his son as replacement on his retirement in 1963.

His area of responsibility stretches from Sunbury in Middlesex to Pangbourne in Berkshire, a stretch of seventy miles containing a couple of hundred swans. Not all of them belong to the sovereign. Some belong to the Worshipful Company of Vintners, and others to the Worshipful Company of Dyers, two very old City of London livery companies. To distinguish which swans belong to which owner, they are all marked during the annual Swan Upping which takes place in the third week of July.

For this the three swankeepers are joined by watermen from the Tideway, who row up river in skiffs in search of the swans. 'When you see a brood of swans you know very well that it's a whole family,' said Captain Turk, 'because they are always together in families. When we approach them we just ease up our speed, try to pick up their speed and get our boats one behind the other. When I think we're in the right position I give a signal to the first and last boats to go in towards the shore, so we make a semi-circle round them until they are between two boats and the shore.

'The Queen's swans are not marked. The Vintners' swans have two nicks, one each side of the upper mandible. And the Dyers' have one nick only on one side of the upper mandible,' he continued. 'We examine the beaks of both the cob and the pen to find out what their markings are, then we mark the cygnets accordingly. So if there was a mixed mating the cygnet markings would be divided equally between the markings of the parent birds, with the owner of the cob bird taking the odd one in the case of an odd-numbered brood.'

Listening to Captain Turk, it all sounded terribly easy, but I've always regarded swans as terrifying birds, hissing and flapping about with their powerful wings.

'We catch them round the neck initially,' he explained. 'And pull them towards us as quickly as we can without too much danger to the bird's neck. We lower our knees over their wings to stop them flapping, because they are very, very dangerous. And then we just ease the legs up over their tail and back, tie the legs up, tie the wings up and the bird is helpless.

35 The Queen's Swankeepers led by Captain John Turk.

'We release the female first and she swims a little way away using the most terrible language. Next go the cygnets, who all swim to their mother, and the cob goes last.'

He told me that it takes four days to go from Sunbury to Pangbourne (they reach Windsor bridge at the end of the first day). Then they work their way downstream again for the following two days.

Apart from the hazards posed by thrashing wings and the ever-present risk of an unexpected swim, Swan Upping sounds a most agreeable pastime. It's colourful, too. All three swankeepers wear naval caps with the badges of the birds' owners. The

Queen's Swankeeper, for example, wears a scarlet coat with white trousers, and his swan uppers wear scarlet jerseys and white trousers.

Marlow's most famous feature must be its suspension bridge, built in 1831 by William Tierney Clark, who constructed a bridge of similar design across the Danube in Hungary linking Buda with Pest. That was destroyed during the last war and the bridge at Marlow is the only surviving example of his work.

Just down-river stands another celebrated Thames-side landmark, the Compleat Angler Inn, named after Izaak Walton's famous book on fishing which he wrote here.

CHALFONT ST GILES, nestling in a wooded valley in the Chilterns, has its own associations with another important seventeenth-century writer, the poet John Milton, who lived in a cottage here during the Great Plague of 1665. Milton's Cottage, as it is now known, is open to the public, and there you can see examples of the furniture and fittings with which he would have been familiar.

The poet was blind by the time he moved away from London to escape the plague and finished writing *Paradise Lost* in the study, one of two rooms open to the public. This was achieved through the efforts of his youngest daughter Deborah, who day after day copied the masterpiece as her father dictated it to her. She was only fifteen at the time, and as girls in those days had a fairly sparse education there were times when she hadn't a clue what her father was talking about and wrote it down parrot fashion, so that someone else could check it afterwards.

Milton came to Chalfont St Giles through the good offices of his Quaker friend and former pupil Thomas Ellwood, who had been looking out for a suitable home for him away from London. Quakers were prohibited by law from practising their faith, and Ellwood and his companions regularly served short stretches in the county jail in Aylesbury after being caught by the justices at illegal services. He was actually locked up for one four-month stint when Milton arrived at his cottage.

As a result, the early Quaker meetings were held in secret and Old Jordans, a little way out of Chalfont St Giles, is an early seventeenth-century farmhouse where they used to congregate. Along with Ellwood, George Fox and William Penn, the founder of Pennsylvania, were among the very early Quakers to attend and their presence and the proceedings of their meetings are recorded in the minutes that survive to this day. (Penn and most of his family are buried near the meeting house at Old Jordans.)

The Mayflower barn here has strong Quaker connections too. By an amazing coincidence it is built of timbers taken from the *Mayflower* when she was broken up in 1624. Research has shown that the timbers are indeed ship's timbers, soaked in salt, and that the bricks in the foundations were made before 1625. Specialist evidence linking the barn with the ship which took the Pilgrim Fathers to the New World includes a beam with a metal patch that corresponds with the account in the diary of William Bradford, the Governor of Plymouth colony, who recorded in mid-voyage that a beam had split and had been repaired by a blacksmith on board. Even more convincing is the ship's cabin door in the farmhouse kitchen, which has mayflowers carved on it.

As the presenter of a radio programme which featured a selection of gramophone records every week, I knew absolutely nothing about how they were made until the programme went to AYLESBURY where we were given a tour of the CBS Record factory. I can't pretend that I came away much the wiser, but the technique was intriguing and the production figures truly awesome – in 1984 they had budgeted to make 45,000,000 records and something like 13,000,000 cassettes.

Fortunately the Quality Control Director at the plant, David Gallstone, was on hand to explain the process to me from the arrival of an artist's tape to the LP on sale in the shops.

The CBS studios in London take the tape and use this to produce what is called an acetate, a thin aluminium disc covered with an acetate film into which the music groove has been cut. To me it looked just like an ordinary gramophone record.

At Aylesbury they spray a very fine layer of silver, five-millionths of an inch thick, on to the surface, making it electrically conductive. This is then placed into a plating bath where a layer of nickel, fifteen-thousands of an inch thick, is grown on to the surface. Instead of having a groove like the acetate, this now has little ridges and as such becomes the master.

It goes back into the plating tank once again to have another layer of nickel grown over its surface, which in turn has grooves instead of ridges. This becomes the 'positive' or 'mother' disc.

The positive is pulled away from the master and is put back

into the plating tank to grow another layer of nickel with little ridges, which becomes the 'stamper' – and that is the mould that is used in the press. With one nickel-positive they can grow fifty nickel stampers to go into the presses.

The record comes from the press in its finished form with trimmed edges, and all it needs after that is its visual inspection before being packed in its sleeve.

I suppose, like many people, I always connect Aylesbury with ducks, and it was rather sad to discover that very few pure Aylesbury ducks are still being bred; cross-breeding with Peking ducks started during the last century and the Aylesburys have been in decline since then. They looked to me flatter than most ducks with their tummies more or less parallel to the ground. They are also a tremendous size, weighing about six and a half pounds and standing fifteen inches high.

Aylesbury ducks had enormous appetites, from all accounts, and it wasn't difficult to get them to become fat very quickly. In Aylesbury they were fed on a special food made from rendered-down offal which built up their flesh without building up their bones, and also contributed to their delicious flavour.

At one time the town was famous for its prune orchards as well, but these, alas, have gone the same way as the ducks.

As a boy I had known about William Cowper mainly through reading his *Diverting History of John Gilpin*. But I found out a good deal more about his life in the village of OLNEY in the very north of Buckinghamshire. Cowper spent eighteen years living in this pleasant little market town, and most of his most famous works, chief of which is *The Task*, were written here.

William Cowper moved to Olney at the suggestion of his friend John Newton, who had been appointed curate in charge of the parish. He took up residence in a fine early eighteenth-century house which now acts as his museum.

Throughout his life the poet suffered from periods of severe depression, and Newton greatly helped him to recover from this. Together they took to writing hymns, some 360 in all, which were published in the collection called *Olney Hymns*. This contains well-known ones like 'God moves in a mysterious way', 'Amazing Grace' and 'There is a fountain filled with blood'. So prolific were they that it was not uncommon for John Newton in particular to sit down and write a hymn for evensong that same day.

Cowper kept three pet hares in his house, named Puss, Tiny and Bess, which are immortalized in his writing. He also had a number of cats, which as kittens he had saved from a viper in the Viper Barn which stands by the house.

Olney's other great claim to fame is its 500-year-old Pancake Race run every year on Shrove Tuesday. Syd Morgan, 'Mr Olney' as he was introduced to me, told me all about the race when we met at the end of 1975.

36 The Pancake Race at Olney.

As one of the official starters he attired himself in a red tunic which had been worn at the battle of Waterloo, and a helmet which had also been worn during the Napoleonic Wars. He carried a pike, too, and the town crier's bell, which was over two hundred years old.

When the race first began the ladies used merely to run across to the church with their pancakes and give them to the sexton with a kiss. Half a millennium later the race, as it has become, attracts large crowds every year and is now an international competition – the ladies of Liberal, Kansas, race on the same day and apparently rather have the edge on their English rivals. In

Olney they say that that is only because the weather is better for training over in Kansas!

Even so the winner's time in Olney in 1975 sounded pretty quick to me. Carrying her frying-pan and pancake, the winner covered the distance through the village to the church in a time of just under sixty seconds. But then Miss Sally Faulkener had had some practice. She had won the race the year before as well.

I didn't enquire about the footwear favoured by the competitors at Olney, but NORTHAMPTON a dozen miles to the north-west probably provided whatever was worn in days gone by. Northampton has always been an important boot and shoe town, and in the Central Museum and Art Gallery there is a collection of boots and shoes which records the town's long association with the trade.

As at Olney, there has always been a certain amount of tanning in Northampton, so boot and shoe-making became a principal industry in the town. In 1213 King John bought the first recorded pair of boots made here and the trade has grown since then, reaching its peak in 1873 when the first National Leather Trades Exhibition was held in Northampton; one or two of the exhibits from that are now in the museum's collection.

There are lots of curious articles of footwear on display. I was shown some huge boots made to fit an elephant taken on the British Alpine Hannibal Expedition in 1959, when the attempt was made to trace Hannibal's route across the Alps. One boot went on each leg and fitting them was quite a performance, taking two hours at a time. In fact it didn't take long to discover that the elephant got on quite well without the boots, so they were quietly forgotten.

Northampton has been providing footwear for the British army since 1642, and samples of military boots from previous centuries, as well as the ones made during both World Wars, can be seen. There are thigh-length sheepskin flying boots from the Great War as well as cossack boots made for the Russian army during the same period.

From the Second World War I was shown one particularly ingenious flying boot, nicknamed the 'escape boot'. This was designed in Northampton in 1943 for aircrews flying over enemy territory, and was sheepskin-lined for use in unheated aircraft. Inside was a little knife which enabled you to cut off the boot's leg to make it look like an ordinary shoe. There was a compass in the heel and a map inside under the sock. The leg could be used as a waistcoat to keep you warm, and there was also a saw in the laces in case you were unlucky enough to get locked up. Although not actually made in Northampton, Queen Victoria's tiny wedding shoes are now housed in the museum. At size four and a half they make a fine contrast to the elephant's 'climbing boot'.

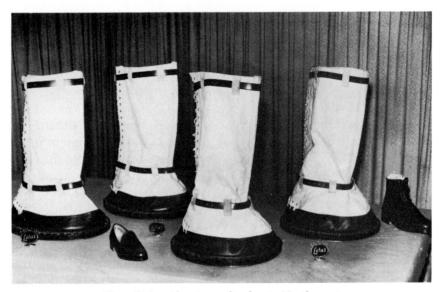

37 The elephant boots on display in Northampton.

Twenty-one miles down the A428 from Northampton you come to BEDFORD, where John Bunyan lived and practised his trade as a tinker before being imprisoned in Bedford gaol for his religious beliefs. It was during the twelve years that he was incarcerated here that he wrote the most famous of his sixty books, *The Pilgrim's Progress*. Within five years this had sold 100,000 copies, which can't have been bad going in the middle of the seventeenth century.

There is a little museum with mementos of his life and work in the Bunyan Meeting Free Church which stands on the site of an old barn where he once worshipped. I was rather struck by the original manuscript of his *Deed of Gift*. Between release from prison and his death in 1688 at the age of sixty there was a period when he feared he might be locked up once again. So he decided to make out his *Deed of Gift* in the form of a will which he placed behind a stone in the cottage where he was living in St Cuthbert's Street. So well was it hidden, however, that it wasn't until 1836 that it came to light!

In the museum there is also an unusual violin made by Bunyan himself out of metal, showing the brazier's art to perfection.

From the museum we turned our attention to one of Bedford's old crafts – lace-making.

'The first lace in Bedford was made in the sixteenth century,' I learned from Mrs June Day, who ran a little shop called Bedford Lace in Newnham Street. 'But it really flourished in the nineteenth century, when lace-makers in the cottages used to make it to eke out their meagre earnings.'

Her shop was lined with lace-making equipment, among them little cushions (which I was told to call pillows) and bobbins all made of wood – tight-grained woods like lilac, box and yew. On the end of each are beds ('spangles' to the well-informed) which add a little tension to the lace and help keep the bobbins in place while you are working.

The pillows rest on little stools, called 'maids', Mrs Day explained. Over this is laid a paper pattern filled with holes into which pins are stuck to create the pattern made by twisting and plaiting the bobbins. On the piece I saw in her shop there were fifty bobbins in use for making a tray cloth which she told me would take a month to make, working at it for a few hours each day.

After being told in Nottingham what great lace-makers they were, I had to ask why the lace-makers of Bedford thought they had the edge.

'We're hand-made lace and they're machine-made lace,' said Mrs Day. 'That's the subtle difference.'

On a crisp snowy day we were back in Bedfordshire once more recording the programme in BIGGLESWADE. This had an aeronautical feel to it because three miles away is the Shuttleworth Collection of Vintage Aircraft, which we just had to go and see. Out on the runway as we drove in, there was something that looked as if it was made of paper – it was so unbelievably frail. Most of the collection is housed in seven hangars and the all-grass aerodrome is fully operational – except when the sheep are grazing it!

Richard Shuttleworth, the son of local landed gentry and a real engineer at heart, began his collection of machines with bicycles and cars, and then turned his attention to aircraft. He bought his first plane in about 1930 and continued collecting until 1939, when he joined the RAF only to be killed at the outbreak of the war.

Virtually all of the thirty aircraft in the collection are capable of flying, manned by an intrepid team of ten experienced pilots who take to the air in them for the flying displays given during the summer months. Insurance restrictions prevent passengers being taken up too, but as Chris Morris, the chief inspector ruefully told me, 'We engineers do fly in them as ballast . . . and flight test observers, I suppose you could say.'

Outside he showed me an aircraft which was built in the year I was born – the oldest English plane still flying, he told me, which was cheering.

There's also a Bleriot aircraft that 'hops' around the airfield, as he put it.

'Hops?' I asked.

'Gets daylight under the wheels. But we don't let it out of the circuit. It's a bit too dangerous to fly it out of the airfield and back again.

The wings of the Blackburn monoplane I saw looked terribly thin.

'They are very flexible,' he said, rather more technically, 'because they have a process of wing-warping. There are no ailerons at all. The wings have to warp in order for the pilot to maintain control.'

The steering-wheel inside the cockpit was minuscule, like the sort you would expect to find in a toy car. Did the pilot actually steer with that?

'Yes,' Chris grinned. 'They hadn't standardized the control of aircraft in those days and each manufacturer had his own method of controlling the aircraft. Blackburn decided to put a steering-wheel on his very early planes to warp the wings.'

In a richly agricultural area (it's one of the main centres for the growing of brussels sprouts, by the way) Biggleswade is very appropriately the home of another mechanical invention, the agricultural tractor. In the town there is a plague commemorating Dan Albone, a bicycle-maker who developed the Ivel tractor, named after the river which flows through Biggleswade.

Biggleswade was also the home of the World Ferret-Legging Champion, Tony Tuthill, who held the record for keeping seven ferrets down his trousers for no fewer than six and a half hours – a feat which he achieved entirely for charity!

He had a ferret with him when we met in the Elephant and Castle down Mill Lane, just off the Market Place. During the course of the interview this little creature cheerfully slipped in and out of the trousers he was wearing and on one occasion popped up through the neck of his shirt. He had never been nipped, he assured me – only scratched a little.

38 Tony Tuthill, World Ferret-Legging Champion.

For competition work Tony wears a special pair of baggy trousers, which he ties just above the knees to stop the ferrets slipping out of the bottom.

But what did he do for the six and a half hours during which seven of them were roaming around his nether regions?

'I played darts, dominoes, anything you like,' he answered casually.

The only ferrets I had known had ponged a little, but this one of Tony's seemed very clean. Did they have fleas?

They didn't, apparently. Just as well, I should think. Having them inside your trousers must be uncomfortable enough. I was amazed that the only person to take Tony on was a young lady who popped a ferret inside her blouse. That must have taken some doing, though it was a lady ferret, so perhaps they had some sort of understanding.

Tony Tuthill only works with male ferrets. 'You can't trust the females,' he reasoned.

Ten miles south of Biggleswade is HITCHIN, a town with a range of important industries, one of which was celebrating its 'bicentannery', as they called it, in 1983. G. W. Russell and Son are makers of chamois leather, producing most of those used in this country. A few modern improvements have been made to the technique, but on the whole the process is much as it was when they started in business two centuries ago.

Chamois leather comes from sheepskin, which was something I didn't know. But why the name 'chamois'?

'Because of the oil tanning of chamois in olden times, which was called "chamoing",' explained the managing director, Ernest Mills. 'When they started oil tannage of split sheepskin, this claimed the name of "chamois".' Today 50 per cent of the skins come from domestic sheep, the other half being imported from New Zealand.

The imported ones arrive in salt and a weak solution of sulphuric acid preserved like a pickled onion. Once they are separated from each other any pieces of flesh still attached to the inside of each skin are removed in a fleshing machine. From there further washing and cleaning take place until they are inflated in a large roller device. Here they are split in a machine that has a band-knife running round the outside of it. The bottom half of the skin, the side nearest the animal, becomes a 'flesher' and is turned into a chamois; the top half will eventually be turned into a 'skiver'.

Cod liver oil is used to tan the chamois, turning it into a chamois leather proper. And the final process seems to roughen it up on a stone. This is actually known as 'wheeling', and it raises a nice even nap which assists the skin in absorbing water.

Chamois leathers look so beautifully clean when they are new that I wondered whether Ernest Mills could recommend a way of cleaning them once they have got dirty from cleaning a car, for instance.

'You should wash them out in slightly warm water with soap,' he said. 'You must never use detergents. If you use detergents they'll take all the natural grease out of the chamois and will spoil it. Use soap. Rinse them well and then hang them out to dry. That way you'll keep your chamois for years.'

The 'skiver', the outside part of the skin, is finally used for bookbinding, making diaries, shoe linings, belt linings, and so on. They even make soft skivers that go into handbags.

Hitchin is also the home of an unusual firm of plant growers, William Ransome and Son, growers of medicinal plants and herbs. Here they produce a range of around seven hundred solutions, tinctures, spirits and other herbal preparations.

These days Ransome's only grow lavender, peppermint and camomile. Hitchin was always a great centre for lavender, used in the preparation of scent and perfumes, so Ransome's are carrying on a proud tradition there. The oil from their peppermint plants goes to confectionary manufacturers to flavour sweets, while camomile oil is one of the most expensive ingredients used in making cosmetics.

That took care of home-grown herbs, but I wondered how they set about using ingredients that came from overseas?

'One quite good example is benzoin, which is obtained from the gum that oozes from a tree in Sumatra,' said Michael Ransome, who is on the production side of the company. This arrives at the factory in large rectangular blocks. The benzoin is then extracted by means of alcohol and, mixed with other ingredients, is turned into friar's balsam.

Although a significant number of Ransome's products leave the factory as liquids, a great many are despatched as 'soft extracts' which have the same consistency as Marmite. These are shipped all over the world to clients who can dissolve them to make their own medicines.

From Hitchin, with its roots in Saxon times, it is only a few miles to STEVENAGE, the first of the country's post-war new towns which was started in 1946. Stevenage is actually two towns, the new one and the much smaller Old Stevenage whose church dedicated to St Nicholas was celebrating its 850th anniversary during our visit in 1985.

The man who really engineered the Stevenage new town development forty years ago was Eric Claxton. When we met he began by telling me that this was really the fifth new town on the site since the Romans first made a settlement here. One of the first things to strike me when I arrived was the road system. I didn't see any bicycles in the streets, and I didn't see any traffic lights but what I did see were an awful lot of roundabouts.

'To me traffic signals are a confession of engineering failure,' Eric explained. 'Roundabouts don't stop people who know how to use them from progressing. And you can cycle from edge to edge of the town in almost any direction without crossing the path of a motor vehicle.'

This makes a terrific contribution to road safety and Stevenage's accident record speaks for itself; set against the national average they only have about 60 per cent of the number of accidents usually recorded for a town of this size.

Safety concerns of a different sort occupy the attention of the scientific staff at the Water Research Centre in Stevenage. Their job is to investigate and develop processes for purifying our water and treating and purifying sewage.

Living in London, I naturally asked where my drinking water had come from and what sort of treatments it had passed through. The answer is that it has probably been through people in Oxford and Reading before coming to me. So I was relieved to hear that it is also purified carefully before coming to my tap.

A range of processes are used, the commonest of which is to add aluminium sulphate, which as a fine dispersant solid absorbs impurities and then sinks to the bottom of the tank. The clear water flows on through sand filters before some sort of sterilising agent, typically chlorine, is added to the water to kill bacteria and make it safe for drinking. In law the requirement for the water authorities is to provide good wholesome water, which means the removal of all bacteria, any toxic substances and any elements that might discolour the water.

Oddly enough, drinking water is not the purest water available – that goes to the Central Electricity Generating Board's power stations.

The water we drink can vary between 50 to 400 parts per million of dissolved salts. These are in no way harmful to you or me; they might even give a little flavour to the water. However, if those dissolved salts are present in the water going into high-pressure boilers used in a power station, they could destroy that boiler within a matter of hours.

To provide some idea of the difference between these two grades of water, I was told to imagine an oil tanker filled with water destined for the power station. That would probably contain about one teaspoonful of dissolved solids. If that were drinking water, on the other hand, the volume of dissolved solids would amount to several sackfuls, which would be entirely acceptable for drinking purposes.

For sixty years HERTFORD has been the home of the Addis company, makers of Wisdom toothbrushes. Their founder, William Addis, is credited with making the first toothbrush in its modern form as far back as 1780.

The obvious question I had to ask was what did people do before William Addis came up with the idea. It seems that they didn't clean their teeth very much. Those who did used little mops made of fabric twisted into wire. In oriental countries people used twigs, too, and sticks from acacia trees are still used in Arabia and eastern countries.

I was quite surprised to hear that two hundred years ago people's teeth were much better than they are today. 'They had hard bread and meat,' I was told by Robert Addis, 'and they chewed their food and kept their teeth in better condition.'

When he started working in the business some sixty years ago all brushes were made of natural bristle, but now nylon accounts for 95 per cent of the 40 million Wisdom toothbrushes that Addis make annually. The small amount of bristle that is used comes from pigs and is mainly imported from China.

He told me that the first toothbrushes had very short heads and looked much like the modern toothbrush. As the trade developed the heads became larger because larger heads seemed to represent value for money. Today dentists are playing their part by advising that shorter headed brushes are more convenient and more efficient.

Perhaps with pigs' bristles coming to Hertford from China, we shouldn't have been too surprised to find the Malaysian Rubber Producers' Research Association in a marvellous early eighteenth-century house in Brickenden Lane. During the war the house had served as the headquarters of the Special Operations

Executive, where many special agents were trained before being sent out for operations in Europe; among the most famous of them was Odette Churchill.

But what was Malaysian rubber doing here?

The answer is pretty obvious once you have been told. With most of the world's natural rubber being consumed in North America and Europe, the Malaysians decided to establish their research facility at the centre of gravity of their main market. Here the staff of nearly two hundred help manufacturers to use rubber more efficiently and to develop new products. In so doing they increase demand and help the small farmers all over Malaysia who produce over 60 per cent of the nation's crop.

One of the most interesting developments to come out of the Hertford centre is the growing use of rubber in engineering, particularly in protecting buildings against noise and vibration. Apparently there are a growing number of buildings in London and other cities standing on rubber bearings which isolate them from a source of noise like an underground train or a nearby railway. The Holiday Inn in Swiss Cottage is one of these; without its rubber bearings, I was told, it wouldn't be habitable as a hotel.

The West Midlands

39 Winchcombe, Gloucestershire.

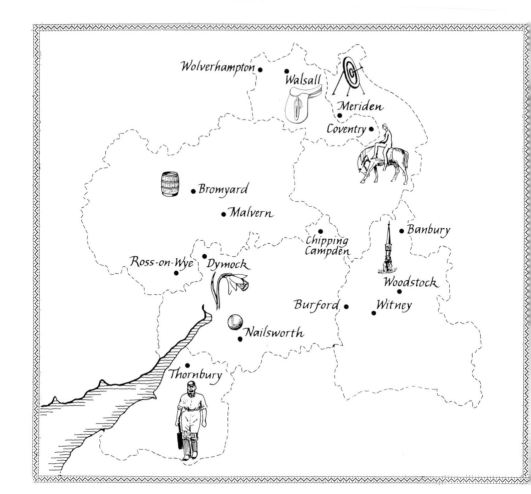

Wolverhampton •

• Walsall

Meriden

Coventry •

• Bromyard

• Malvern

Chipping
Campden

Banbury

Ross-on-Wye • Dymock

Woodstock

Burford • Witney

Nailsworth

Thornbury

I was lucky enough to go to New College, Oxford, so know the city and the surrounding countryside well. I had a wonderful three years at the university, but I'm afraid played more than worked. Cricket and rugby were my games, and all the colleges had wonderful grounds.

I think I am unique in having scored a try at rugby whilst wearing a mackintosh. Someone had pulled and torn my shorts off when tackling me, and I rushed to the touch line and asked someone to get me another pair. Meanwhile, a kind spectator lent me his mackintosh to help cover my confusion! As I was standing waiting, the ball came down the three-quarter line and when it reached the wing I joined in the line, took a pass and ran in to score under the posts. The referee should not have given a try, but he was laughing so much he couldn't blow his whistle.

In the summer we used to have a minor boat-race, supping at the Trout Inn and then racing down to the boat-houses. I always stroked my eight, as I found it easier to keep in time with the others.

Also whilst at Oxford I rode in my first and only point-to-point. I hired a horse called Tip-Top, a half brother of April the Fifth, which had won the Derby the previous year. Tip-Top could have stopped when he liked, but luckily he had the racing instinct and ran gamely to finish fifth. And amazingly I stayed in the saddle. I also begged for the first and only time of my life. I placed some pictures against a wall, put a cap on the pavement, and as I sat there whined to the passers-by – 'Thank you, guvnor – I've got a wife and four kids – please give generously.' It was after a concert in the college, so there was quite a trail of people. Luckily none of them asked the price of the pictures. They did, however, throw in the odd penny, encouraged by the example of some friends of mine, who ostentatiously tossed in half-crowns and shillings (which of course I had to pay back afterwards).

So I have many happy memories of Oxford, and, although I had to cut down my cricket to four days a week, I managed to get a third-class degree in history. But now, alas, about the only date I can remember is 1066.

Gloucestershire, Herefordshire and Worcestershire form a triangle in the South Midlands. For four years from 1924 to 1928 my family lived in the middle of this triangle, in the quaintly named village of Much Marcle. It was in the heart of lovely countryside, with the apple orchards for the cider and the hop fields for the beer. We used to take part in all the village activities and even had the audacity to have a family jazz band with my mother 'on the keyboard'.

We also put on sketches in the annual village concert. One of these was called 'George's Ghost' and it ended in disaster. Just before the dramatic climax and the appearance of the ghost I had to strike a match to light a cigarette for my brother Michael. He was wearing a large fake moustache and unfortunately my match lit the moustache instead of the cigarette. It went up in smoke and my brother had to try to pull it off, to the accompaniment of gales of laughter from the delighted village audience. So the intended drama turned into farce.

We lived a typical country life, with village cricket, rat-hunting and even the occasional 'day' with the rather posh Ledbury Hunt. One of the main attractions at the meets was the Master's wife, a beautiful lady riding side-saddle and dressed in an immaculate blue riding-habit with top hat and veil. She was none other than the famous musical comedy actress Lily Elsie of *The Merry Widow* fame. She had married Major Ian Bullough, the Master, and felt no doubt that she should support him. But she didn't take a very active part in the hunt and often disappeared after trotting down the road to the first covert.

We went to Gloucester to watch rugger and to Cheltenham for cricket. It was there in 1926 that I saw the Australians for the first time in their baggy green caps. I can especially remember Jack Gregory bowling fast, the gnome-like Grimmett bowling his round-arm leg-breaks and googlies, and the 'Governor-General' Charles Macartney perfecting delicate late-cuts.

And then of course there was Worcester, with its beautiful ground in the shade of the cathedral, dominated by the Foster family. Seven brothers played for the county – four of them together in one match – so that it became known as Fostershire.

There were some beautiful houses, one of them called Stoke Edith in Herefordshire. It was the only house I knew which had its own fire-engine, but ironically it had a big fire and was burnt down.

Warwickshire represents hunting and cars for me. In the fifties it was the heart of the Roots Empire, which made Humbers, Hillmans and Sunbeams. At that time I used to report on the Monte Carlo Rally and got to know all the motor-industry people. One year Sheila Van Damm won the ladies' prize in a Sunbeam Talbot, and there was much celebration in the English camp, with champagne corks popping freely. Rather unfortunate timing, as it turned out. Roots were going through a financial crisis and had sent their financial director down to Monte Carlo to see where economies could be made, especially in the hospitality field. We were in the middle of an uproarious party when in walked a gentleman, straight from London in his pinstripe suit. There was a nervous silence as he entered, as we had been warned he might be coming. Norman Garrad, the *chef d'équippe* of the Sunbeam Team, said: 'Gentlemen, I would like to introduce to you our financial director, Mr Goat.' I admit that I had had too much champagne but I just couldn't resist shouting out: 'You must be kidding.' There were gales of laughter, but luckily Mr Goat entered into the spirit of the occasion. He was soon toasting Sheila in champagne, and I'm sure he felt that the Roots money was being well spent.

Standing at the junction of six important roads that lead to and from all the points of the compass, the ancient market town of BANBURY in north Oxfordshire is known throughout the world for its cross and the rhyme associated with it:

> Ride a cock horse to Banbury cross
> To see a fine lady on a white horse,
> With rings on her fingers and bells on her toes,
> She shall have music wherever she goes.

Like most people, I knew this from my nursery. What I had
never been clear about was how it originated, and it was Ted
Clark, former editor of the *Banbury Guardian*, who clarified this
for me.

'The rhyme probably goes right back to pre-Christian times,' he
suggested, 'when the primitive people living in the area held an
Earth Goddess festival in the spring. They chose a young girl to
represent the goddess and, except for decorations of flowers and
foliage, she rode nude through the surrounding fields to bring
fertility to the crops. The horse, of course, represented the sun.'

Until 1600 Banbury had four crosses, but these were all destroyed in a wave of Puritan zeal and the present-day cross
standing at the road junction at the bottom of the Oxford hill was
erected in 1859.

Much of the fighting in the Civil War took place around
Banbury, and the castle which stood in the town until the middle
of the seventeenth century was first garrisoned by Cromwellian
forces, before being taken by Royalist troops who held on to it,
in spite of repeated attacks, until the end of the war. With the
fighting over and the forces of Parliament victorious, the castle
was given to the townspeople, who were invited to dismantle it
and use the stone for their own purposes. Looking round Banbury
today, you can see stone from the old castle walls in many of the
older buildings.

Pre-dating these are Banbury's two famous and finely timbered
Tudor pubs, the Unicorn in the Market Place and the Reindeer
in Parson Street. A third hostelry worthy of mention (and a visit)
goes today under the name of the Whately Hall Hotel, though it
was formerly called the Three Tuns. Jonathan Swift stayed here
while he was writing *Gulliver's Travels*; indeed much of the book
was written at the Three Tuns, and I learned that Swift took the
name Gulliver from a tombstone in Banbury churchyard.

Broughton Castle, two miles away on the Shipton-on-Stour
road, played an even more significant role in the Civil War, for it
was here in the ancestral home of the Lords Saye and Sele that
the prime movers in the rebellion against Charles I met to plan
his overthrow. Lord Saye and Sele deeply disapproved of the
King's autocratic style of government and collected like-minded
men of influence in the castle's Council Chamber to plot against
him.

Broughton Castle had been standing for 350 years when the Civil War broke out, and since 1451 it has been the home of the Fiennes family, bearers of the title Lords Saye and Sele.

It may well be more than coincidence that the family's surname (pronounced 'Fines') occurs so close to Banbury with its nursery rhyme about the 'fine lady on a white horse'. As the present Lord Saye and Sele put it, 'There was a Fiennes lady who rode on a horse, and I think it's a fair assumption to think there's a connection between the two.' I think so as well.

Half an hour's gentle drive south from Broughton Castle brings you to WOODSTOCK and another ancestral home steeped in national history, Blenheim Palace. There had been a royal hunting park at Woodstock since medieval times and following John Churchill's historic victory at the Battle of Blenheim in 1704, Queen Anne made him Duke of Marlborough and presented him with the park and funds to construct the magnificent palace we see today.

It was in the room which had been formerly occupied by the first duke's private parson that Sir Winston Churchill was born a century and a half later on 30 November 1874. Small as it is, this room is one of the principal attractions for the thousands of visitors that come to Blenheim every year.

Inside there are one or two mementos of the famous event which took place here. Sir Winston's baby vest is on display, together with some of the curls trimmed from his head when he was five, and over a looking-glass is a letter from his father, Lord Randolph Churchill, to the local doctor, Mr Taylor, thanking him for his 'careful attention to her ladyship during her confinement'.

'My late father wrote to Sir Winston when we were about to open the house,' the Duke of Marlborough told me, 'asking if there was any clear indication of how and why he happened to be born here. There were two stories going around. One that Lady Randolph was out with a shooting party in the park and, being bumped around in her carriage, felt unwell and came back. Another theory is that there was a ball going on at Blenheim and, again, she felt unwell and was taken into this room.

'So he wrote to Sir Winston and the following reply came back, "Although present on that occasion I cannot recall the facts leading up to it"!'

Work on the palace started in 1705 and it wasn't until 1722

that it was completed, which isn't suprising when you consider that there are in the region of 365 rooms. In the course of their visit to the rooms open to the public these visitors walk along more than a thousand square yards of carpet.

40 With the Duke of Marlborough in the room at Blenheim Palace
in which Sir Winston Churchill was born.

The grounds and lake surrounding the palace were landscaped by Capability Brown, who created the wonderful vista as you enter through the triumphal arch from Woodstock which, according to his Grace, 'has been quoted as "the finest view in England"'. One of the nice traditions that is still retained is the free access to the park enjoyed by all the citizens of Woodstock and the nearby village of Bladon, where Sir Winston lies buried, 364 days a year.

Very often when we visited places people would tell us that we had to go and visit so and so, and they did just that in Woodstock where we were told that we had to go and see Miss Florence Budd, who lived in the house in the High Street where she had been born in 1904. In her younger days she used to cycle up to the palace every morning with a few scones and a small loaf for the 'Great Duke', as she referred to him, which she handed over to Madam Lammedy, the cook, 'a well known personality, who was twice round the gas works and always arrayed in white with a lovely large white apron with a huge button at the back to hold it together.'

'Did you ever by any chance see Sir Winston when he was younger?' I wanted to know.

'Yes,' she beamed, 'it was quite a little adventure. I was coming up from the stoke hole, where I'd been having a long chat with Tommy Jakeman who did the stoking. There was a long plank you had to walk up, and I was half-way up this on Christmas Eve 1918 when I saw Sir Winston with a large cigar in his mouth coming down.

'He stopped short and said, "Little girl, I want to go down there." '

'I said, "Mr Churchill, I want to go up there," and neither of us would give way. So in the end he said, "I suppose I shall have to."

'He advanced a few steps, caught me in his arms and literally twirled me round. "There," he said, "that will suit you and that will suit me."

' "But Mr Churchill," I said, "I'm sorry, but I had two mince pies given to me and one of them is sticking to your coat collar!"

' "I shall have to ask Madam Lammedy to clean me up," he said in reply.'

Another place we were told we shouldn't miss in Woodstock was the King's Head pub, which has a sign showing Charles I outside, a date, '1734', and underneath a sub-title, 'The Potato Pub'. Inside, in the quiet of the dining-room, mine host Brian Rendle explained that when he first took over the King's Head he hadn't a clue what sort of food to serve. So, deciding on something wholesome and simple, he settled for baked potatoes served with twenty-one mouth-watering fillings. These proved to be very popular, and when we visited there was one chap employed solely to clean a ton of potatoes a week – and they looked pretty big potatoes to me.

It takes three-quarters of an hour to bake these, and once they are cooked they can be filled with goodies like chopped bacon and egg, curried chicken sauce, baked beans and tomatoes, and – a particular favourite with American visitors – chicken and sweetcorn served with a nice white sauce.

Moving westwards from Woodstock into the lovely valley of the river Windrush, you come to the old market town of WITNEY. For anyone who knows the song 'There's an old-fashioned house in an old-fashioned street in a quaint little old-fashioned town', it is interesting to discover that Witney is in fact the town in question. We were able to go one better by visiting the very street and the very house also mentioned, and there we met Miss Muriel Harris, whose grandparents ('the old-fashioned pair' in the song) lived at number 48, West End.

Miss Harris's father's cousin, Ada Leonora Harris, wrote the song with its lovely melody simply because she loved the house so much from her many visits.

According to Miss Harris, she was 'a dear little old-fashioned lady' herself. 'She wore long skirts right down to her feet and if she wanted a handkerchief she used to lift up her skirt and go right up to her waist to get it.'

As long ago as the Domesday Book, Witney was mentioned for its blanket-making and, lying on the edge of the Cotswolds, it has become famous the world over for the quality of the blankets still made here today. This industry grew up around the river Windrush, which originally provided power for the little fulling mills where the woven blankets were shrunk and washed. The quality of the river's water helped in the fulling process, too, and before the introduction of factory production methods in the Industrial Revolution there were sixty master weavers with 150 looms all over the town. The master weaver was the kingpin in the process. He bought the wool and blended it in his own home with the help of his family. He would then take it out to spinsters in the Cotswolds and as far away as Wiltshire, where the yarn was spun. The weaving took place on hand looms, again in the master weaver's own home, following a process that continued until the introduction of machines like Hargreaves's 'spinning-jenny' and Crompton's 'spinning-mule'.

Eight miles westwards along the A40 is the popular tourist destination of BURFORD, sometimes called the Gateway to the Cotswolds. References to the town date back as far as three hundred years before the Norman Conquest, but it was the arrival of the Normans and the growth of the wool trade in the Middle Ages which really established its prosperity. Nell Gwynne is reputed to have been born here (though the city of Hereford might dispute this), and only a few years before her birth Cromwell's troops are believed to have executed a number of prisoners up against the walls of the church.

You might not expect a small town like Burford to be the place where a magazine is edited, but it doesn't come as much of a surprise when you know that the magazine is called *The Countryman*. This is based in a former coaching inn in Sheep Street, called the Greyhounds, and here the magazine is prepared for its 72,000 readers all over the world.

The Countryman was started in 1927 at a time when the whole countryside was in a great period of depression. Robertson Scott, probably the first argricultural journalist in the country, was horrified at the conditions in which the people of his own village of Idbury, a few miles north of Burford, were living. So he began the magazine to campaign for improvements to their standard of living and, looking around half a century later, I think he would be pleased at the changes that have been made. Today, as Crispin Gill the editor told me, the emphasis is on ensuring that the prosperity which has come to rural areas doesn't itself destroy what we all cherish and value in our countryside.

The magazine also keeps an ever-open door to visitors. As we were making our way in to see Crispin Gill, we met a reader from Australia who asked whether he could have a look round the lovely garden. 'It's a steady flow,' Crispin confirmed. 'We had two from Japan the other day, and oddly enough this summer we've had the third largest contingent of overseas readers from Holland.'

From *The Countryman* in print it was only a short walk to visit one of the country's most popular countrymen in real life, Bob Arnold, known to millions of listeners to *The Archers* as Tom Forrest.

Bob was born just over two miles down the Windrush valley in the little village of Asthall, where his father ran the local pub. 'It had its advantages and disadvantages,' he told me, when I asked what it was like as a boy brought up in a pub. 'One of the disadvantages was that I had to go to bed very early. My bedroom was right above the tap room and these dear old boys, they'd got no entertainment – the gramophone was a luxury, radio didn't exist – so night after night they used to sing the same old songs, droning away. I couldn't go to sleep, so I had to learn those songs as they sang them.' And these are the songs we hear Tom Forrest singing all round Ambridge.

The Archers was about four months old when Tom reared his head, and from January 1952 he has been introducing the weekly omnibus edition on Sundays, which I was amused to hear is supposed to be given over the bar in the Bull with Tom talking to anyone who is prepared to listen.

It seemed to me that whenever I listened to *The Archers* Tom was always on it, but Bob reminded me that for four weeks he was absent from the programme while on remand in prison. 'I shot a poacher,' he continued. 'Terrible accident, but he died and Tom was put in gaol until the case came up. Regrettably, I had to stay longer than I should have done because one of our script-writers realised the Easter recess was on and Tom would have to wait until there was another court.

'Listeners sent postal orders along. They started a fighting fund: "Get this man out, he's innocent." I remember when the wife and I were in Witney shopping one day, a lady in the street stopped in her tracks and said, "What is thee doing? I thought thee was supposed to be in prison."

'I had to think very quick and said, "And so I am."

' "Well, what's thee doing out here, then?"

' "It's a bit cold up there today, they've got no coal, so the sergeant says to go and have a walk round and get myself back in half an hour."

' "Well, wasn't that good on him," she said and off she went!'

Until the Industrial Revolution shifted the centre of the woollen industry to the newly mechanised looms of the north, the Cotswold hills prospered for hundreds of years on the backs of their sheep. Witney became famous for its blankets, and other towns like NAILSWORTH, which had nearly thirty woollen mills at one time, became renowned for making West of England broadcloth. Those days have long since passed, and when *Down Your Way* went to Nailsworth we found only one working mill left, and that had turned its attention to an unusual present-day speciality – making the cloth for tennis balls.

Since the early 1970s Longford's Mill had been exporting this all over the world, with the one exception of the USA, where a prohibitive tariff barrier was in force. The cloth made at the mill varied according to conditions and playing surfaces in different countries and it struck me that the finished tennis balls were quite rough on the outside. Bill Smith, the managing director, explained that until the late 1920s balls were covered with a very smooth cloth made from fine merino wool. As tennis got faster and faster and the balls were hit harder and harder, they became very difficult to control in the air and also wore out very quickly. So a very much rougher, coarser cloth was developed, which made the ball easier to control through the air and off the ground, as well as giving it a much greater abrasion resistance.

Another development in recent years has been the introduction of coloured tennis balls, of which there seemed to be all sorts of shades at Longford's Mill.

'The fluorescent yellow colour was developed mainly when indoor play became more general,' Bill Smith told me. 'The fluorescent yellow dye is much sharper to the eye under conditions of artificial light and also in conditions of poor daylight. White balls are better in conditions of sunlight.'

I wondered how the cloth was attached to the ball, especially when I picked up a couple of pieces which looked rather like large egg-timers.

First comes the rubber ball, Bill explained, which is composed of two half spheres which are joined together. The rubber ball is coated with adhesive, as is the back of the cloth. Then the two 'egg-timer' shaped pieces of cloth are wrapped around the ball and stuck to it. Amazingly, this was still being done by hand.

And how much cloth were they making, I asked?

'At the moment,' said Bill, 'we produce enough cloth to cover about 1,200,000 balls a week!'

Whenever I did cricket commentaries at Bristol I used to stay at the Ship Hotel at Alveston because I could look out of my bedroom window over the cricket ground on which W. G. Grace played. So when *Down Your Way* went to THORNBURY I took particular pleasure in revisiting that hallowed spot in the company of a Derek Hawkins, who played for Gloucestershire in the 1950s. He told me that the Thornbury Cricket Club moved to the ground in 1871 when the two existing cricket clubs in the town amalgamated.

Dr E. M. Grace was the first captain of the club. He was also captain of the country side, as well as being secretary, so he had a busy cricketing life. W. G. Grace was his younger brother, who played at the Ship at Alveston as a guest for Thornbury on half a dozen occasions. But since those first two Grace brothers a further twenty-five members of the family have played for the club, including Dr E. M. Grace's son (also initialled E. M. and also a doctor). Derek recalled fielding for him as a youngster when the doctor used to nip off for evening surgery, which consisted of some fairly swift consultations, as you might expect. He carried the Grace legacy well into the post-war years and helped put Thornbury Cricket Club on the flourishing path it follows today.

When we lived at Much Marcle for a few years one of the delights of spring was the mass of daffodils that sprang up around the village of DYMOCK, a few miles from home just the other side of the county boundary in the north-west corner of Gloucestershire. These are not the tall daffodils one commonly sees, but slighter, delicate little flowers about eight to ten inches high. They grow wild today and are carefully protected as a result, but they were once gathered to be used to make dyes.

For a small village (it hasn't grown a great deal since the Middle Ages), Dymock has been home to some notable people. Foremost among them was Sir John Dymoke, who was the King's Champion to Richard II at his coronation in 1377. Sir John had gained the title through his marriage to the heiress of the Marmion family, who had been the hereditary Royal Champions from the time of the Norman Conquest until their line ran out in the middle of the fourteenth century. The function of King's Champion was last performed by Henry Dymoke at the coronation of George IV, but members of the family have carried the Royal Standard at every coronation this century.

Just before the Great War Dymock was also the brief home of a rather nostalgic group of poets centred around Lascelles Abercrombie, who moved into the Gallows Cottage in 1911. With him came Wilfred Gibson who lived in the Old Nail Shop. They were joined by the American poet Robert Frost, followed soon after by Edward Thomas. It was while living at Dymock that Abercrombie decided to publish a new quarterly poetry magazine called *New Numbers* and he, John Drinkwater and Rupert Brooke wrote for this in that last Edwardian summer before they were scattered by the outbreak of war.

Hop fields and cider apple trees were familiar to me from the borders of Herefordshire and Gloucestershire, but I have to admit that I didn't expect to find a vineyard. Since 1973, however, the Three Choirs Vineyard has created over twenty acres of vines on the south-sloping face of the undulating hills on the way to Ledbury. These are pretty hardy vines, developed for the cool climate of West Germany. They can tolerate temperatures as low as minus 17 degrees Centigrade before they come to harm, I was interested to hear.

41 Tom Day showing off the harvest at the Three Choirs Vineyard.

They seem to thrive on the red sandy soil, as well. Within two years of starting up, the Three Choirs Vineyard was able to produce 1000 bottles of wine. And in the glorious summer of 1976 one field of only two and three-quarter acres produced a staggering 17,000 bottles! Nearly fifteen years later annual production is up to around 110,000 bottles. Nearly all of these are white wines, with a small but growing proportion of very pale and attractive rosé. I had a glass after the interview, and delicious it was, too.

In contrast to Dymock, with its timber-framed, thatched

cottages, CHIPPING CAMPDEN is a Cotswold town built from lovely Cotswold stone, which made it one of the most attractive in the country.

We were fascinated to find out that Chipping Campden holds every year something called the Cotswold Olympic Games, which were started in about 1612 by a chap named Robert Dover, who was a local attorney. He is supposed to have had the active support of King James I in this venture. At any rate the King presented him with a suit of his old clothes to wear as his regalia as master of ceremonies at the games.

42 Chipping Campden's Cotswold Games.

By 1636 the event was well enough established for a book to be written about it, and this shows competitions in pretty brutal activities like cudgel play, in which the victor was the first to draw blood, and the even more unpleasant sport of shin-kicking. The games died out for a century until their revival for the Festival of Britain in 1951, when a couple of local fellows bravely gave a demonstration of shin-kicking, aided by a good deal of padding, I am assured. In days gone by the competitors had no protection on their legs. They concentrated instead on fitting metal plates to their boots to add to their kicking power.

Since the early 1960s the games have been held every year on the evening of the Friday after the Spring Bank Holiday up on Dover's Hill. There are running events, leaping, tugs-of-war and all sorts of side-shows. They end with a grand bonfire and fireworks, after which everyone lines up with torches to be led by the band down into the town square, where there is open-air dancing until after midnight.

The day after the games, Chipping Campden celebrates the crowning of the Scuttlebrook Queen as the centre point of its Scuttlebrook Wake, a celebration named after the stream that runs through the town and one that grew directly from the festivities surrounding the games. This sounds every bit as colourful and lively as the previous evening, with Morris dancing, decorated floats and fancy-dress processions.

Archery is another time-honoured pursuit of rural England and the Warwickshire village of MERIDEN, which lies slap-bang in the middle of England, as a medieval stone cross on the village green proudly announces, is the home of the country's oldest archery society, the Woodmen of Arden. The exact origins of the society have been obscured by time, but it was revived in 1785 when the surviving records begin. There are eighty members, all of whom have connections with the district, which lies at the centre of the old Forest of Arden.

From Colonel John Horsfall, one of the secretaries, I enquired whether any qualifications with respect to archery skill were required.

'No,' he answered candidly. 'Some of us never hit anything. I'm a very bad archer myself. Years and years ago I thought I was quite good, but I no longer think so. I merely enjoy it now.'

His modesty belied the fact that the members still shoot with the traditional long-bow and practise their skills in the traditional way by loosing off their arrows at 'clouts', small targets about two and a half feet in diameter which are set between 180 and 240 yards away. To me this seemed a tiny little target to have so far away. The fact that the clouts in use are a couple of hundred years old shows that they are not hit that frequently.

'Some of our better archers will actually hit it quite often,' said Colonel Horsfall, 'though none of us will hit it more than a few times a year.'

Instead they mark rings around the clout at distances of up to two bows' lengths from the centre; you score by placing your arrow within them.

The Woodmen of Arden have a very handsome uniform which they wear once a month on their Wardmote days. With white trousers, dark green tail coats, white waistcoats and distinctive green hats they look 'quite decorative', to borrow their secretary's description.

It sounded a very friendly, uncompetitive society, where the members simply practise their archery because they like it. The setting of their lovely shooting ground, surrounded by trees and graced by Forest Hall, the pavilion that acts as their headquarters, must be another benefit of membership.

While we were at Forest Hall we went inside to meet Charlie Warmingham, the official bowmaker, and to find out from him how you actually make a long-bow.

My first question was about length – how long is a long-bow?

'Round about six feet for a gent's bow and five feet six for a lady's,' was the answer.

Following the tradition of bow-making which reaches right back into the Middle Ages and beyond, the bows are made of yew, though unlike those from times gone by the modern bows are made from yew imported from America. Something I hadn't realised is that the bow is spliced in the middle from two shorter lengths, to make it a full-length one. At either end are hooks ('nocks' to give them their correct terminology), where the bow-string is fastened. These are made of buffalo horn.

'Cow's horn wouldn't be any good for this,' Charlie explained, 'because it's hollow right up to the tip. The buffalo horn is solid.'

Bowstrings today are made from the man-made fibre dacron, which has largely replaced hemp. When the bow is strung the bowstring is pretty tight, with a distance of about seven and a half inches between the handle and the string.

I had a go at drawing one of Charlie's bows and I don't mind admitting that I found it pretty difficult. They average a tension of anything from forty-five to sixty-five pounds, with target bows having the lesser tension and flight bows the greater.

Cedar or straight-grained pine provides the wood for the arrows, which like the bows vary in length depending on whether they are being used by men or women. Ladies' arrows measure around twenty-five inches overall, while those for men are longer, reaching up to about thirty inches.

All Charlie's work was so precise that I was somewhat suprised to see him measuring the weight of an arrow by coinage, but this is traditional, he assured me. 'Ladies' arrows are usually the weight of three and sixpence [pre-decimal, of course],' he said, 'a gent's target arrow four and sixpence, a flight arrow three and threepence.'

The feathers are those from a turkey's wing, ideal for the job because they always return to their shape even if they get a bit ruffled up in use. And down at the other end is the steel point, or 'pile'.

In addition to its medieval cross, Meriden's triangular-shaped green has at its apex another stone monument about twenty feet high which commemorates cyclists who fell in the two World Wars. The monument was formally unveiled by Lord Birkenhead in 1921 after over £1000 had been raised for its construction. The late Duke of Windsor was instrumental in getting the appeal going, selling his own bicycle, I gather, and donating the proceeds towards the memorial fund.

Every year a service is held at the memorial on the Sunday nearest 21 May, the anniversary of its unveiling. Between the wars this used to attract cyclists from all over the country, with numbers reaching 15,000 in some years. They have fallen since then, but on average 500 still come to Meriden to pay their respects to the fallen at this unique memorial.

Meriden lies close to the western fringes of COVENTRY, which is without question the road-transport Mecca of this country and, in the eyes of Barry Littlewood, manager of the Museum of British Road Transport, the world. 'Coventry has been home to about 125 car manufacturers, 300 cycle manufacturers and about 90 motor-cycle manufacturers,' he told me proudly. The museum has examples from most of these, beginning with early bicycles. Among the cars, the collection ranges from an 1897 Daimler up to one of the last E-type Jaguars, the Lotus Sunbeam which won the 1980 RAC Rally and Richard Noble's Thrust 2, which set a world land-speed record of 633.468 mph.

The list of car manufacturers connected with Coventry is almost a roll-call of the British motor industry, with Rover, Humber, Lea-Francis, Hillman, Armstrong-Sidley, Riley, Singer, Standard and Jaguar – to mention the best known names. I spotted a car which brought memories flooding back – the Humber Snipe which Monty used in Normandy and from which I remember seeing him distributing cigarettes to the troops. 'Monty's known for having two Humbers during the war,' Barry said, ' "Old Faithful", which he used in the desert campaign, and the Victory car, which he used in the European campaign.' I knew that this had met with a slight accident at Mulberry harbour, and Barry confirmed that it had been dropped off the end of the pontoon while being unloaded. However, the engineer in charge of the car had it all stripped down and back together in working order within twenty-four hours, and it was some time before Monty found out that his car had taken an unplanned dip while coming ashore. They have searched far and wide to find exhibits for this museum. In 1957 they came across a 1907 Standard which was being used as a chicken run in Australia at the time. This was completely restored by Standards of Australia and came to the museum in 1960.

I suppose the two things about Coventry that spring to everyone's mind are Lady Godiva's ride through the streets and the expression about sending someone to Coventry. I had never been sure about the origin of either of these, but Derek James, who bears the splendid title of Senior Keeper of Social History in the city's Herbert Museum, was able to explain both to me.

Lady Godiva's husband Leofric was the Earl of Mercia, one of the top half-dozen men in the country, and as lord of all of the Midlands he decided to impose unfair taxes on the people of Coventry. His wife didn't approve of these and threatened to ride naked through the streets unless he repealed the taxes. An interesting detail mentioned by Derek was that by threatening to ride 'naked' Lady Godiva may have actually meant naked of dress of rank, putting a slightly different gloss on the famous story. The legend of Lady Godiva is very important to Coventry, and at the turn of the seventeenth century she became a figure of great local importance, symbolising Coventry's stand against unfair taxation.

There is still some debate about why people should be 'sent to Coventry', but Derek James reckons that the most convincing argument is that during the Civil War the city was a strong Parliamentary centre, and Royalist prisoners of war held there were totally ignored by the people, who refused to speak to them and were generally fairly unpleasant, so giving rise to the time-honoured phrase.

Of course it was the Second World War which wrought such horrific changes to Coventry when the whole of the city centre was devastated by the air raid of 14 November 1940. There wasn't a single building within a mile-and-a-half radius of the centre which escaped damage, and symbolic among those destroyed was the medieval cathedral. We made two visits there on *Down Your Way*, on the second of which I sat on a bench in the old cathedral talking with the Provost, Colin Semper. I wanted to know the significance of the east end, where the altar carries a cross made of charred roof timbers and a small cross made from three medieval nails found by a soldier among the ruins, above which are the words 'Father forgive'.

'This is really all about reconciliation,' he began. 'After the air raid, my predecessor but one, Provost Howard, said, "Let there be no enmity, let there not be hatred. Let's build a more Christ-like world." And so from out of this place came a world-wide ministry of reconciliation, of crossing one another's boundaries.'

Provost Howard was actually on fire duty on the night of the air raid, but the incendiaries set fire to the roof while other bombs put the hydrants out of action, so the poor man could do nothing about the fire. However, he did manage to retrieve a beautiful silver cross and two silver candlesticks, which are used in the modern cathedral.

It came as a surprise to find that WALSALL, twenty-five miles north-west along the M6 from Coventry, has long associations with the saddlery and leather industries. As I learned, this is probably because of Walsall's position on the periphery of the Black Country with its traditional small-forge crafts of making saddlery hardware like bits, spurs and buckles. What interested me was that so much of the work here was still being done by hand.

'It doesn't change,' said Oliver Morton, the saddlery director of the firm Cliff Barnsby. 'It isn't mass produced in the way that boots and shoes are mass produced. It's still a comparatively small and intimate trade, although we sell all over the world.' The saddles they make are used for every type of horse from race horses to children's ponies, and from show jumpers to the horses of the Household Cavalry. Oliver told me that Walsall supplied the tack used in the Jameson Raid in 1895 – six or seven hundred saddles made and despatched to South Africa in a very short time. Some saddle-makers bought pianos from the proceeds of that order, he told me. I saw one colossal saddle in the works when we went on our tour, one made to fit the drum horse of the Household Cavalry. This weighed half a hundredweight, in contrast to a racing saddle of a pound and a half which I could lift with my little finger.

43 Oliver Morton watching the finishing touches being given to one of their award-winning saddles.

After being told that Willenhall now forms part of the Borough of Walsall, we couldn't miss a drive out to visit the Lock Museum, which records its history of making locks and keys. There Sarah Elsam, the curator, showed us a vast range from a reconstruction of the simple wooden locks made by the ancient Egyptians to the sophisticated locks of the present day. Interestingly, the Egyptians employed the so-called 'pin-tumbler' system in their designs, which wasn't rediscovered until Linus Yale of the famous lock firm hit on it again in the nineteenth-century.

Locks and keys have been made in Willenhall since the reign of Elizabeth I, and generations of the town's craftsmen have stooped over their vices for centuries hammering, filing, sawing and drilling. By the end of the day they must have been looking pretty hump-shaped, and Willenhall has become known locally as 'Humpshire' because of this. It is even said that a lot of the pubs had special seats to accommodate the clients' humps.

Among the unusual locks on display I spotted something called a 'bottle lock', which was described as having been 'used in Midland homes to prevent servants from stealing wine'. This was fitted with little claws which grasped the cork when the key was turned, so that no one could pull it out. Another I spotted was a 'seaman's lock', which originally secured a seaman's chest and was fitted with a bell that rang when the key was turned, to warn the owner if anyone was trying to break in. There was a combination padlock which opened when you turned the letters to spell 'Amen'. And most unlikely of all was a padlock made of leather. This seemed to be of rather dubious value, especially as its key (also made of leather) had broken across the shank. I suppose its one merit is that it neatly combines two of the principal local trades, but why it should have been made in the first place is anyone's guess.

WOLVERHAMPTON, like Walsall, has long been famous for its iron and brass foundries, as well as its lock-making. Sadly, the foundries have all but disappeared, but lock-making is still an important industry and, from talking to John Hunt, the senior research engineer at Chubb and Sons, I can understand why. Chubbs have been in the business since 1818, and the locks and safes they produce today have usually been designed in the first instance to keep out John Hunt, who must be one of the few men who goes about his lawful business trying to pick locks. Thanks to the work done by him and his team, the company have developed a number of important security features which they have incorporated into their products. That must be reassuring to their customers, and so must be the exhaustive tests they put them to. He told me that the British Standard test requires 60,000 complete cycles with the key, that institutional types of lock are tested 250,000 times from each side and really sophisticated locks like the electronically controlled door I saw are tested a million times.

I asked what was the most successful test they had carried out. 'I suppose one of the most successful was a test on fire-resisting equipment. After we had developed an internal box to fit into a standard drawer, we demonstrated it to some Scottish bankers. In this box we put a bottle of Scotch and a bowl of ice cubes as well as floppy discs and things like that. The cabinet was put into the furnace at 1100 degrees Centigrade for an hour until everything was red hot. The handles had melted off, of course, but it was fetched out, dropped thirty feet on to rubble, tipped upside down, put back into the furnace for half an hour, and then fetched out glowing red to be hosed down. When it was opened, the papers in the standard drawers were still in excellent condition and the box was taken from the special drawer up into the laboratory. When it was opened in full view of the bankers, the ice cubes were still ice.' And what of the bottle of whisky? They drank that!

Nineteenth-century Wolverhampton also threw up a notable inventor of a rather eccentric disposition, Colonel Thorneycroft, a successful ironmaster in the town. His more bizarre inventions included portable London dancing saloons, which were designed to be extended across streets from the first-floor windows of houses. He also invented a sock-warmer made from heating pipes bent into a U-shape. Not that all his inventions were in this mode – playing cards for the blind counted among some of his more worthwhile ideas.

I'm sure that for many people Herefordshire immediately brings cider to mind, and when *Down Your Way* went to BROMYARD, mid-way between Worcester and Leominster, we visited Bill Symonds at the cider mill at Stoke Lacy where his family have been in business since 1727. From him I learned that the process of cider-making is more or less the same today as it has always been; only modern machinery has introduced improved production techniques. Whereas in the past the apples used to be crushed by a stone crusher pulled by a horse, hydraulic presses are used today.

Most of the apples that go into Symonds cider come from orchards within a radius of twenty miles of Stoke Lacy. I asked Bill whether he could cross his heart and swear he could tell the difference between Herefordshire cider, Devonshire cider and that from Somerset.

'Yes, that's quite simple to an expert,' was his answer. 'Herefordshire has the finest soil in the world for producing cider. It produces a nice red drink. The other soils, like the ones in Devonshire, produce more of a whey colour.'

(The other cider areas might have something to say about that, I expect.)

'When do the apples begin to arrive from the orchards?' was my next question.

'They start to come in in the first week in October,' said Bill. 'They are what we call the sweet variety. Those apples are pressed and put into a vat on their own because they make the sweet ciders. They contain more sugar and less acid. As you go on into the season you get a later variety coming in in the middle of October, which make the medium ciders. They are a little bit sharper with a little tannin. Later on at the end of November and into the second week of December come the late varieties of apples. They contain plenty of tannin, which produces the dry ciders.'

I saw one big barrel marked with the ominous-sounding name Scrumpy Jack.

'It's a very strong cider,' Bill cautioned. 'I can tell you something about Scrumpy Jack. On Easter Monday we had a fellow come in who said he wanted to take some scrumpy home because he was going to do some gardening. He said he'd take half a gallon home, saying he used to work on a farm when he was a boy and knew about scrumpy. But as he went out of the door I told him to have only two small glasses, mind. Of course, he went home, and half an hour in the garden, got a sweat on, went into the house and had two half-pint mugs. A bit later on everything went quiet. His wife went to see what was happening and found him on his back in the trench. He'd passed out!'

At least that isn't a problem when you sample MALVERN's most famous drink – water, about as pure as you can get it. The oldest records of the special properties of Malvern water go back a good 900 years. The purity of Malvern water is such that it is practically balanced between acid and alkaline; it will not change the colour of litmus paper. To prove the point I was told a delightful rhyme:

'Malvern water,' said Dr John Wall,
'Is famous for containing just nothing at all.'

It is said that whereas the Battle of Waterloo was won on the playing fields of Eton, the Battle of Britain was won on the playing fields of Malvern College, where the Royal Signals and Radar Establishment moved to develop radar at the start of the Second World War.

As it is part of the Ministry of Defence, I realised that the military work which goes on there today is not the sort of thing to be broadcast on the radio. However, there are plenty of fascinating spin-offs from radar which affect an amazing range of goods and activities in civilian life. The liquid-crystal displays that many people have in their watches are made from a material developed jointly by the Malvern establishment and Hull University. Here they also design radars for air-traffic control, laser radars which can be used to find clear-air turbulence that can be such a hazard to aircraft, but which can also play an important part in detecting the early stages of blindness.

I was impressed to hear that the silicon chip was first proposed as a concept by a member of the Malvern establishment. In the development of infra-red technology there were six or seven major inventions which made thermal imaging possible, all but one of which were made at Malvern. Among the many important developments from this research was one that greatly amused me.

In the course of developing infra-red technology the Malvern scientists were particularly interested in producing a hard infra-red optical coating. In the fullness of time such a material was produced, and one of the Malvern scientists wondered whether this might not be a better material for a durable non-stick frying pan than the coating currently in use. So in the best traditions of experimental science, he coated a frying pan with this stuff, broke an egg into it and fried it, but unfortunately found that it stuck rock solid to the pan.

The clever bit of his thinking came next, because he concluded that biological material obviously stuck to the coating and realised that in the medical area there was a particular difficulty with surgical pins which get rejected by body tissue. So by a commend-able process of lateral thought he approached the medical pro-fession with his discovery, and the upshot has been that in various areas surgical pins coated with the Malvern optical material have proved to be very useful. That's the way inventions are made.

At ROSS-ON-WYE, twenty miles down the A449 from Malvern, we came across another ingenious development which struck us as being particularly interesting. These were specialised timber structures designed and made by a company called Structaply, which were destined to provide living and working accommodation in Antarctica. If that was not challenge enough, the base they were building had to be completely self-sufficient as supply ships would only be making the journey down to the Antarctic once a year.

The model I was shown consisted of a round tube, inside which was the rectangular building itself that contained the living and working accommodation. As Graham Boyce, one of the firm's directors, told me, 'Most of the other bases in the Antarctic are located on rock, whereas this one is located on ice. This means that we have had to build a structure which can be put on the ice safely, can withstand the initial weather problems of high wind speeds and very low temperatures, and then after two or three years, as the temperature is so low down there, can withstand the pressures created as snow and ice builds up over it and buries it.'

When I asked how far down they might be buried, his answer was as much as thirty feet below the surface after five years, increasing up to sixty feet after fifteen years. That's a lot of snow and ice.

In the early stages of the installation the cylindrical structure, or the 'tube' as I referred to it, was set into a six-foot trench in the ice, to prevent it from being blown away by the 80 mph winds. The tube was cleverly made up of a series of compression rings designed so that each one could move against its neighbour. This was done, Graham said, to let the building settle without breaking, rather as a caterpillar moves over an uneven surface.

The finished size of these tubes was pretty impressive. Structaply were making four in all. Each had a diameter of thirty feet; two were a hundred feet long, the other couple about eighty feet long. The buildings inside were the same length and they comprised two-storey accommodation to make the best use of the space.

The permanent complement of the base being built was eighteen people, I was told, though the buildings were capable of supporting a lot more. I saw lounges, a bar, a surgery, sleeping accommodation and offices – all of which seemed staggering to me when I thought about eighteen people living there under the ice for up to eleven months of the year.

It was all a far cry from the gentle autumn countryside around Ross-on-Wye.

Wales

44 Caernarvon Castle, Wales.

Conwy

Dinorwig

Betws-y-Coed

Ruthin

Llangollen

Portmeirion

Borth

Tregaron

Lampeter

Newcastle Emlyn

Hay-on-Wye

Brecon

Fishguard

St David's

Carmarthen

Monmouth

Laugharne

Chepstow

Caldey
Island

Wales has always been a bit of a mystery to me. It is a land of fantasy, song, strange customs and unpronounceable place names. The Welsh are fiercely and passionately proud of their country in a way no Englishman ever shows that he is proud of England.

The Welsh relationship with England is not unlike the love–hate feelings which Australians have for Great Britain. Think of Wales and you see in your mind mountains and valleys, mine-shafts, coal tips and innumerable castles. You can hear male-voice choirs, rugby crowds singing and the bards and poets at the eisteddfods. And in spite of the inroads of mining and industry, Wales has some of the most breathtaking scenery in the United Kingdom. Breconshire is a special favourite of mine.

So it has always been an adventure to step over the border into Wales. There *is* something different about it. But the welcome is warm and friendly, and I only have happy memories of my visits. The first one was in 1927 when I went to stay with some friends near Builth Wells for a cricket match. I remember that I had to change trains at a junction with the exotic name of Three Cocks. We played the match in a permanent drizzle and at the end of the game our host proudly said how lucky we had been that the rain had held off and that we had had such a nice fine day! I must admit that whenever I go to Wales, it does seem to rain rather a lot.

A year or two later I went to stay with a friend at Chirk Castle, the first time I had ever slept inside one. It had been, and still is, a family home since the early fourteenth century. It is set on a hill surrounded by parkland and was my first experience of a stately home. I was allowed to *try* to shoot grouse on the moors.

At the end of the day round the dinner table everyone was saying what their bag for the day had been. When it was my turn I had to blushingly confess that my bag was NIL.

During the war we took our tanks by train from Warminster for shooting practice at Linney Head on the lovely Pembrokeshire coast. It was 1943 and the weather and scenery were gorgeous. The tanks were broader than the railway wagons on which they travelled. We were told that the railway people had to make sure that two trains carrying tanks never passed each other – otherwise there would have been an almighty crash.

When I joined the BBC after the war my Welsh visits became more frequent. There was cricket commentary both at Cardiff and Swansea, where on one occasion we operated with just *one* camera – nowadays they have six or eight at Test matches. But sadly I never went to a Glamorgan match at Ebbw Vale in the heart of the mining area. It is claimed that a batsman was once patting down the pitch there when he heard an answering tapping coming from *underneath* his feet!

This reminds me of the only pitch in the world – so far as I know – which has an elephant buried underneath it. We discovered this at the ground of Queen Elizabeth's College in Carmarthen – of which more presently.

One of my most outstanding memories of Wales was the day when the Barbarians beat the All Blacks at Cardiff Arms Park. The celebration went on long and noisily in the club-house after the match – so much so that a sporting quiz which we were recording there for a later broadcast was not an outstanding success. The audience, armed with pints, seemed to want to sing rather than listen to the quiz. But a packed Cardiff Arms Park, especially when the home side wins, is surely the most typical and inspirational example of the fervour and national spirit of the Welsh.

It would be wrong to leave Wales without recalling some of my many Welsh friends who have brought so much laughter, enthusiasm, exuberance and effervescence into my life. People like the much missed Wynford Vaughan-Thomas, Alun Williams, Cliff Morgan, Peter Jones, Harry Secombe and so on. They are all – or were – a joy to meet, and always bring with them a tremendous feeling of fun, laughter and friendship. What's more, they all talk more than me – which is saying something.

To my way of thinking there's nothing quite as Welsh as the eisteddfod, and it was the civilising influence of the National Eisteddfod that inspired the founders of the International Musical Eisteddfod to inaugurate their worldwide gathering in LLAN-GOLLEN in 1947. According to Nowel Bowen, the chairman of this truly international event, the founders' aim was 'to bring about a level of understanding, respect and tolerance amongst the people of the world, particularly amongst those who had been fighting one another for five long, dreary years'.

Ten countries were represented at the very first of the eisteddfods held at Llangollen, and for many years now up to thirty-four different countries have taken part from all over the world. Back in those early years immediately after the war the International Musical Eisteddfod was held in an ordinary marquee on the recreation ground. Ten years on, in 1957, the event had far outgrown that early location and the organisers had the opportunity to purchase the present-day site, a field peacefully grazed by sheep when I saw it in the middle of June. It is a steep field, ramped upwards from the stage area a distance of 75 yards to the top of the auditorium. The marquee that covers this area looks like an enormous aeroplane, and with its two wings measuring 200 feet from one side to the other it is able to hold 5–6000 seated spectators or 8–9000 if the rear seats are removed to allow people to walk about freely in fine weather.

The eisteddfod at Llangollen lasts five days, always beginning with a ballet, usually a folk ballet, from one of the visiting countries – when we were there it was the turn of the Bulgarians. The remaining days are filled from nine in the morning until five in the afternoon with competitions forming an endless chain of musical entertainment.

While the International Musical Eisteddfod may have firmly planted Llangollen on the international map in the last forty years, nearer home the town and in particular its bridge over the Dee has attracted attention for considerably longer. The bridge is unofficially listed as one of the Seven Wonders of Wales. The original was built in about 1284, with arches that have remained irregular to this day owing to the location of the rocks in the river bed on which they are sited. I noticed that the last arch on the north side is square, built that way to accommodate the railway, which came and went within a hundred years.

About a quarter of a mile up Castle Street from the bridge leading up to the canal we came across a sign advertising the premises of Charles Day, a goldsmith. Now, I remember a long time before on *Down Your Way* talking to a couple of silversmiths, but Charles was the first goldsmith we had come across. He makes rings and jewellery, trophies for the eisteddfod and probably anything else you require in that line. His gold arrives in nuggets, in sheet form, as wire or as a tube, depending on the purpose he wants to put it to.

One detail about his craft I had never understood was the carat classification – the difference between twenty-two-carat gold and nine-carat gold for example, and I asked Charles to explain it to me.

'One carat is one twenty-fourth of the quantity of metal in the alloy,' he said. 'Twenty-four-carat gold is pure gold. Eighteen-carat gold is eighteen twenty-fourths, or 75 per cent pure gold; the rest will be an alloying metal, and that will depend on the requirements of the alloy.' Pure gold is very soft, of course, which is why it isn't used to make jewellery, because it would wear too quickly. The softest gold usually used is twenty-two carat, which is used for wedding rings but little else.

We were visiting Llangollen only a few weeks before the Prince and Princess of Wales were married, and knowing that the then Lady Diana Spencer's ring was said to be made of Welsh gold, I was interested to learn exactly what that was.

'It's mined in a little mine near Dolgellau,' Charles answered, 'and the actual quality of the ore is extremely rich. South Africa will mine down to perhaps one-tenth of an ounce per ton, which is almost invisible in the ore, whereas Welsh gold can be as high as 500 ounces to the ton, which is the richest yield in the world. In fact that last batch of refinement yielded 30 ounces of gold for 200 pounds of ore, which is roughtly 300 ounces to the ton.'

Because of its scarcity and the fact that it is all hand-processed from beginning to end, Welsh gold commands a premium over worldwide gold of about 25 per cent.

Visitors to RUTHIN, sixteen miles north of Llangollen up the A525 never find themselves very far from visible evidence of the medieval world. In the centre of the town is the picturesque St Peter's Square with a number of fine late thirteenth-century timber-framed houses. I had also heard that Ruthin claims to be the only place in the world where the curfew has been rung every night at eight o'clock since the eleventh century, and this indeed proved to be the case. With the exception of the Second World War, when all bell-ringing was suspended, a night hasn't gone by when the curfew hasn't been rung from the church of St Peter's. As an interesting detail, the curfew bell also chimes the month and the date. On the night of 10 March, for instance, the bell would ring three chimes for the third month (March) and after a brief pause ten chimes to mark the day.

St Peter's itself is a lovely example of late thirteenth-century architecture, with one particularly interesting detail – the roof donated by Henry VII which contains five hundred ornately carved panels. It came as quite a surprise to learn that there is no vicar or rector of St Peter's, and that there hasn't been one since the eleventh century. In his place is the Warden, a post created by the Norman lords who built Ruthin Castle and which still remains to this day.

The Old Court House in St Peter's Square, erected in 1401, was one of the two hanging sites in Ruthin, and the old gibbet can still be seen on the side of the building (which acts as a bank today). In 1679 a Jesuit priest who was hanged, drawn and quartered was the last victim to perish here. Alongside, stands another fine timber-framed building (again a bank), which used to be used as a grandstand for the bull-baiting that took place in the square. Beneath its steps is a stone full of legendary significance in the story of King Arthur. For tradition holds that over it Arthur executed one of his rivals in love.

Rather later in history and rooted in concrete fact, as opposed to the mists of Celtic romance, is Ruthin Castle itself, which dates back to the late thirteenth century like many of the castles built in North Wales by Edward I to keep the Welsh in the hills. The only time in its history that the castle was captured was during the Civil War, when it fell to Parliamentary forces after a three-month siege. As was Oliver Cromwell's practice with the majority of the castles he captured, the walls were destroyed, and for three hundred years Ruthin Castle remained a ruin until it was rebuilt in the nineteenth century in the mock-Gothic style popular with many Victorian gentry. Until the 1920s it was a private home, after which it became a clinic of worldwide renown, remaining as such until the 1960s, when it became a private hotel and the site of today's splendid medieval banquets.

Out along the Corwen road from Ruthin we went to visit an artist who specialised in one of the most difficult media I can imagine – Patricia Evers-Swindell paints on spiders' webs! As she explained, inspiration came to her after seeing a picture near the choir stalls in Chester Cathedral which had been painted on cobwebs in the eighteenth century, and she decided to have a go herself for fun. The delicate process begins by collecting cobwebs on a cardboard frame until they form a surface firm enough to paint on. The next stage is to coat the area she wants to paint with milk. This stops the brush sticking to the cobweb and also provides a smoother surface on which to paint. Once the painting is completed, it is framed in the same way as a picture, though space is left to keep the glass away from its surface. Sometimes glass is mounted on the back as well, so that when the painting is held up to the light you can see through the cobweb and so achieve a sort of three-dimensional effect. And I must say that when I held up a picture of a dog she had painted on cobweb,

45 Patricia Evers-Swindell painting on a cobweb.

the effect was quite remarkable, even if there were the remains of a few flies and dead insects still wrapped up with the spider's threads!

From the Vale of Clwyd in which Ruthin lies a move west takes you into neighbouring Gwynedd, where we visited the mountain resort of BETWS-Y-COED situated at a point at which three rivers and five valleys meet in some of the most magnificent scenery in Snowdonia. This provides a perfect setting for the National Centre for Mountain Activities at Plas y Brennin ('The House of the King' in English, so named after a visit made by King George VI when it was a hotel in the 1930s). Since 1956 it has been a mountaineering centre offering rock-climbing, hill-walking, snow and ice-climbing, orienteering, skiing and canoeing. Visitors take courses either in one specific activity, or a general course that allows them to sample most of what the centre has to offer, depending on the season. With the snowfall being unpredictable, the winter courses are often run in Scotland. However, the artificial ski slope at Plas y Brennin is in constant use throughout the year and provides a very acceptable substitute for the real thing.

If you want to try your hand at going up mountains as opposed to coming down them, Plas y Brennin can offer indoor courses in rock-climbing which also make use of artificial surfaces. We were shown a terrifying-looking climbing wall dotted with notches and crevices where reasonably experienced climbers come to gain further experience on a 'rock face' which I'm told is fairly challenging. What amazed me is that many people brush up their technique by moving right round the room by climbing along the wall about four feet from the ground, clinging on like flies. Traversing the wall, to give this activity its proper name, is a popular pastime, partly because falling off is relatively painless at that modest height.

One detail of climbing, and a rather important one at that, which I had never fully understood is why climbers don't pull their companions down with them when they fall. To answer this Dave Walsh, the senior instructor of Plas y Brennin who acted as our guide, gave a simple account of how a climb takes place.

'The more experienced climber normally leads the climb. He ties on to the rope and the second climber ties on to the rope as well. The leader will climb a certain distance up the rock and then find a convenient ledge on which he will stand to tie himself (belay) securely to the rock. Climbers carry little mechanical devices called wedges and chocks which they insert in cracks to form anchorage points. If you've arranged these anchorage points correctly and you are unlucky enough to fall, you shouldn't fall very far before one of them stops you. The rope is made of nylon, normally 11 millimetres in diameter, measuring 150 feet long. It's very strong, having a breaking strain of about 2 tons, and it will stretch 30 or 40 per cent of its length before it snaps.'

The nightmare I think I would always have would be to fall over a ledge and have my legs dangling with nothing to grip on to. 'How would I get out of that one?' I asked.

'With some difficulty,' replied Dave. 'Unless you've practised the technique, you'd find it quite an awkward position to be in. Climbers do have quite a lot of tricks up their sleeve and they can climb ropes fairly easily once they've mastered the skill. They don't pull hand over hand up the rope – it's very difficult to do on a thin rope. But they use little knots that they tie around the rope, called prussic knots, which enable them to slide the knot up the rope and stand in a loop which grips the foot when they tread in it, and they haul themselves up in this fashion.'

Coming down into the village we passed a house which looked like a shamble of stone thrown together and was aptly named the Ugly House. Seemingly, this owed its existence to a form of squatter's rights in the area which held that if you could build a house in a day and a night and have smoke coming out of the chimney by the following morning the land on which the house stood and as far as you could throw an axe was all yours. The trick, of course, was just to build the chimney to qualify! This particular house had a story attached to it of two brothers both courting the same girl, who promised herself to whichever of them could give her a home. So one of the brothers set to and built the Ugly House in the set time, but she went and married the other one!

I noticed that several of the houses in the village have very small panes of glass, which I gathered is a result of the lack of good roads in the past. In fact, until the coming of Telford's road and his cast-iron Waterloo bridge, built in 1815, it wasn't possible to carry breakable material in wheeled transport, so only small panes of glass brought by pack animals or porters could be used in glazing.

Down at the mouth of the river Conwy in the medieval town of CONWY itself stands a house that would be well suited to the early glaziers of Betws-y-Coed. For built into the wall of one of the towers of Conwy Castle stands the smallest house in Great Britain. It is a tiny red house measuring just ten feet by six with two little rooms, one above the other. The last tenant was a man six feet three inches tall who must have found living there something of a challenge. There is a delightful tale that during the summer months he used to sleep with his feet poking out of the window to keep cool. In the floor of the downstairs room there is a hole where he kept his supply of coal, and the room still has the settle he would have sat in by the fire on winter

46 A fisherman repairing his gear outside the smallest house in Britain.

evenings. Looking up at the chimney I noticed some stones across the top of it. That is a witches' rest, I discovered, where witches used to take a breather when they were out and about on their broom-sticks. In return for this they promised that the little house would never be demolished, and although it has been under the threat of removal at least twice, it has managed to survive so far and looks set to continue so.

Altogether there are eight towers forming the defences of Conwy Castle. Construction work started in the spring of 1283 and was practically finished in four and a half years, a remarkable achievement. During the height of the building season some 1500 workmen were employed and the total cost was something in the region of £15,000! In addition to the castle, there are walls running all round the town, which was built at the same time. The town walls are about 1400 yards in overall length, rising to a height of thirty feet with twenty-two towers and three of the original gateways remaining. They lie in an interesting shape, too, resembling a Welsh harp.

In 1627 Charles I sold the castle for £100 to Lord Conwy, who later leased it out to various Conwy families on condition that whenever he visited the town he was given a dish of fish. Accordingly, when his descendant, the Marquis of Hertford, visited Conwy in 1958 he was presented with a dish of salmon by the mayor, who is also the Constable of the Castle.

We were very interested to find that Conwy was also the site of another important military construction dating from my own lifetime – the famous Mulberry harbour which played such an important part in the Normandy landings of the Second World War. This was designed and the prototype built at Conwy by a civil engineer named Joris Hughes, whose brother Sior Hughes told us about his vital contribution to the war effort. Joris had worked with Sir Owen Williams, the engineer who had invented concrete barges during the First World War, and the basis of Joris Hughes's design was also a series of concrete ships or barges, each weighing 6000 tons. These were built on the beach at Conwy by a team of local quarrymen before being towed up to the west coast of Scotland, where they underwent their sea trials. The labour force had no idea what they were building, but they must have had some fun trying to guess what use their concrete constructions would be put to. Following the successful trials of the prototypes, the main sections of the Mulberry harbour were built down on the south coast near to their final destination off the coast of Normandy. I actually drove across one in a scout car when we landed at Normandy, and it was quite a surprise to find that they floated.

I had to confess to Sior Hughes that I had never known that the prototypes had been built here, nor that they had been designed by his brother. However, the Conwy council have erected a memorial stone to record the fact, and I hope this important detail of our recent history will become more widely known as a result.

Some twenty miles over the mountains to the south-west of Conwy stands the Dinorwig Pumped Storage Electric Scheme. Six times larger than the first such hydro-electric power station in Britain, at Blaenau Ffestiniog fourteen miles away, the Dinorwig plant took ten years to complete at a cost of £450 million. Unlike most other forms of energy, electricity cannot be stored in large quantities; you have to use it as you produce it. At Dinorwig the idea is to store electricity indirectly by pumping water from a lower lake to an upper lake when there is a surplus supply, so that the water can be allowed to flow down again when there is a need for more power. A considerable amount of work had to be undertaken on both lakes before they met the power station's requirements. Some ten million tons of slate waste had to be moved from the lower lake, much of it being used to fill in old quarry holes, returning it to where it had originally come from. In the upper lake the CEGB have increased the capacity considerably, so that both the high-water and low-water levels are above the level of the original lake.

Apart from these two lakes there is little outward sign of the power station, since the majority of the workings lie inside the mountains. There the CEGB has tunnelled about ten miles in all, and some of the tunnels are large enough for two double-decker buses to pass. The underground area that caught my imagination was the surge pond that has been created to contain water rushing in at 400 tons a minute at times when the units in the power station go into action. This subterranean pond has the same surface area as Wembley Stadium!

In all there are six units in Dinorwig, the first producing electricity from the end of 1981, the others coming on stream over the next three years. The plant has apparently been designed to go from no load to 1320 megawatts of load in just ten seconds. In addition to providing this very rapid supply of electricity, Dinorwig can be used as a highly sophisticated tool to absorb surplus energy when that is available. In this way Dinorwig will be helping to maintain a constant supply of electricity in the UK by coming on or off load as demand dictates, and either pumping water into the upper lake if there is surplus power or releasing it

47 The Dinorwig Hydro-Electric Pumped Storage Power Station,
with its lower reservoir in the foreground.

to flow down again to generate electricity when there is a fresh
demand.

Unlike the Dinorwig plant, which is largely hidden from sight,
the holiday village of PORTMEIRION is an architectural feast of
colonnades, pavilions, towers, domes and statues set against a

steep wooded hillside on a lovely promontory covered with sub-tropical gardens. Portmeirion was the creation of the architect Sir Clough Williams-Ellis, who started work on the site in 1925. There are no permanent residents, but at the bottom of the village is the delightful Portmeirion Hotel, where we met Sir Clough's widow, Lady Williams-Ellis, who explained that her husband had set out to prove that you could develop a beautiful site without spoiling it. He was a conservationist, but not a conservationist who believed that you could freeze everything and never make any changes.

The site had belonged to an uncle of his who had leased it to a woman who had lived on the promontory as a complete hermit. During her stay the grounds had become so overgrown that when she died a man with an axe had to walk in front of the hearse clearing a way through the undergrowth to reach the house. In fact, Portmeirion had become so completely cut off by vegetation that in spite of living only six miles away Sir Clough had never explored it. Instead he searched all over the world, including islands off the coast of New Zealand, trying to find the right site for the creation of his architectural dream.

When he finally ventured into Portmeirion, of course, he knew immediately that he had found what he had been searching for. As a successful architect and town planner he had the vision and resources to work gradually and sympathetically at Portmeirion, blending his buildings with the natural environment. Once it was appreciated what he was doing, other sympathetic people began offering buildings that were being demolished in different parts of the country. Some, like a colonnade originally erected in Bristol and delivered to Portmeirion as numbered stones on the back of a lorry, could be accepted. Others, like the Euston Arch, were clearly too large for Sir Clough's scale and had to be politely declined. From those that were incorporated into the overall scheme, Portmeirion became affectionately known by its creator as 'a home for fallen buildings'.

Walking round, there is strong evidence of the influence that Italy had on Sir Clough – the village of Portofino, in particular. But the outdoor frescoes you see, and the use of ironwork, also suggests the important part that Bavarian architecture played in his conception.

I asked Lady Williams-Ellis whether Sir Clough was satisfied

when he had finished. Did he want Portmeirion to grow, for
instance? In reply she told me: 'What he said was, "I don't want
it to get any bigger. It's a nice agile little mouse and I don't want
it made into a great big cow." ' Well, it certainly isn't a cow, and
like most visitors before me I found it quite enchanting.

The name of Portmeirion is also well known in this country
and overseas because of the very colourful Portmeirion pottery
produced in the village. The firm was founded in 1962 by Susan
Williams-Ellis, as she then was, with its main factory sited in
Stoke-on-Trent, from where the finishing studios in Portmeirion
received the white glazed pottery ready for decoration and final
firing. Designs like the 'Botanical Garden', the 'Birds of Britain'
and 'Oranges and Lemons' have made Portmeirion pottery popular worldwide.

We went to some rather unusual places on *Down Your Way*
and seven miles north of Aberystwyth we found BORTH Bog in
the Dyfed National Nature Reserve, an expanse of a thousand
acres or so forming something I had never heard of before – a
raised bog, so called because its highest point is in the middle.
The bog is actively growing in the centre, in fact, and there the
peat reaches to a depth of over thirty feet. Dead and lifeless the
bog may appear, but once you start looking closely you find that
it is teeming with plant and animal life. I saw a heron taking off
as we arrived, and the ditches around the perimeter are favourite
haunts for teal and mallard. I had been told to look out for
dragonflies and though I didn't spot any that day, twenty species
of dragon and damsel flies have been found on Borth Bog, making
it rather an exceptional site.

There was a pleasant smell not unlike thyme near where I was
standing, which Glynn Jones, who has the marvellous title of
Assistant Regional Officer of the Nature Conservancy Council,
identified as coming from a small green shrub in front of us, the
bog myrtle. When the leaves are crushed they give off a very fine
aromatic smell, leading to their use in wardrobes for keeping
clothes fresh.

I asked about a yellow plant not far away with starlike yellow
flowers and a flattened green leaf – the bog asphodel Glynn
informed me. Its Latin name is *Narcethium ossifragum. Ossifragum* refers to brittle bones and Glynn told me that the farming
fraternity used to hold that if cattle grazed this plant their legs

would collapse. Well, he reckoned that the plant grows in habitats which are deficient in calcium. The environment of Borth Bog is indeed very acid, and it is possibly from this lack of calcium that the plant derives its name.

Another that caught my attention was the sundew, an insectivorous plant which has a round leaf with spikes and nice little glistening spots of sugary liquid at the end of its leaves. Insects are attracted to these sugary droplets, and once they are stuck fast the leaf rolls over and digests them.

On an earlier *Down Your Way* visit we had been to the nearby bog at TREGARON, fourteen miles south-east of Aberystwyth down the A485, where we met Peter Davies, who until a fortnight before had another exotic title – Warden of the Bog. When we met him he had recently become a scientific officer to the Nature Conservancy Council.

'The story of Tregaron Bog goes back about 20,000 years or so,' he told me. 'At that time Britain was covered with ice and an enormous glacier filled the Teifi valley. As it melted slowly at the end of this Ice Age it left behind great dumps of clay and boulders across the valley, and this barrier ponded up an enormous lake six or seven miles long at that time and perhaps two miles wide. The bog is the result of this original glacial lake gradually silting up and growing over with vegetation.'

For the last three hundred years the bog has been preserved as a sporting area for duck shooting, which has protected it from the process of drainage that has removed so many of the original bogs from the British Isles. The nature reserve which occupies most of the bog today is about five miles long by a mile and a half wide. Like Borth Bog, the main area is really just a large deposit of peat about twenty-seven feet thick. From a scientific point of view this is a fascinating time capsule: the peat pickles all the plants that grew in it, so that if you dig a hole down through it and look at the lowest layers you are seeing recognisable plants which actually grew there 6000 years ago. Present-day plant life includes three species of sundew, which we learnt about at Borth Bog. There are several types of orchids and a group of rare mosses including one called *Sphagnum balticum* which is only found at three other sites in the UK.

Tregaron Bog is rich in bird life as well. There is a large duck population. In winter a flock of Hooper swans migrate south from

Iceland. And the red kite, a bird of prey with a wing span of five feet, glides over the bog in search of mammals like mice and voles and sometimes larger ones such as otters and polecats.

We came across wood-carving of a distinctly Welsh variety in LAMPETER, eleven miles down the Teifi valley from Tregaron. Here Stan Watkins, who retired from teaching because of a weak chest and consequently had to give up turning wood on a lathe, had tried his hand at carving – specialising in love spoons in particular. One he showed me, carved from a light wood, had a handle with two little cavities containing what looked like tiny wooden marbles inside them, and at the end was a chain with a locket.

Love spoons like this used to be given in much the same way as gold and jewellery are given today. The greater the skill of the suitor's carving and decoration, the greater his love was reckoned to be. The two little marbles, I gathered, were an indication that the would-be husband was hoping for two children; three wooden marbles implied three children, and so on. These spoons seem to be unique in Wales. There has been mention of some form of Scandinavian connection, but Stan hadn't found any evidence for this in his investigations. The spoons date from the end of the seventeenth century and apparently gave rise to the word 'spooning', which was something I never knew.

I learnt the origins of another common expression during a tour of the water mill at Felin Geri, two miles outside NEWCASTLE EMLYN, twenty miles from Lampeter down the river Teifi. Among the pieces of milling equipment, I was shown an American machine dating from 1872 which was used for sifting and grading the grains when they arrived at the mill. This was called a Temse, and Michael Heycock, the partner who showed us over the mill, explained that it was this machine which gave rise to the saying that 'a lazy man will never never set the Temse on fire'. You worked the machine by shaking it backwards and forwards, and presumably if you worked it hard enough and fast enough the friction caused could build up quite a temperature.

The grinding stones interested me too. These had been installed round about the 1870s, when the equipment had last been given a major overhaul. They came from France, where the best milling stones were quarried from freshwater quartzite at a quarry south of Paris. Even in those days they would have cost £200. The gap between them sounded astonishingly fine. The old miller's rule held that the space between the stones at the centre, or eye, where the grain enters, should be the thickness of brown paper. At the edge, where the flour emerges, the gap should be tissue-paper thick.

Milling has to be a slow process, I was told, because the faster you mill, the more heat you generate. And since heat destroys the wheatgerm which gives flour its flavour, you lose much of the taste from milling it too quickly. Wheatgerm also has the highest concentration of vitamin E, Michael Heycock told me. So at Felin Geri they ground about 300 pounds of flour an hour.

Today the port of FISHGUARD, twenty-three miles west of Newcastle Emlyn is an important ferry link to Southern Ireland; two hundred years ago, when Britain was at war with America and later France, both adversaries hoped that it might be a key point in their campaigns. The Americans came first in the form of the infamous John Paul Jones, the founder of the American navy. During the American War of Independence he was wandering the Irish Sea causing trouble, in the course of which his ship fired a shot over Fishguard. The shell exploded and the traders of the town were forced to pay a ransom of five hundred pounds. Vowing that this would never happen again, they raised a subscription to build the fort. This fired only one shot in anger during its history, during the celebrated invasion of 1797.

Again there was an American involved in this escapade – William Tait, a general of Irish descent, who led a French army of 1400 in a landing near Fishguard, hoping that the disaffected Welsh would rise against their English oppressors. Unfortunately for him, the good people of Fishguard had other ideas. One shot from the fort scared off three French warships, and the women of Fishguard, led by Jemmy Nicholas, whose gravestone can be seen by the church railings, gathered on the heights above the town to march down on the invading troops. Looking up from the sands the French soldiers saw the advancing mass of figures in tall black hats and red petticoats, apparently mistook them for a battalion of British redcoats and promptly surrendered to a man.

Whatever truth there is in this story, there can be no denying that the Pembrokeshire Yeomanry were awarded a unique honour for their action at Fishguard. They still carry the name on their standard, and as such it is the only battle honour ever awarded to a British regiment for an engagement fought on British soil. This ignominious French campaign was also the last foreign invasion of Britain.

In the Globe Inn in Fishguard's main street we came across another unusual story from the last war. Leaning on the bar was George Taylor, a regular at the Globe who had served in the navy during the war and was bombed off Tobruk in a Stuka attack on HMS *Zulu*. Thirty years later he moved to Fishguard and in the course of a pint in the Globe started talking to Heinz Kersling, one of the joint landlords. Heinz had served in the Luftwaffe, and in their exchange of reminiscences happened to mention that he had attacked a destroyer off Tobruk in September 1942 – none other than the *Zulu*! George admitted that he was a good shot too, dropping his bomb right down the ship's funnel into the engine-room – mind you, that's what the Luftwaffe no doubt expected from a pilot who holds a decoration as distinguished as the Knights' Cross with oak leaves. Heinz was presented with this by Adolf Hitler himself, but thirty years on it was marvellous to see that he and George were the very best of friends.

At the western extremity of Wales, close to the St David's Head mentioned in the regular shipping forecasts, lies the city of ST DAVID'S itself, probably the smallest city in the world with its population of 1700, but a city none the less by virtue of its magnificient cathedral. Standing in the centre of St David's in Cross Square, by the old market cross, you can only see the 116-foot tower of the cathedral. It is only by walking down a steep narrow street through one of the old city gates that you suddenly come across the cathedral nestling snugly a hundred feet down in a deep dell, with steep grassy wooded slopes forming a unique site for any cathedral.

The present cathedral is the third building on the site, all of which have acted as shrines to St David himself, the patron saint of Wales, whose own monastery stood here in the sixth century. If you go inside the cathedral and look down the nave you will notice that it slopes from west to east and the pillars down the sides appear to be sloping backwards. In fact they *are* leaning backwards. They are twelve inches out of the perpendicular, but no one is terribly concerned since they have been like this for hundreds of years. As for the slope, the floor of the Lady Chapel at one end of the nave is at the same level as the top of the west door at the opposite end, a height of ten feet.

In addition to the shrine to St David, the cathedral also contains Abraham's Stone, which is kept safely out of harm's way in the wall of the south transept because of its historical significance. The stone records that when the cathedral was burned down by the Danes, the raiders killed Bishop Abraham and his two *sons*. The fact that the bishop was not celibate is an important key to the history of Christianity in this part of Wales, according to the Dean, the Very Reverend Lawrence Bowen, confirming that it was Celtic in origin and not Roman.

48 St David's Cathedral.

St David's is also the only cathedral in the country in which the reigning sovereign is automatically a member of the chapter. This unique state of affairs dates back to the reign of Henry VIII and his Dissolution of the Monasteries and their associated foundations. Among those under threat was the cathedral school in St David's. The headmaster was himself a member of the chapter and he suggested that if the King was also made a member, he might not carry out his threat to dissolve the school. So Henry VIII was made a canon, though it did not prevent him from carrying out his threat. However, the royal stall has been in the cathedral ever since.

Around the coast, off the western shore of Carmarthen Bay, there is another site of great religious significance – the monastery on CALDEY ISLAND. The first monks settled there in the sixth century, and today fifteen Cistercian monks live and work there permanently, aided by visiting monks from other monasteries and lay workers who help during the busy tourist season. It is very much a tradition of the order that each monastery has to be self-supporting, and the community of Caldey is no exception. Like most monastic communities this has a farm, though like most of the others, too, it no longer produces sufficient income to sustain the community. So the monks have to direct their talents to other enterprises, and on Caldey Island the monks run a perfumery, using local flowers in scented sachets and in some of the oils from which the perfumes are made, blending these with imported materials. As another sideline the monks also make delicious chocolate.

Unlike most working people, they begin their day at 3.15 in the morning, with the first of seven religious services around which their daily routine is structured. I wondered if they ever had the chance to relax and enjoy any sort of sport, and I was delighted to hear that a cricket match is played every summer between the islanders and the monks – which the monks usually win in spite of their age, the youngest being in his forties!

The post office is one of the interesting features on the island, especially in winter when the mail has sometimes to be stamped 'Delayed by rough seas'. You can get Caldey Island stamps too, not that they are legal tender; you have to add a GPO stamp to have them carried by the Royal Mail.

Laver bread is a delicacy specifically associated with this part of Wales and in LAUGHARNE, which lies on the estuary of the river Taf, to the north-east of Tenby, we met Elliot James, who makes part of his living collecting the seaweed from which laver bread is made. To be honest the laver bread served in our hotel looked more like mince than bread, but Elliot told me that it is a traditional breakfast dish in Wales, served with bacon or a sausage, or anything else that takes your fancy in the frying pan. The seaweed itself is much smoother than the sort of coarse weed I am used to seeing when I visit the coast and, as Elliot told me, it is a weed that is quite distinct from any other. It is also scarce, and you have to travel a long way to find it. It is seasonal, too, only growing from March until the end of October.

In addition to gathering laver weed, Elliot James is also the last licensed cockle-gatherer in Laugharne and these two occupations have him working round the clock following the tides to catch low water, whether it comes in the middle of the normal working day, or at two o'clock on a bitter winter morning. Raking and sieving the sand to gather a hundredweight of cockles is jolly hard work, judging by his description, and I wasn't surprised that he was the only licensed gatherer left. I assumed that he must work by artificial light at night, but Elliot reckoned that the water provided its own illumination, making it twice as light on the sands as inland. He also told me that a trained ear can hear the cockles singing – especially on a spring morning!

For many visitors Laugharne's greatest attraction lies in its association with Dylan Thomas, who spent the last five years of

49   Dylan Thomas's boathouse at Laugharne.

his short life in the boathouse below the cliffs. Walking to this
little whitewashed house, you pass the small work-shed where
he spent the most prolific period of his life, writing some of his
most famous works including *Under Milk Wood*. The views from
this little hut and from the house are breathtaking, and now that
both are owned by the local authority visitors are able to attend
poetry readings on the patio on summer evenings, enjoying the
scenery which gave Dylan Thomas himself inspiration and reliv-
ing his life in Laugharne through his verse. Dylan Thomas died
in America when he was only thirty-nine, and his body was
brought back to Laugharne to be buried in St John's churchyard,
marked by a simple wooden cross that overlooks the estuary
where the herons he used to watch and write about can be seen
on most days walking across the sands at low water.

On the river Tywi in nearby CARMARTHEN I had a fascinating
introduction to the ancient art of catching salmon from coracles.
Present-day coracles are made of fibreglass, and modern nets are
spun from nylon, but in their design both reflect the traditional
craft and gear used for centuries by coracle fishermen in this part
of Wales.

Originally the cow played an important part in coracle fishing.
Its hide was stretched over a framework of ash laths to form the
skin of the coracle, its fat waterproofed this, the cow's horns were
cut into rings at the top of the net, and its tail was used to make
ropes to which the net was attached.

Although the materials may have changed with the advance of
time, the method of fishing remains unaltered. The coracle men
work in pairs, drifting down-river on the ebb tide with their
thirty-three-foot net stretched between them and trawling the
bottom eighteen inches of the river.

Coracles are individually made to suit their users, but generally
they are a little under three and a half feet wide and five and a
half feet long. They are shaped like halves of chocolate Easter
eggs (paddled blunt end first and moved sideways on to the
current), and even with only one seat across the centre looked
incredibly unstable to me. In skilled hands it is a different story.
These little boats are so manoeuvrable that a coracle man can
hold the net with a twenty-five-pound salmon struggling in it
with one hand and paddle his boat with the other.

There are certain limitations to fishing in this way. For one thing, it is very unusual to catch more than one salmon at a time because the fish get so entangled in the light net. Most of the fishing is also done at night, even though the men are licensed to fish the river on any tide and at any hour. It is not surprising, then, that there are just a dozen coracle pairs fishing the Tywi today, in marked contrast to the time when Carmarthen was an important fishing centre employing as many as two thousand men as both fishermen and suppliers of their equipment: the farmers who bred the cattle and grew the flax and the workers in the rope works which turned this into net yarn. Yet in spite of this decline, the coracle fishermen in present-day Carmarthen are still able to maintain a traditional industry followed by their forefathers for centuries.

50 Coracle fishing.

There is one feature about Carmarthen which I know I am hardly likely to forget, and that is the elephant which is supposed to be buried beneath the cricket pitch of the Queen Elizabeth Grammar School! The playing field, known as the Prisoners'

Field, was given to the school by the gaol authorities, but at some time in its history it also played host to a visiting circus, one of whose elephants died during the Carmarthen stop-over and was buried under what is now the square. No one has ever found any trace of it, but I gather that the difficulties they have in creating a decent wicket seem to confirm its presence.

Ben Brown, landlord of the Five Alls pub in CHEPSTOW, was someone else with long experience of the waters around the Welsh coast – though not in coracles, I hasten to add. After serving in the Merchant Navy he became skipper of the *Severn Queen*, one of the Aust ferry-boats which used to carry vehicles and passengers across the river before the Severn Bridge was built in the mid-1960s. On the wall of the pub there is a photograph of the ferry going through some very rough water which I had never associated with the Severn, but Ben told me that on occasions when a strong south-westerly wind met an ebb tide the service might have to be suspended for the day because the conditions were too rough. He told me it wasn't unusual to see people made seasick even in that short crossing.

The ferries stopped running the day the bridge opened, on 8 September 1966, but by that time Ben had turned his hand to running a pub. Its name interested me – I hadn't come across a Five Alls before – but he said that there are at least three others in the country: in Chippenham, Marlborough and Cheltenham. The sign over his entrance outside explains the name. There is a picture of a soldier ('I fight for all'), a parson ('I pray for all'), a king ('I rule all'), a lawyer ('I plead for all') and the last one is John Bull holding two large money bags ('I pay for all'). The last used to be a spade with the caption 'The grave-digger digs for all', but that was a bit too morbid, so John Bull was introduced instead.

Up the river Wye from Chepstow in the town of MONMOUTH, you come across a rather unexpected museum devoted to Nelson – unexpected to me at least because I didn't know that he had any connection with the town. However, Andrew Helme, the museum's curator, explained that Nelson made a couple of visits to Monmouth one year, most probably to see the naval temple built on a hill outside the town – at that time the only naval war memorial in the country. Today the temple belongs to the National Trust and is open to the public. The nearby Forest of Dean was also an important source of ship-building materials, and Nelson wanted to see what the stock of timber looked like. He couldn't have thought very much of it because he wrote a scathing report afterwards.

The museum's collection really began to be amassed in the early years of this century after the centenary of the battle of Trafalgar, and dozens of mementos from Nelson's life are to be seen. There are interesting details about his appearance from the many pictures of him. For instance, he is often thought of as wearing a patch over his right eye, but in fact he never lost this eye. The wood splinter that blinded him at Calvi detached his retina, but the eye was never removed. Nelson was a small man, between five feet three and five feet four and a half, and his height is marked on one of the museum's cases for children to measure themselves against. After losing his right arm at Tenerife he had difficulty in drawing his sword from its scabbard and in the museum you can see his service sword, the only genuine fighting sword of his that exists, which has had six inches cut off the end to make it easier for him to draw with his left arm.

Following his death the Nelson myth really took off, and hundreds of forgeries were produced to satisfy the demand for Nelson relics and memorabilia. There is a case in the museum marked forgeries containing some of these, including his 'glass' eye, which of course he never actually owned. Lady Llangattock, who lived near the town and began the collection in Monmouth, actually commissioned several of these fake pieces which helped to attract people to the museum, but the majority of her finds, including many of the letters, are genuinely associated with Nelson. I was fascinated to hear that her son, the Honourable Charles Rolls, was the Rolls of Rolls-Royce fame. He was also a pioneer aviator and was the first pilot to be killed in a flying accident in Britain when he crashed near Bournemouth in the summer of 1910; a monument to him stands outside the Shire Hall in Monmouth.

Over the hills and up the Usk valley in the town of BRECON, one of the first attractions to catch a visitor's eye is the museum of the 24th Regiment South Wales Borderers, the Royal Regiment of Wales. It is a fabulous military museum, with the usual collection of flags and other soldiering paraphernalia, and it has got a number of unique elements which make it doubly worth visiting.

One of these is a cabinet full of Victoria Crosses. The regiment won a total of twenty-three VCs, which ranks it among the leading VC-holders of line regiments. Five were won in unique circumstances at the Andaman Islands in the Indian Ocean in 1867, when they were awarded for a feat of life-saving that didn't involve engaging the enemy. Gary Marshall, who looks after the museum, elaborated on the rather unusual chain of events.

Apparently a ship had been lost off the Andaman Islands, and a second Royal Navy ship with a detachment of the 24th aboard were sent to investigate what had happened. A small navy unit landed on one of the islands and was immediately attacked by the islanders. At the same time a hurricane blew up which made a rescue virtually impossible. However, Surgeon Douglas of the 24th and four other men immediately volunteered to take a skiff to see if they could reach the beleaguered sailors. Against all odds they did manage to reach land and return with the stranded shore party, for which they each received the coveted decoration.

Zululand also played an important part in the regiment's history. Two VCs were won at the battle of Isandhlwana in January 1879 and seven in the famous defence of Rorke's Drift a few days later.

The Zulu room in the museum also contains the bullet-holed Union Jack which flew over Rorke's Drift, brought back from the campaign by one Private Evan Jones of Welshpool. On the centenary of the battle his great-great-granddaughter, the Miss Jones who was a former Miss Wales and Miss United Kingdom, presented it to the museum.

There is another Union flag on display here with more recent historical connections. This was the first ever to be flown over Greater Berlin, and was presented by a former brigadier in the regiment.

If you are motoring through this part of Wales and happen to be keen on books, sixteen miles to the north-east of Brecon lies HAY-ON-WYE, a Mecca for book enthusiasts the world over and the only town in the world with secondhand books as its major industry. Richard Booth, who has masterminded the trade in Hay, told me that his shops stock in the region of a million books on a total of fifteen miles of shelves. To my surprise he said that his principal source is the east coast of the USA, which he visits half a dozen times a year to buy stock. By the same token American visitors form a substantial portion of his trade, so many of the books find their way back to the States from Hay.

In amongst this vast range of stock there are still real treasures to be found by the canny searcher. Richard cheerfully admitted that his shops frequently sell books for a few pounds which are later sold in auction rooms for several hundred pounds. He quoted the case of a book of old Canadian letters found in a dustbin which was sold in Hay for a pound or two and later made five hundred in a saleroom. Someone else found a James Joyce manuscript in an old grammar which they bought for a pound in Hay and sold for £1500 at auction. As Richard Booth admitted, 'I'm afraid that in the secondhand book business the customer's much cleverer than we are.'

I asked why he had chosen Hay, miles from anywhere. 'I think it's very important that somewhere in the world there's one town where the bookshops are bigger than the supermarkets,' he answered. 'In a way Hay's got a bigger market than London: it's got the whole of the South-West and Bristol, and the whole of the Midlands and Birmingham, and buyers have a beautiful drive of an hour and a half over the Welsh hills to come to the book town.'

I must say I can't think of a more pleasant way of hunting for secondhand books.

The North Midlands

51 Chatsworth House, Derbyshire.

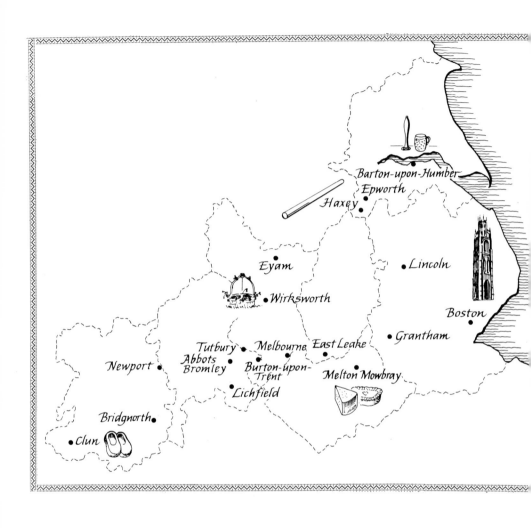

Barton-upon-Humber
Epworth
Haxey
Eyam
Wirksworth
Lincoln
Boston
Tutbury
Abbots
Bromley
Melbourne
East Leake
Grantham
Newport
Burton-upon-Trent
Melton Mowbray
Lichfield
Bridgnorth
Clun

Shropshire is a beautiful county and said to have been the spot which P. G. Wodehouse chose for Blandings Castle. I have personal reasons for liking it. My daughter-in-law's family live there and we had a delightful country wedding in July 1986. My youngest daughter spent three very happy and productive years at Derwen College for the Disabled just outside Oswestry. I cannot speak too highly of what they did for her and it was always a pleasure to find an excuse to visit her – especially as there is now a motorway to Shrewsbury instead of the narrow, crowded A5.

Shrewsbury is one of the most attractive county towns in Britain, with the river Severn, views of the Wrekin and lovely old black and white timbered buildings.

Staffordshire to me means pottery, especially the Toby Jugs and those lovely blue and white mugs with top-hatted cricketers on the side. I also owned one-tenth of a horse, which was trained by Reg Hollingshead at his training stables at Rugeley. I was part of a syndicate of cricketers and as the sire of the horse was Grey Mirage we named our horse W. G. Greys. It actually won once or twice.

My first visit to Stafford was during the war, when as a technical adjutant I was sent up to English Electric, who were then making the Covenanter and Crusader tanks which we were using. I was told a story about their new PRO who shall remain nameless, as he has since denied the story. Anyway, he was on a short list for selection as PRO, and there was to be a final appearance before the Board in which applicants would be required to make a short speech to prove that they could speak well. Much would depend on their clarity and delivery. Just before it was his turn to go into the boardroom he went to spend a penny, and thought he would give a final clean to his false teeth. So he took them out, but he was so nervous that he dropped them down the loo. He only had a minute or so before he was due. So what could he do? What would you have done? All I can say is that no one knows what he *did* do, but he passed the test and got the job!

A final memory of Staffordshire is of the old lady of eighty-three in Penkridge who was still doing a daily milk-round when I interviewed her. But even more remarkable was the fact that she had slept *every night* of her life in the same house where she still lived. She had been on day trips to Great Yarmouth and London, but she had always come back home every night to sleep in the same house.

I always think that Derbyshire offers more variety than any other county. There is the spectacular scenery of the Peak District National Park, the peaceful beauty of the Dales of Darley and Dove, the river valleys, the cliffs of Matlock, the caves and potholes of Castleton, the Blue John stone which makes such fine jewellery, the stately homes, the crooked spire of Chesterfield, Bakewell tarts and the busy industrialism of Derby itself.

The spa town of Buxton will always be famous in the cricket world. In the long hot summer of 1975 the county match against Lancashire was stopped by a snowstorm on 2 June!

I have fond memories of one of the best and most beautiful cricket grounds in England – Queen's Park, Chesterfield. I'm not so fond of the old race course ground at Derby, though it has been much improved recently, but on a cold day it can be distinctly draughty! We all know the old story of the horse which went automatically to the roller when the number eleven batsman went in to bat. But at Derby it is more up to date. The groundsman actually starts up the engine on the roller, and sits there waiting – usually not for long.

I have always had a special liking for the city of Nottingham. It's a vibrant place full of life, and contains so much in the way of entertainment, sport, education and industry. Like most boys I first got to hear of it from the Robin Hood legend, where the Sheriff of Nottingham was a particularly nasty 'baddy'. There is still a Sheriff. I met him recently and am glad to report that he bears no resemblance in character to his predecessor.

My first real acquaintance with the city came in 1950 when,

because the transmitter at Sutton Coldfield had just opened, BBC TV were able for the first time to cover a Test match at Trent Bridge. I remember it well. It was against that great West Indies side, with Ramadhin and Valentine causing so much havoc with their contrasting spin. West Indies had just won their first ever Test match in England at Lord's, where there were the famous scenes of calypso singing and dancing in front of the Pavilion. Now again at Trent Bridge they won easily thanks largely to a magnificent partnership of 283 in 210 minutes by Weekes and Worrell. Norman Yardley was captain of England, and when the stand had reached over 200 I said on TV, 'I wonder what Norman Yardley is going to do to stop this flow of runs. Let's have a look at him, he's standing at mid-on.' The camera panned on to him, and unfortunately at the particular moment he was scratching himself in a rather awkward place! The camera swung swiftly away from him as I murmured, 'Obviously it's a very ticklish problem!'

After Lord's, which is something special, Trent Bridge has always been my favourite Test ground. It is a friendly place with a warm welcome for everyone, and as it is so compact one has the feeling of being in the game among the players. Its famous landmark, Parr's Tree, is now, alas, no more, being the victim of a gale. It was chopped up and made into little miniature cricket bats, which were sold for charity.

I mustn't forget the rest of the city, with its theatres the Playhouse and the Theatre Royal, the two football league clubs both adjacent to Trent Bridge, the rowing on the Trent and the racecourse. Truly a city of variety.

And just one last memory of Nottinghamshire. When we visited Radcliffe-on-Trent we went to the home of a lovely old lady – Mrs Emily Brewster. She had just celebrated her hundredth birthday. I asked her if she had had a happy day. 'Yes', she said, 'I had a lovely party.' 'Did you' I asked, 'get a telegram from the Queen?' 'Oh yes,' she replied, 'but I was a bit disappointed – it wasn't in her own handwriting!'

Along with its cricket and *Down Your Way* connections, Leicestershire brings to my mind magnificent hunting country and Glorious Stilton cheese. When travelling in a train through Leicestershire I often look out of the window and imagine myself following one of their famous packs of hounds. It's fun to pick the spots where I would try to jump the fences, and, being in the safety of a railway carriage and not in the saddle, I usually choose the most terrifying of jumps.

Until my sister went to live in Lincolnshire I thought that it was all flat, but I found her house right on the edge of a high windy escarpment looking down on the city and a wide fertile valley. Of course most of Lincolnshire *is* flat, with long straight roads and ditches and canals. Much of it is only just above sea-level, and over the years a wonderful job of drainage has been carried out. There are acres and acres of rich dark soil ideal for agriculture and horticulture. Sugar beet, potatoes, peas, vegetables of every kind, flowers (especially tulips), and fruit – I associate them all with Lincolshire. And I must not forget the many airfields, especially Scampton, once the base for the famous Dambusters and now the headquarters for the Red Arrows – the best aerobatic and formation team in the world.

In contrast to the fens is the wooded spa town of Woodhall Spa, strangely continental in appearance with its tree-lined roads. I used to stay there during the weekends of Trent Bridge Test matches and was particularly struck by the cinema *in the woods* – the only one I know so situated.

The coast-line offers another contrast, with Grimsby in the north and a number of holiday resorts to the south, such as Cleethorpes, Mabelthorpe and Skegness. They certainly live up to their reputation of being 'bracing', and I always pack a sweater whenever I go there.

Lincolnshire is one of the largest counties in England and you will probably see more windmills there than anywhere else. You get the impression of the Dutch influence wherever you go, and when you turn right off the A1 it is the beginning of a journey into a very different part of England.

During the border troubles which flared up all through the Welsh Marches in the Middle Ages, towns like CLUN in Shropshire had a pretty turbulent time. Today, however, Clun is a very quiet and remote agricultural community tucked away in the south-west corner of Shropshire. To the west, running up to the Welsh border, is the old hunting ground of Clun Forest, an area of heather-clad hills which gives its name to the popular breed of Clun forest sheep. You will find woodlands around Clun, but these form part of the larger area known as Mortimer Forest, which straddles the boundaries of Shropshire and Herefordshire and crosses the border into Powys. Here the Forestry Commission grow Douglas fir and larches, the high-yielding species which are ideally suited to the local soil and produce twenty tons of timber per hectare per annum.

In days gone by local timber, maybe oak or beech, was used to make the distinctive upright Clun chair which has now become a popular collector's item because so few have been preserved. Clog-making was another local industry which once thrived here as the almost exclusive preserve of the Lunn family, in fact the last of the Lunn cloggers had died only a few months before we visited Clun. They used alder to carve their clogs, setting up camp beside the river bank where they would fell a tree and cut the trunk into various lengths to suit clogs of different sizes.

Split hazel was another wood with a specific use in this rural area. This was woven into what are known locally as 'whisket' baskets, sturdy containers used to carry cattle feed out to stock in the fields, each holding the best part of half a hundredweight of mashed swedes.

Set alongside these traditionally robust rural crafts, it came as quite a surprise to find a violin-repairer tucked away in Clun, but Ralph Greiphan set up in business in the village in 1975, undertaking repairs for a large firm of musical-instrument specialists in London. Violin woods, he explained to me, were mainly derived from the mountainous regions of Europe. Maple is traditionally used to form the back of the violin and the instrument's neck, where it is inlaid with ebony. The thinner wood at the front of most violins tends to be spruce. The bulk of Ralph's work is concentrated in the restoration and repair of old instruments: cleaning and mending cracks, filling and colouring his and earlier repairs and carefully revarnishing the instrument to restore it to mint condition. However, he also makes instruments as a hobby and showed us a viola he was working on – the fruit of a month's labour, if his restoration work allowed him to spend time on it continuously.

Two miles outside NEWPORT in Shropshire we visited one of the most unusual establishments that I ever went to on *Down Your Way*. This was the National Foaling Bank at Meretown Stud, a unique equine adoption service, the only one of its kind in the

world and the inspiration of Miss Joanna Vardon who runs it.
Here she and her team provide a twenty-four-hour service for
breeders, helping them find replacements for dead foals or blood
mares. The service was in its eleventh season when we went to
Newport, and during its first ten years 5000 adoptions had been
successfully made. The ratio of lost foals to mares is about three
to one, Miss Vardon told me, which makes her task marginally
easier. In most cases both the orphaned foal and the brood mare
who has lost her own foal are brought to the National Foaling
Bank for the process of adoption to take place. Apparently a mare
will only accept a foal on smell, so in order to deceive her into
adopting an orphan, it has to have the dead foal's skin draped

52 Chatting to Joanna Vardon and friend at Meretown Stud.

over it for the first forty-eight hours of their time together. After
two days the mare's milk will have passed right through the
orphan foal naturally giving it her own smell. With luck this
makes it indistinguishable from the foal she has lost.

Foals arrive at Meretown from all over the country at any time of the day and night and in any manner of vehicle. Not long before our visit a Shire foal turned up on the back seat of a Mini! Sometimes it is possible to put the owners of an orphaned foal and foalless brood mare in contact without the need for them to come all the way to Newport. Miss Vardon's greatest coup had been to put two owners who lived only a couple of miles apart in touch with each other when neither knew that the other was in trouble and needed swift help.

In Beaumaris Road, Newport, we came across another first for me – a firm that specialises in making feathered flights for darts. To my untutored eye the flights seemed to be little bits of wood about an inch long to which four bits of feather were glued – technically, I was told, they are called 'wings'. All around the factory I saw sacks filled with large feathers which had come from turkeys bred in America; apparently the average American bird is twice the weight of the ones we breed in Britain, so their feathers are correspondingly larger and firmer.

Roughly 250,000 flights were despatched from the factory every week. A certain amount were sold in threes to be used as replacement flights for existing sets of darts, and the rest went to the company's factory in St Albans, where complete sets were assembled.

At the time of our visit they had just launched a new flight on to the market called the 'springback'. This had been designed with a small spring at the base of the flight which made it flexible and allowed players to get better groupings on a board than they could with the conventional rigid flights.

Dart flights from Newport were being exported all over the world and even into outer space; the factory provided flights for one group of American astronauts who whiled away free time in their capsule by playing darts, though the ones they threw were fitted with rubber suckers in place of steel points.

A visit to BRIDGNORTH, down in the south-east corner of Shropshire, is a real feast day for railway enthusiasts, and on *Down Your Way* we used to find it very difficult to resist anything to do with steam engines. So we were delighted to find the Severn Valley Railway alive and well and still running, despite railway nationalisation and the cuts made to British rail services by Dr Beeching. This is a private railway run almost totally by volunteers, who man the locomotives, sell the tickets, clean the carriages, work the signals, and carry out most of the maintenance and repairs to the permanent way as well as the rolling stock. In addition there is a small core of full-time staff who perform the essential administration and commercial functions. Together they operate over twelve and a half miles of track between Bridgnorth and Bewdley, where the line is connected to the British Rail network at Kidderminster.

Here we found a fleet of thirty-four locomotives, nearly half of which are operational at peak times in the season. These cover all types and classes from 4-6-0s down to tiny little shunting engines. I wondered if they had any of the old Great Western King class locos, the biggest and the best. But as Michael Draper, the General Manager, told me, they couldn't get a 'King' over the bridge.

The service concentrated on major holiday periods and bank holidays, as you would expect, and on the Severn Valley Railway you can even treat yourself to a 'Father Christmas Special' or a 'Mince Pie Special' at Christmas. To take care of the inner man at other times of the year you will find a buffet car on every train, and pride of the operation is the Severn Valley Limited Wine and Dine Train which offers a first-class four-course meal in the hour it takes to travel from one end of the line to the other. My eyes lit up at the thought of this very agreeable way of passing a journey through such lovely countryside.

There is another railway in Bridgnorth which brings passengers up from the Low Town on the eastern bank of the Severn to the High Town on the western bank. This is a cliff railway, rising 111 feet up a very steep incline. In fact the total length of the rail is only 201 feet, which makes it the shortest and steepest funicular railway in the country. Before it was built, the only means of transporting goods from the busy river port below was by the Cart Way, up which donkeys used to plod with packs on their backs.

Back in the Middle Ages there used to be a castle at Bridgnorth dating from the eleventh century. But Oliver Cromwell captured this during the Civil War and blew it to pieces. All that is left today is one tower which stands two hundred feet high and leans at a precarious angle of seventeen degrees – considerably more than the Leaning Tower of Pisa!

Among the industrial centres of the Midlands the city of LICHFIELD is something of an oasis of peace and tranquillity, owing in good measure to its lovely 1300-year-old cathedral with its three distinctive spires known as 'the Ladies of the Vale'.

Lichfield is a city which saw a lot of fighting during the Civil War, and of course it was the birthplace of that towering eighteenth-century figure Dr Samuel Johnson. Johnson is famous for his great dictionary, a work which took a decade to compile and a copy of which can be seen in his old home. But we came across a brand new but equally valuable dictionary of the English language being written in his home town. This work was being undertaken at the Maple Hayes School for Dyslexics, a mile or so outside Lichfield, where children with dyslexia go for special education to help improve their reading and writing difficulties. Dr Neville Brown, the principal, and his research team have devised a revolutionary method of teaching dyslexics which they reckon puts them at the forefront of this special education.

The method sounds rather complicated at first hearing but consists of dividing up words into groups of letters which are marked by special signs referred to as 'icons'. I gave Dr Brown the word 'construction' as an example, and asked how that would be divided up.

'First of all, we wouldn't divide it up into syllables,' he began. 'The "con" happens to be a syllable, but what we're more interested in is what it means when we take it over a range of words. So we mark it by two arrows coming together, showing that whatever it is, it's coming together to make one. The "struct" part we indicate by three Lego blocks being assembled, conveying the meaning of "building". And the "ion" at the end, wherever it occurs, means one picture idea in your mind, so we show this by a thought balloon like the ones you see in comics.' By highlighting these 'icons' the dyslexic reader is able to visualise the meaning of words as an important aid to remembering the sound that each 'icon' represents and the order in which the letters occur.

The dictionary Dr Brown and his team were three-quarters of the way through preparing comprised these 'letter strings', like the 'con', the 'struct' and the 'ion' which have the same kind of meaning wherever they occur. The dictionary covered the English language and as far as he knew it was the first time that such a dictionary had ever been compiled for any language – a long way from Dr Johnson's, perhaps, but I'm sure he would be the first to give his wholehearted support to such a valuable contribution to this specialist teaching.

Twelve miles up the A38 from Lichfield, BURTON-UPON-TRENT immediately brings beer and brewing to mind. At one time there were over thirty breweries in the town, and the skyline was dominated by brewery chimneys. Today you can count the chimneys on the fingers of one hand, and the number of breweries has dropped to three. The first brewers were monks who settled in the area in 1002. It was they who discovered the special properties of the water which reaches the surface at Burton after passing through gypsum-rich rock for centuries. It is very pure and contains mineral qualities that cannot be found anywhere else in England.

The ideal place to find out more about brewing is the Bass Brewery Museum, where we met Maurice Lovett, the author of a book on the subject. He told me that the distinctive Bass red triangle is the oldest trade mark in the world. This is believed to have originally been the shipping mark used by William Bass when he was sending his beer into the Baltic ports and dealing with dock workers who couldn't read or write. Bass adopted the trade mark officially in 1855 and when trade-mark registration became compulsory in 1875 it became the first.

I was amazed to hear that in the middle of the seventeenth century the river Trent was navigable all the way to Burton from the sea, and when the breweries started it was quicker to carry the beer to London by sea rather than by road. Later Bass established an important market in Russia and north Germany, and even before 1800 they had forty agencies in the Baltic countries. Of course the beer carried quite a premium in those days, and there are stories of Russian nobles at court drinking bottled Bass from silver spoons because it was considered such a delicacy.

When the railways arrived Bass alone built a network of twenty-seven miles of track just inside the brewery. Bass also owned twenty-one locomotives, and in the museum there is a model of the town showing all the chimneys and the intricate railway layout that once existed within the brewery. There are sufficient records to enable the museum to fix the 'scene' of their model to a particular time and date in 1921, so it shows a small fire that broke out in the brewery, and even a rent collector at work on this particular Monday morning. From the model you can see that all these railway tracks must have mucked up road transport in the town quite a bit. There were thirty-two level crossings in Burton, more than anywhere else in the country; the High Street alone had four.

William Bass founded his brewing company in 1777, and it was his son and grandson who built it up during the nineteenth century to the point where it was the largest company in Britain by the 1880s. Michael Thomas Bass, the great entrepreneur of nineteenth-century brewing, was a noted radical, and did a lot for the town and especially for his employees, for whom he provided a Sports and Social Club in the 1860s, including a cricket club – Derbyshire had played on the ground on the week before our visit. He also started the Bass Trip, taking all his employees and their families to the seaside for the day, having arranged for the whole line to the coast to be closed to other traffic. On one trip he took 12,000 for a day out by train! His interests in the railways and their employees even led him to set up the forerunner of the NUR, paying its first general secretary out of his own pocket.

Before leaving Burton I gleaned one fascinating piece of sporting history that I for one never knew, and that is that the rules for water polo were first written down in the Star Inn, which still stands in the High Street. Obviously there is more to Burton water than the special properties it gives to beer!

The gypsum seam which is responsible for this water is mined a few miles away at TUTBURY, from where the rock is sent to be turned into plaster or alabaster, in the case of the finest grades. During the last war the Air Ministry took over one of the old gypsum mines to use it as an underground bomb store. On 27 November 1944 one small section of this blew up. Estimates put the total of explosives at four million pounds of TNT, making this the largest man-made explosion in history to that time (the atom bomb the following year was to eclipse it, of course). Structural damage was recorded as far away as Burton. There was considerable damage in Tutbury itself, and the gypsum workings were completely blown away. In all, about seventy-eight people were killed and today the crater – half a mile wide and a hundred feet deep – lies just behind the new mine.

If you go west from Burton-upon-Trent, following the B5234 through Needwood Forest, you will come to the attractive old village of ABBOTS BROMLEY, where each year on the Monday

following the Sunday after 4 September the celebrated Horn
Dance takes place, one of the oldest folk customs in the country.
From Dr John Salter, who lives in the village, I learned that no
one knows when the dance originated, although all the authorities
agree that it dates from a long way back in our history. Neither
does anyone know for certain why it originated. Some books
describe it as a fertility rite. Some reckon it may have had something to do with the granting of forestry rights in the old forest of
Needwood, and then there are those who suggest that people just
started dancing for the pleasure of it, perhaps after a deer hunt
when the horns became part of the hunters' rites.

53 The Abbots Bromley Horn Dance
in the grounds of Blithfield Hall.

The only definite date that can be given comes from carbon-
testing of the horns themselves. When a portion of horn was
broken several years ago carbon-dating suggested a date of 1065.
The horns are actually reindeer horns, and the reindeer has been
extinct in Britain for a very long time. So no one knows where
they came from, nor why they came to Abbots Bromley.

Today the six sets of horns can be seen hanging in the parish
church. On the day of the dance they are carried by six dancers,
who process initially in a straight line. From this they break into
a circle, then into two lines facing one another, as in a number of
English folk dances. The two lines, with three horns on each side,
come forward like rutting stags with their heads down. They back

off for a few paces and then pass through the line on the other side before repeating the same movements. In addition to the six horn dancers there is the musician who accompanies them on an accordion, a boy with a triangle, the 'man woman' who appears in a number of early dances, a boy with a crossbow, a hobby horse and a fool with his pig's bladder.

We could see wild fallow deer grazing in the distance when we went to visit the broadcaster, naturalist and countryman Phil Drabble in his lovely house just outside the village. The wood in which we were watching the deer belongs to Phil's house, and he had two rides cut into it so that he can see animals crossing when he is working at his desk and knows where to go and look for them in the wood. 'It's quite a good area for wild fallow deer,' he confirmed, and when we were with him he was hoping to introduce a few little muntjac deer as well, bred from a couple he had raised in his garden.

Horns were much in evidence in Abbots Bromley, and over the porch to Phil Drabble's house there are seven goat's heads and inside others decorate the chimney. I wondered what their significance was. 'This house was originally built for the goatherd of a very famous herd of goats – the Bagot goats,' he explained. 'Tradition has it that they were brought over from the Crusades by Richard I, and that his son Richard II came up into Needwood Forest to have a day's hunting and enjoyed himself so much that he gave a herd of goats to the Bagot family. There is a lot of substance in this because the Bagot family has had a goat's head on its crest since Richard II's time.'

Phil showed me some pictures of them, and the billies in particular have very big horns. They are also very distinctive-looking goats, with black heads, necks and front legs, but white behind. They almost look like a black goat with a white saddle cloth thrown over it. Unfortunately, you won't see any Bagot goats in Phil's wood today, nor in Abbots Bromely. Their numbers dropped to the point where they were in danger of disappearing for good, and in an effort to preserve them and introduce some fresh blood into the herd the whole lot were moved to the Rare Breeds Survival Trust headquarters in the Cotswolds, where I hope they are making a good recovery.

One of the largest and most attractive of the Peak District villages is EYAM, which lies just off the A623 about ten miles south-east of Castleton. Eyam became famous in the middle of the seventeenth century for the selfless way in which the villagers deliberately isolated themselves from neighbouring villages when the plague spread among them in 1665. Today there are plaques on many houses and cottages in Eyam recording their seventeenth-century inhabitants who died. Along Church Street is Plague Cottage itself, where the devastating outbreak first struck the village. We called there to meet Mrs Clarice White, whose home it is today, and to find out from her what happened in her house in the autumn of 1665.

'Apparently a travelling tailor named George Vickers lodged here with a Mrs Cooper, a widow with two sons,' she told me. 'According to legend he sent down to London for some material, which I presume was to make a wedding dress. But when it came he thought it smelt musty, so he spread it out in front of the fire to dry. A couple of days later he was taken ill and died quite suddenly.' George Vickers was the first victim of the plague of Eyam. Three weeks after his death one of Mrs Vicker's sons followed him, and a week after that she lost her remaining son to the disease.

Clarence Daniels, a local historian who was the author of a book about the plague in Eyam, took up the story when we visited his small museum in the village. 'According to the letter sent by the rector, William Mompesson, to his uncle after the plague was over, seventy-six families were "visited" and 259 people died. It was Mompesson who persuaded the villages to cut themselves off from the outside world for the duration of the plague. He wrote to the Earl of Devonshire asking him to arrange for provisions to be brought to the perimeter of the village, and in return Mompesson took it on himself to make sure that no one from Eyam strayed beyond a prescribed boundary. And so it was that food and simple medicines were left at marker stones on the parish boundary, known today as Penny Stones or, in the case of one between Eyam and Stoney Middleton, the Vinegar Stone. This is a boulder pierced with a series of holes which were filled with vinegar into which the people from Eyam put their coins in payment for what they had been brought; the belief was that the vinegar would disinfect them, though this was not in fact the case.

'The effect of Bubonic plague depended very much on the

state of health of the victim before the disease struck,' Clarence told me. There were quite a number of men in Eyam who worked as farmers and lead miners and were fit enough to fight off the disease. However, those with less stamina, like William Mompesson's wife, who suffered from tuberculosis, were less fortunate. Catherine Mompesson died quite rapidly after the initial signs of infection. These, Clarence told me, were very similar to a common cold with coughs and sneezes. Even today I say 'Bless you' when someone sneezes, and this, he assured me, stemmed from a little prayer which used to be offered when there was always a possibility that the sneezer might have more than just a head cold.

In Clarence's museum I spotted a couple of little cones, which he told me were pomanders that visitors to plague areas would hold to the their noses to ward off infection. And the 'pocket full of posies' in the nursery rhyme 'Ring a Ring of Roses' refers specifically to pomanders like these. In fact the whole nursery rhyme describes the onset of Bubonic plague.

Among the other exhibits is a ring called Richard III's ring, a silver one given by the King to his mistress. What makes it particularly interesting is the tiny fragment of wood set into it which is claimed to be a piece of the true Cross. In the days when Richard wore the ring it was common for the sick and infirm to seek his permission to touch the wood of the Cross, hoping for a miracle cure, and it is from this practice that the superstition about touching wood evolved.

Derbyshire is famous for its old custom of well-dressing, of which Eyam is one of the principal villages. Originally a pagan rite, this has long been a Christian practice too, in both cases giving thanks for a plentiful supply of water. In earlier times it simply consisted of sprinkling flower petals on top of the water in a well, but today the dressing is an intricate process of pressing individual petals on to a bed of clay to form a mosaic of flowers in a religious picture. The well-dressing week in Eyam comes at the end of August, so we had missed it when we were there on a gloriously hot and sunny September day. However, Mrs Sue Elkins, who had been involved in the design, was able to describe it to us. The theme is different each year, and in this particular one they had chosen the Nativity. Around the central panel showing a typical Nativity scene, Mrs Elkins had depicted all the trappings of a modern Christmas, the tree, the presents, the crackers, the holly, and the pudding, all carefully picked out in petals, sometimes mosses, lichens and evergreens.

54 Well-dressing at Eyam.

The tradition of well-dressing takes place on a rather larger scale in the town of WIRKSWORTH, which lies south of Castleton on the southern edge of the Peak District National Park. There are usually around a dozen well-dressings placed at strategic points in the town over the Spring Bank Holiday, and organisations within Wirksworth are entitled to create their own to raise money for charity. When piped water first appeared the dressings were placed round public taps, and there are still a few people in the town who know them as tap-dressings.

There is another lovely old tradition which still takes place twice a year in Wirksworth in April and October. This is the sitting of the Barmoot Court, which controls the staking of claims for lead-mining in the King's Field, that is to say the area surrounding the town which belongs to the Duchy of Lancaster. According to Horace Ellam, the unofficial organiser of the court, anyone is entitled to go prospecting for lead provided that they don't try digging in a churchyard, a public highway or an orchard. Provided you can prove that you have found lead, you are entitled to stake a claim at the Barmoot Court, in return for which the Duchy of Lancaster will take one-thirteenth of your find. This is measured in a long, narrow brass dish kept by the court and presented to it in 1512 by Henry VIII. Election to the court is by invitation, and after the Bar Master, Stewards and members of the jury have finished their official business they repair to the Hope and Anchor in the town for traditional refreshment. As mine host of that particular hostelry, Horace Ellam is party to the secret recipe of the special punch they drink, which I regret to say he did not divulge to me.

Down in the south of Derbyshire is the old town of MELBOURNE, probably best known for Melbourne Hall, the home of two of Queen Victoria's prime ministers. Compared with Chatsworth and the other stately homes in the area, this is a comparatively small house, but it is filled with the most lovely furniture and pictures and is built in a charming blend of architectural styles. The north side is the oldest part, dating from the thirteenth century. This was owned by the bishops of Carlisle, who used it as a rectory. In 1628 the house was leased from the bishops by Sir John Coke, and his grandson the Rt. Hon. Thomas Coke bought the freehold and became the first lay owner. Then some time later, came the second Lord Melbourne, Queen Victoria's first prime minister, with his wife Lady Caroline Lamb. After Lord Melbourne, the house passed to his sister, whose second husband was Lord Palmerston, the second of the prime ministers to have lived at Melbourne Hall.

Beautiful gardens were laid out by Queen Anne's head gardener, and they remain a perfect example of an early eighteenth-century English garden. The centrepiece standing in front of the lake, or basin, is the very famous pergola, much better known as the wrought-iron birdcage. We went to sit in it, and you really do feel rather a like a canary looking out through all the gold leaf and intricate patterns created by Robert Bakewell, the famous Derbyshire wrought-ironsmith, whose other marvellous work includes the gates in Green Park in London. The garden also contains a number of fine lead statues, of which the best known is the large one depicting the four seasons. This was Queen Anne's gift to the Rt. Hon. Thomas Coke, her Vice Chamberlain, to mark the completion of his garden. One other feature to note is the two-hundred-yard yew tunnel, which really is a tunnel and was planted as such over four hundred years ago.

(If you go to Melbourne, have a look at the cross in the middle of the village. It was erected to mark the accession of King Edward VIII and must be one of the very few, if not the only, memorial of its kind in the country.)

Beside the deserted station at EAST LEAKE, just across the county boundary in Nottinghamshire, there is a long, rather curious-looking building with steel windows which can be clamped right down and a solid steel door. This was built in 1939 as an emergency control room for railway traffic on the Eastern Region line in the event of the main control centre in Nottingham being knocked out. Nowadays the building houses the firm of bell-rope-makers run by Alf Ellis and his family. The steel shutters might be a little excessive, but the length of the building makes it ideal for making the church bell-ropes, some of which have a finished length of 110 feet, and that is after 30 per cent of the original warp length has been lost in the process of making the rope – all of which is done by hand. There are four variations of rope thickness, Alf told me, depending on the weight of the bell they will be ringing, and these have an average life of five years.

The nice fluffy bit at the bottom which the bell ringers actually pull is called the 'sally', I learned. This is made of pure wool which is cut into short lengths to be inserted into each individual strand in the rope. There are three or four strands to each rope, and once these have been twisted together the wool is combed to bring out all the ends and raise its 'pile' before it is trimmed neatly with a pair of electric shears to its finished length.

A journey of a dozen miles down the A6006 brings you to MELTON MOWBRAY, which for many people is surely associated with fox-hunting, Stilton cheese and pork pies.

From the eighteenth century onwards Melton has been the Mecca of English fox-hunting, attracting in its heyday the crowned heads of Europe together with the leading lights of the British aristocracy.

It wasn't only in the hunting field that they enjoyed their sport. Melton Mowbray was the birthplace of the expression 'to paint the town red', a turn of phrase which came into being after a former Marquis of Waterford and a group of companions, who must have been feeling at a bit of a loose end one evening, hit on an unusual pastime. Starting at the Tollgate at one end of the town, they worked their way through Melton with red paint and brushes literally painting everything red – including the watchman. This didn't please him greatly, as one might imagine, and the Marquis and his friends spent the rest of the night in Melton gaol for their trouble.

By the time the Marquis of Waterford got up to his antics Melton Mowbray had already established itself as the centre for the making of Stilton cheese, which derived its name from a village on the old North Road just to the south of Peterborough. The story goes that a farmer's wife in Wymondham, a few miles east of Melton Mowbray, used to make this and supply it to her brother, who was landlord of the Bell Inn at Stilton. Travellers staying at the inn spread word of the delicious cheese that they had eaten there, and the cheese became known thereafter by the place where it was first *sold*.

What was a farmhouse industry three hundred years ago is now a large-scale dairy industry, although still closely linked to its place of origin. Milk is delivered to the Stilton cheese factories every day from farms all around Melton Mowbray. The cheese-making process begins at half-past three in the morning, when the milk is pasteurised and poured into a vat. A substance called 'starter' is added, which I was told is not dissimilar to yogurt in nature. Once that has started to sour the milk, rennet is added and after about ninety minutes the curds are set solidly enough to enable them to be cut.

The curd is then allowed to settle out in the whey until the surface whey can be drawn off and the curds separated off properly and placed on trays, where they remain overnight. The following day salt is added, and the salted curds are placed in the cylindrical moulds, or hoops, where they are allowed to knit together under their own weight. They are turned end-over-end every day for a week, by the end of which the cheeses are firm enough to be taken from their hoops to be sealed over the whole surface; at this stage the makers don't want any mould development. As soon as the crust has formed and the cheese inside has firmed to the required degree it is pierced with stainless-steel needles, allowing oxygen to get inside. This is what starts the mould growth which gives Stilton its distinctive blue veining and taste.

Melton Mowbray's famous pork pies developed as a direct result of Stilton cheese-making in the 1830s. Local pigs fed on the whey which was a waste product from the cheese industry gradually acquired a slightly different flavour from the pork produced in other parts of the country. The hunting fraternity acquired a taste for this pork and the pies made from it, and it wasn't long before the demand for Melton Mowbray pork pies had spread to London.

The ingredients of a Melton Mowbray pie are deliciously simple: pork, salt, pepper and pastry. To make a pie the pastry is raised up a block rather like the side of a jam jar and the meat is put into the hole in the middle. A lid is put on top of this and the pie is baked.

These are the various stages, but making a Melton Mowbray pork pie is a little more time-consuming than it sounds, because between each stage the pie has to be cooled in a fridge to prevent the pastry losing its shape.

The last ingredient to be added is the jelly, which is poured in through a hole in the top of the pie while it is still hot. This serves two purposes, I gather: it keeps the meat moist, but more importantly it keeps air out of the pie and prevents mould forming on the meat – quite the opposite to the process of making Stilton cheese, in fact.

Fifteen miles north-east of Melton Mowbray the A607 arrives at GRANTHAM, the birthplace of Mrs Margaret Thatcher and formerly an important coaching halt on the Great North Road. We began our tour outside the Beehive Inn in the High Street beneath something I had never seen before and which I am sure must be unique – a living inn sign. The sign for the Beehive really is a beehive, complete with bees buzzing inside to make their honey. It has its own little tale which runs:

> Stop, traveller, this wond'rous sign explore,
> And say, when thou hast view'd it o'er and o'er,
> Now Grantham, now two rarities are thine,
> A lofty steeple and a living sign.

And from outside the Beehive you can see the spire of St Wulfran's church standing high above the town about two hundred yards away. It is the sixth highest spire in the country and the third highest among parish churches.

Inside St Wulfran's there are a number of charity boards on display, and we had been told to look out for one in particular in which Michael Solomon gave forty shillings a year to the Angel Inn to have a sermon preached once a year against drunkenness. Great play used to be made of this in the last century when the temperance movements were at their height, but over the years the Solomon bequest sermon has gradually mellowed, and very mild references to the evils of drink are included in it today.

Thirty miles along the A52 from Grantham you come to the busy port and market town of BOSTON, famous for its Stump, the medieval lantern tower which rises 272 feet above the parish church of St Botolph's. As its name suggests, the Boston Stump looks like a tree trunk shorn of its branches. Towering above the Fens, it is visible from twelve miles away when you approach Boston from the north, and you can also see the Stump from the other side of the Wash at Hunstanton. Not that the Stump is the only remarkable feature about St Botolph's. The church is the

55 The Boston Stump.

largest parish church in the country, with a nave 172 feet long and pillars which are only slightly shorter than those in York Minster. It can seat a congregation of 1200, and frequently has to cater for even greater numbers at the main religious festivals.

The name of Boston immediately brings to mind the great American city of the same name, but I was surprised to discover that the town has other historical connections with the New World through the Pilgrim Fathers, whom I always associate with Plymouth. However, down in the cells below the town's ancient Guildhall there is a plaque which states: 'William Bradford, William Brewston and others, otherwise known as the Pilgrim Fathers, were imprisoned on 23rd September 1607 after attempting to escape to religious freedom.'

David Barston, custodian of the Guildhall Museum, was on hand to fill in the gaps in my knowledge. He explained that under James I it was illegal for anyone to leave the country without his written permission. It was also illegal to be a non-conformist, so when the Pilgrim Fathers were apprehended trying to slip out of Boston harbour that September night they ended up in prison. There they were held for three months before being released after paying a substantial fine. In the following year, 1608, they were successful in making their escape to the Netherlands, where they lived until 1620. In that year the English company of Merchant Adventurers fitted them out with two ships, the *Mayflower* and the smaller *Speedwell*, to cross the Atlantic and found a trading colony. From the Netherlands, where they embarked, the emigrants crossed the English Channel to Southampton Water and then sailed west along the south coast of England. Where does Plymouth come into the picture? Apparently this was their last landfall in England before setting out across the Atlantic. (Two other interesting items from the seventeenth century on display at the museum are the Boston cannon, the only two outside the Tower of London cast by John Brown, cannon-maker to Charles I. Ironically, they were used to defend Boston against his forces in the Civil War.

Walking round the market in Boston, we came across the butcher's shop belonging to Herbert Dawson which advertised stuffed chine, a cut of meat with which I wasn't immediately familiar. Inside, Herbert told me that the chine is a cut of pork taken from the back of the carcase by means of two cuts either side of the backbone. It is an old-fashioned way of butchering a pig which he still practices for customers who like their pork prepared in this way. Stuffing the chine consists of cutting slits on either side of the meat and filling these with fresh parsley. The chine is then wrapped in cloth to keep the parsley in place while it is boiled, for up to five hours in the case of large joints. Stuffed chine is always eaten cold and when I tried some it was absolutely delicious.

If you climb to the second gallery of the Boston Stump on a clear day and look towards the north-west, you can see the three majestic honey-coloured towers of LINCOLN Cathedral almost thirty miles away. Today the Great Tower is 230 feet high, though until 1549 it was topped by a spire which must have made it even more spectacular. In that year the spire was blown down in a storm and to date there are no plans to replace it. The first cathedral was built in 1072 and was burnt down within a century. In 1180 the tower of the second cathedral collapsed in an earthquake, making way for the magnificent third cathedral which survives today. Lincoln Cathedral contains one of the earliest medieval windows in England, still in its original position, and the magnificent carved stalls in St Hugh's choir.

The Angel choir, the last part of the cathedral to be constructed in 1280, is home to the Lincoln Imp, one of twenty or thirty grotesque carvings of little demons around the building symbolising the spiritual warfare between good and evil. This little character has become enormously popular with visitors over the years, though not necessarily with the cathedral authorities. 'The Lincoln Imp is rather an albatross round our necks,' it was confided to me. 'People always ask where the imp is when they come into the cathedral, which is so sad because there are far better things to be seen closer at hand.' I had to confess that we had asked exactly the same question when we arrived.

Attached to Lincoln Cathedral is a library which contains one of the four original copies of Magna Carta (two of the others are in the British Library; the fourth is at Salisbury). The Lincoln one has a special claim to fame as its address is shown, saying simply 'To Lincoln'.

At much the same time as the present cathedral was being built at Lincoln, a local tradition came into being in the village of

HAXEY in Humberside, thirty miles to the north-east. It was here on a muddy January day that one Lady Mowbray lost her hood while she was out riding. There were thirteen men working in the fields nearby and they had a terrific scrummage to have the privilege of returning it to her. Inevitably, the largest and strongest of them ended up with the hood, or what was left of it. But he was too shy to return it to her ladyship and gave it to one of the others. Faint heart never won fair lady and Lady Mowbray, who had enjoyed the tussle enormously, named the shy man a fool and the one who had returned the hood a lord. These titles have been retained ever since by two of the principal figures in the Haxey Hood game, which is played every year on 6 January. Neither war nor weather has forced the game to be cancelled once in its 700-year history.

The third principal in the game is the Chief Boggan, who leads a team of ten Boggans making up numbers to match the original thirteen, against all corners. I wondered why they were called Boggans. Probably from the state they got into scrumming in the mud, I was told by Stan Bore, Lord of the Hood for the past thirteen years when I met him in October 1980. Stan went on to tell me that the game begins outside the church, where the Fool makes his speech of welcome. When he has finished, everyone troops up to the fields between Haxey and the village of Westwoodside, where play takes place. Twelve dummy hoods made of a roll of stitched sacking are played for first, leaving the main 'Sway' hood made from a cylinder of leather, twenty-four inches long, two and half inches in diameter, to be played for at the end of the afternoon. The Boggans are spaced out round the field of play, surrounding their opponents, and the dummy hoods are thrown into the ring, where the other players have to try to break through the ring of Boggans carrying a hood. Anyone who does manage to break out and make his way to a public house is rewarded with a pint of beer. In the end, all the dummy hoods are carried past Boggans by their opponents, and at about a quarter to four the Sway hood is thrown into the air and everybody who wants to take part gathers round in an enormous rugby scrum containing anything from fifty to two hundred people. The hood is in the middle of this so-called Sway and is pushed along until it too reaches one of the three pubs in the area. The choice of pub depends on how many of its regulars are pushing in the

Sway. No matter which it reaches, the hood remains there until New Year's Eve.

Haxey lies within an area of Humberside called the Isle of Axholme and, driving the three miles north from there to the little town of EPWORTH, we noticed that the fields are divided into strips. From Harold Woolgar, secretary of the National Farmers' Union in the area, we learned that the Isle of Axholme is one of the last two areas of England where the old medieval practice of strip farming is still followed. Even today some of the strips are 300 to 400 yards long, though the ideal length in the Middle Ages was around 200 to 240 yards. Harold told us that when he came to the town in the mid-1960s the Epworth Field, which has an area of about 200 acres, was owned by 250 or so individuals and farmed by 80 or 90 different farmers. Fifteen years on, the same area of land was owned by 80 or 90 people and farmed by perhaps 20 or 30 different farmers. With farming of this type it is common for farmers to own strips in different fields, which has led to a certain amount of swapping taking place to make the best use of modern machinery. I saw one five-acre strip growing corn which Harold told me may have had as many as twenty owners, with all of whom the farmer would most likely have had a tenancy agreement.

Twenty miles to the north-east of the Isle of Axholme lies the river Humber and the town of BARTON-UPON-HUMBER, which was an important port and ferry crossing as early as the Domesday Book, which records a population of 900 to 1086. Throughout the Middle Ages the ferry from Barton provided the principal means of travelling between the great medieval centres of Lincoln and York. Then came the development of Hull across the river, and Barton's importance declined. However in the mid-1970s construction work began on the Humber Bridge, and when it opened in June 1981 it transformed travel and trade in this eastern part of England.

From the office of the Bridgemaster, Malcolm Stockwell, we looked out at this extraordinary feat of engineering one cold misty day in the middle of February 1986. The bridge took almost nine years to build, he told us, at a cost of around £100 million, though with interest charges the debt had risen to nearer £240 million and was increasing at the alarming rate of a pound a second! Some of the construction statistics are pretty mind-boggling too.

There are 44,000 miles of wire in the main cables alone; add to that the wire in the hanging cables and you can comfortably say that you could stretch the total length round the world – twice. There is getting on for half a million tons of concrete in the bridge. And the span between the two 500-foot towers is nine-tenths of a mile, making the Humber Bridge the longest single-span bridge in the world. With a wind of eighty miles an hour, Malcolm told me, it moves ten feet sideways at the middle, though he added that the day it stops moving he and his staff will be in trouble.

56 The Humber Bridge.

In the middle of the eighteenth century, when shipping was still an important source of employment in Barton, a ship-owner from Hull by the name of Hall set up a rope works to make use of the large quantities of flax which were grown in the surrounding district. That works was still in business when we visited it, and it operates one of the longest rope walks in the world. Apart from the introduction of man-made fibres alongside traditional materials like flax, sisal, manila, coir and cotton, the technique of making rope here has changed little in two centuries. The raw material is combed into fibres to remove irregularities and impurities. These are then spun on machines which revolve at about 2000 revolutions a minute before being taken to rolling machines where the raw sliver of straight fibre is twisted into the yarn from which the ropes are made. Man-made materials like nylon, polyester and polyethylene are turned into yarn by means of extrusion, a process which was explained to me as being like mincing meat at the butcher.

The rope walk we visited consisted of a couple of railway rails which seemed to disappear away into the distance. A truck running on the line makes rope in the traditional fashion by drawing fibres into a tight tube to create a strand. Halls' ropes can have three, four or nine strands. In each case the truck returns up the rails, twisting the required number of strands in the opposite direction so that one strand locks against the other, and leaving the finished rope behind to be coiled. The terrific length of this rope walk, 250 fathoms or 1500 feet, allows ropes 200 fathoms (1200 feet) to be made. I was astonished that anyone would want a rope that long, but in the American market in particular, I was told, 200-fathom ropes are in great demand. I was also surprised to learn that 40 per cent of the rope made at Barton still comes from natural fibres.

The North-East

57 View from Roseberry Topping, North Yorkshire.

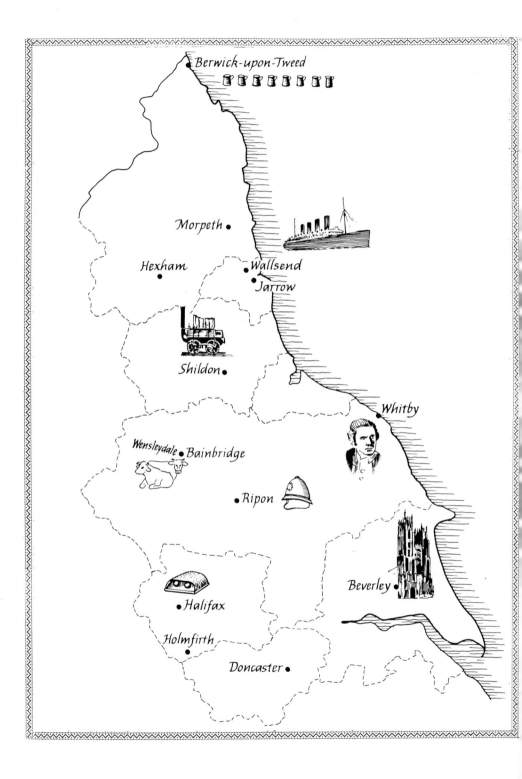

Berwick-upon-Tweed

Morpeth •

Hexham
•

Wallsend
•
Jarrow

Shildon •

Whitby •

Wensleydale • Bainbridge

• Ripon

Beverley •

• Halifax

Holmfirth
•

Doncaster •

I have always been told that there are more acres in Yorkshire than there are letters in the Bible. Whoever carried out this time-consuming research I don't know. Nor do I know whether it is true. But no matter, Yorkshire *is* vast and the biggest county in Britain. And so, as you might expect, it has a tremendous variety of scenery and landscapes with the big industries of coal, steel and wool contrasting with the beauties of the wolds, moors and dales. In West and South Yorkshire especially town is joined to town without any obvious boundary. Factory chimneys, mine-shafts and old mills are the main features. But always somewhere just round the corner comes a splendid view or picturesque landscape. A Southerner has to be careful what he writes about Yorkshire. People from Yorkshire are intensely proud of their heritage and, more than those from any other county, have common characteristics — bluntness, obstinacy and toughness. But, unless one criticises any aspect of Yorkshire, they are friendly and outgoing, and always give a visitor a warm welcome. I should explain why I can claim to be such an authority. I married a Sheffield girl, whose father was the Master Cutler in 1936. We have been happily married for forty-two years, which I hope proves my point about the friendliness and welcome.

I first journeyed north to Yorkshire in 1930. We lived in Cornwall at the time and I motored in a second-hand open Austin Seven which had cost me £17. I had several breakdowns on the way and had plenty of time to admire the countryside as I progressed slowly up the A30 and A1. I stayed with a school friend near Boston Spa, and I was soon involved in winter activities such as a Hunt Ball in Harrogate and a terrifying day out with the

Bramham Moor Hunt. I remember the Princess Royal was also out hunting and came back to tea afterwards. (No more name-dropping, I promise!)

I went back in the next few summers when we played cricket at Escrick, a delightful ground just outside York. It was here that a young raring-to-go fast bowler called Trueman is said to have excelled himself. It was about 1950 and in those days Yorkshire used to play a few pre-season practice matches against local clubs. On this occasion they were playing the Yorkshire Gentlemen, and with a succession of bouncers Fred had knocked out four of these Gentlemen, who had been carted off to hospital. A grey-haired figure emerged from the pavilion with I Zingari cap, silk shirt buttoned at the wrist, and a white bristling moustache. He looked a trifle apprehensive. The Yorkshire captain Norman Yardley went up to Fred and said, 'This is Brigadier so and so – go easy on him. He's an important patron of Yorkshire.' So Fred went smilingly up to the Brigadier and said, 'It's all right, Brigadier, off first ball I'll give you one to get off the mark.' The Brigadier's face relaxed into a smile, only to freeze with horror as Fred went on. 'Aye,' he said 'and with second I'll pin you against f—g sightscreen!'

I'm ashamed to say that at the same ground on a cricket tour before the war, we put some kippers on to the cylinder block of one of our opponents' cars. When the engine got hot the resulting smell was unbelievable. So much so that when the unfortunate owner got home, his spaniel leaped on to the bonnet of his car and scratched away with his paws, trying to get at whatever was underneath. We weren't too popular the next day!

When I was at Oxford I had a Sealyham called Blob, who always came round with me to every cricket match. I went off to Brazil for eighteen months in 1936 and left Blob with my friends at Boston Spa. One day he disappeared, and although they searched everywhere they couldn't find him. Later in the day someone brought him back. He had been found quietly sitting watching the local village cricket match.

I returned to Yorkshire in 1943 when our battalion was stationed at West Lutton Camp and the village of Helmsley. We used to go into Scarborough for our 'recreation', and I'm afraid that we drank the cellar of the Pavilion Hotel dry. This was the hotel owned by the Laughton family, and before the war they had accumulated some superb wines. We were not too popular with the wine-drinkers of Scarborough, since the cellar could not be re-stocked during the war. Our battalion cricket side were also lucky enough to play on the famous Scarborough Club cricket ground, and one of the pleasures of my cricket commentating life has been the festival at the end of every season. It has a wonderful atmosphere, with the marquees, the town band and the noise of the 'naval battle' fought every afternoon on the lake below the ground. One of my proudest moments was in 1984 when I was honoured to be asked to be the President, which involves hosting the lunches and teas at the festival.

Since 1952, when because of the opening of the Holme Moss transmitter the Tests were able to be broadcast on television. I have been a yearly visitor to Headingley. I have many memories of the thirty-seven Tests since then. The outstanding match was undoubtedly that sensational Test in 1981 when, thanks chiefly to a brilliant hundred by Botham and some superb hostile bowling by Willis, England won by 18 runs. Australia had only been set 130 to win, and it was not surprising that the bookies offered odds of 500–1 against England winning. What was surprising though was the fact that both Lillee and Marsh of Australia were so tempted by the odds that they each put a fiver on England – and won!

It was on this ground that Henry Blofeld claimed to have seen a butterfly walking across the pitch. 'And what's worse,' he added, 'it's got a limp!' There was one mystery there that I have never solved. When Jim Swanton and I were doing the TV commentary a man walked past with a ladder over his shoulder and a lavatory seat round his neck. He disappeared under the football stand. Ten minutes later he emerged, still with the ladder but minus the seat! I have never worked out why he needed a ladder. Surely no seat could be that high off the ground?

I am lucky to have a great friend who lives in a large house with beautiful gardens about six miles out of Leeds. I made one of my worst jokes when staying there. We were having breakfast when one of the daughters came in with her dog, which she said wanted a drink. She looked around for a moment and then said, 'Has anyone seen the dog bowl?' 'No,' I said, 'But I've seen him play some fine innings!'

Before I started to do *Down Your Way* in 1972 I seldom had

occasion to visit the north-east. But from what I had seen from trains on the way to Scotland I particularly enjoyed Northumberland, with the sea and ragged coastline on one side and the moorland and valleys on the other. I also stayed once in a castle near Hexham for a cricket match and learned that it was one of many which had been built originally as fortresses against the Scots.

I also had a very happy connection with Durham. When I was at Eton the headmaster was the distinguished grey-haired figure of Dr Cyril Alington. Soon after I left he was appointed Dean of Durham. His daughter Elizabeth had been a friend of mine at Eton and she later married Lord Dunglass (now Lord Home).

It was because of her presence in Durham that I 'adopted' a family called Corbett. They lived at 90 Cuthbert Avenue and there were at least four children plus Mr and Mrs Corbett. This adoption came about in 1938 when I went to morning service in St Michael's, Chester Square, just near where I was living in London. The vicar was a famous preacher, Canon W. H. Elliott, and on this particular day in his sermon he appealed to his congregation to help families in the north-east who were suffering tremendous hardships because of the unemployment situation.

I used to write regularly to Mrs Corbett, who kept me informed of the progress and activities of her family. I also sent the odd present and a food hamper at Christmas, and Elizabeth kindly visited them on my behalf. It was, as I said, a very happy association with the city of Durham.

Before the creation of the new county of Humberside the town of BEVERLEY, eight miles north-west of Hull, was the capital of the East Riding of Yorkshire. Beverley is famous for its racecourse and its superb Gothic minster, a minster as opposed to a cathedral, I was told, because no bishop has sat at Beverley for any length of time. In place of a bishop was a warden and chapter, and this accounts for the handsome appearance of the building, built over a period of two hundred years between the thirteeth and fifteenth centuries. I commented to Dr Ivan Hall, who showed us round, on what an excellent state of repair the minster is in. 'Beverley people have always looked after their minster through the centuries,' he replied. 'You can give an instance of this when John Wesley came to Beverley expecting to find a rather run-down building. He said in 1766 that it was better kept than most of the English cathedrals he set foot in.'

As we spoke a bell was striking in one of the two magnificent towers that crown the minster. 'They are built so close together that they look like one,' Dr Hall pointed out, and looking at them you do indeed get an impression of power surging upwards to the sky. He also told me that these towers were chosen as explicit models for the present towers on Westminster Abbey. I had heard something about a treadmill at the top of one of them, and Dr Hall confirmed that there is an extraordinary wheel in the central tower like a gigantic version of the sort mice run round in. This is still used for raising and lowering all the building materials like lead, timber and stone needed for repairing the upper works of the minster. The wheel is operated just as it was in the medieval period, with a man walking inside to raise his load on the end of a seventy-foot rope.

Beverley's minster may only be a fraction of the size of the one at York, but the architects so arranged their design that optical illusions, or delusions, increase its apparent dimensions. If you go inside, for example, the minster gives the feeling of being very long and narrow. Your eyes are drawn upwards, giving the building a sense of being far bigger than it really is.

There are two other important points of interest to visitors. Firstly, the Percy Shrine, a masterpiece of medieval carving which rivals any in Europe, Dr Hall assured me; and, secondly, the Sanctuary Chair, where anyone who had done wrong or who was thought to have done wrong could claim sanctuary. Outer sanctuary, as it was called, could be claimed within the boundary marked by posts still standing in surrounding fields and by roadsides. To claim full sanctuary you had to get right into the Sanctuary Chair in the minster. Apparently there are still families in Beverley who know that their ancestors claimed sanctuary in this way hundreds of years ago.

From the minster we went out on the York Road to visit the racecourse and talk to Chris Thompson, a local farmer who was then chairman of the Pasture Masters, twelve freemen elected to control the pastures owned by all the freemen of Beverley. These Pasture Masters fix the rents for grazing on the common land. The racecourse stands on their land too, as does the golf club, so their dues are set by the Pasture Masters as well. 'They are elected each 1 March between the hours of nine and four,' Chris said, 'but the funny part of it is that the mayor presides and he has the power to close the poll if no one votes within twenty minutes.' If no one has turned up by nine-twenty, he can call it a day. It is an open ballot and bribery is not frowned on. It is perfectly legal to take voters across the road to the pub opposite the Guildhall and buy them a pint or two. Though, as Chris pointed out, the cost of beer today has virtually put paid to this practice.

Before leaving Beverley we thought we ought to go out to see Skidby Mill, a famous landmark about four miles south of the town on the Hessle Road. The tar-black tower of the windmill and the four white sails have been a prominent feature of the landscape for miles around since the early years of the last century, when it was built. What I liked about it is that Skidby Mill is still a working mill, thanks to its owners, the Beverley Borough Council, who have fully restored it and have regular sessions when they grind corn and sell the flour produced.

From the ground to the top of the tower is a height of fifty feet, on top of which the white cap rises a further fourteen feet. The cap is constantly turning under the control of the fan tail, which sticks out behind to make sure that the sails are always facing into the wind; it can be quite dangerous if the wind gets behind the sails. Each of the four sails has a number of vanes which are feathered, or opened, when the mill is not in use. Once these are closed, the sails start to turn and grinding can begin – even in a breeze as gentle as five miles an hour, I was surprised to hear.

The floor below the cap is the dust floor, where dust blown up through the mill can collect. Below that are two floors which are simply bin stores, where grain is kept waiting to be ground. Then comes the stone room, with its three pairs of stones for grinding different types of corn. A pair of French stones are used for grinding wheat. The others are a pair of traditional Derbyshire Peak stones and a pair of carborundum stones which were probably installed in the last war when the other types may not have been available. I wondered if this was a very slow method of grinding corn, but on a good day you can grind a ton, apparently – slow by the standards of modern roller mills, but perfectly adequate during the nineteenth century and well into this one. Skidby Mill was worked commercially until 1946.

Under the stone room is the meal floor, where the flour is bagged and where a certain amount of control of the mill is carried out. For instance, there is a gear there that enables the miller to control the gap between the stones and set the degree of fineness for the flour being ground.

The reorganisation of local government in the mid-1970s which placed Beverley in Humberside also created the metropolitan county of South Yorkshire, of which DONCASTER is one of the principal towns. Throughout history Doncaster has always been one of the main stopping-off points on the journey between London and Scotland. The Romans were here, and by the eighteenth-century traffic through the town had grown to the point where it was decided that the mayor should have a large, imposing house in which to entertain distinguished travellers who were passing through. The result of this was the magnificent Mansion House, one of only three in the country (the others are in London and York). The architect James Payne was commissioned to design and build it, and work commenced in 1745. The Highland rising led by Bonnie Prince Charlie interrupted the work and the Mansion House was not finished until 1748. By 1750 it was completely furnished and fitted, and the bill for the whole lot was £8000 – an amazing figure when you see what is inside. The furniture was designed by Hepplewhite, Sheraton and Chippendale, and all the fireplaces were designed by Robert Adam – pretty good choices in the light of history.

You can see examples of their exquisite work throughout the Mansion House and there are other pieces on display with a peculiar interest of their own. In the mayor's parlour, a lovely cosy room, my eye was caught by an extraordinary black chair standing in one corner. This is made from bog oak, a material that comes from a tree which is halfway towards becoming coal, I learned. Several of these trunks were found in the nearby village of Arksey during swamp-clearing work in the last century. The local squire asked a carpenter to carve him a chair from one of them, and the finished chair was sent to the Great Exhibition in London in 1851. The squire didn't have any further use for it after that, and on the coronation of Edward VII in 1901 the chair was presented to the Mansion House.

On the mantelpiece are two rather nice silver goblets with handles on either side, known as whistling cups. They were used for drinking either champagne, claret, port or sherry at civic banquets, and when the drinker had drained his cup a little whistle was provided in the bottom to call a footman to come and fill it up again. Apparently the expression to 'wet your whistle' comes from cups like this.

To me Doncaster has always meant railways, and one of the places we visited was the British Railways Engineering Works, the Plant as it is known here, which covers an area of eighty-four acres beside the station. The works opened in 1853, making the old eight-foot single locomotives with their massive driving wheels measuring eight feet in diameter. These could travel at 70 or 80 mph, I was told by Eric Marshall, the quality control manager. The *Flying Scotsman* was built at the Doncaster works, as was the *Mallard* which broke the world speed record with an average speed of 120 mph in 1938. When we were there they were busy building a dozen Class 58 standard freight locomotives.

A considerable amount of repair work takes place at Doncaster, too, and in one of the shops we saw a huge diesel-electric engine being overhauled. The diesel part I could understand, but I didn't see where the electric part fitted in. Eric Marshall explained clearly and simply how it worked: 'The diesel engine itself provides the mechanical power. That drives an alternator which provides the electricity, which in turn puts the power into the traction motors, which move the locomotive and rolling stock along.' So there you have it!

HOLMFIRTH, thirty miles west of Doncaster, is known to many people as the setting for the long-running BBC series *The Last of the Summer Wine*, which has brought a growing number of visitors to the town each year. The cast have made friends throughout Holmfirth during the dozen or so years the series has been running, and most of the buildings have been seen on television at one time or another.

Perhaps less well known is the fact that Holmfirth was one of the earliest places in this country where films were made. These developed from lantern-slide shows created and given by the founder of the local firm of Bamforth's. When moving pictures arrived, he quickly cottoned on to them and began making short comedy films. These frequently involved local people as well as a few professional actors brought in from theatres in Huddersfield.

If the scene of a bank raid was needed, for example, the local bank manager and his staff would be drafted in to take part.

The film-making side of Bamforth's business lasted until the First World War, when shortages of film brought an end to it. The end of the Great War also finished off the highly successful run of sentimental postcards which Bamforth's had developed out of their earlier lantern slides. Where sentiment died, however, comedy took over, and from song cards of winsome lasses Bamforth's turned their attention to saucy seaside postcards which have been their hallmark ever since. These haven't changed greatly over the years. The ladies are still more than amply proportioned and the jokes always on the risqué side, which I adore. (I love sending Bamforth's cards to my rather pompous friends and imagining the expression on their faces when they find these have been delivered by the postman.)

I had been told to look out for 'wuzzing holes' as I went round Holmfirth, and Frank Burley, who gave us a description of the village in general, explained that these were connected with the early textile trade in the town. 'With the hand industries they had very little machinery and they wanted ways to dry the yarn,' he said. 'So a hole was made in the wall. The yarn was put into a basket. A stick was placed through the handles of the basket, with one end in the hole, and then twirled, making an eighteenth-century spin drier. You can see "wuzzing holes" all over the district.'

Mention HALIFAX to most people and they will immediately think of the Halifax Building Society. So when we were visiting the West Yorkshire town in July 1984 we paid a call on John Spalding, the Chief General Manager at the Society's imposing headquarters, to find out about building societies in general and the Halifax in particular. Until then I hadn't talked to anyone about their history and although you see familiar names up and down any High Street, I was curious to know how they came into being. 'They were clubs,' I was told. 'Originally working men's self-help clubs – part of the Industrial Revolution and the general development of Friendly Societies, Burial Clubs and Holiday Societies – which people created for themselves by clubbing together to save money, in order to buy houses.

The first building society was formed in Birmingham at the end of the eighteenth century, but they don't talk much about that in

Halifax. Today the Halifax itself is the largest in the country, and
at the time of our visit its assets exceeded £18,000,000,000, 80
per cent of which is in mortgage balances. It is a mutual building
society in that nobody owns it except its members; there are no
shares. Everyone who has an investment in it nominally owns
part of the society and is entitled to a vote at the Annual General
Meeting.

Around the town the Halifax Building Society is known as the
'Bank' and John Spalding went on to tell me that it has actually
had a cheque-book service since 1917, though with the arrival of
plastic-card technology this form of traditional 'banking' is perhaps less of a priority than it used to be.

'Catseye' Halifax is the telegraphic address of Reflecting Road-
studs Ltd and gives an immediate clue to the famous product
they make, those marvellous reflectors which line the centre of
our roads and have saved so many hundreds of thousands of
lives. Percy Shaw, the inventor of the catseye, developed his idea
in the early 1930s and went into production in 1935. During the
war the catseye really took off when cars had to travel with

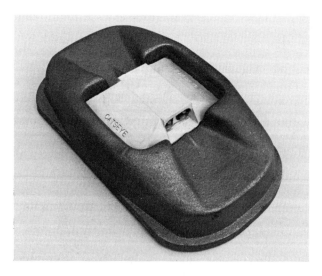

58   A catseye
as it is seldom seen.

masked headlights. The company was ordered to produce 40,000
a week and they haven't looked back. Even now production tops
one million a year.

According to Percy Shaw's nephew, Trevor, who runs the firm

today, he got the idea walking home at night from his favourite hostelry in Queensbury, which was shrouded in mist for three-quarters of the year. While the trams were still running Percy followed their highly polished rails, but when the trams began to disappear, taking the tramlines with them, he decided that the time had come to do something about getting home. One night he saw a cat sitting on a wall and also spotted a tin can shining in the gutter. As an engineer, he took these two features and set about devising a way of placing a reflector in the middle of the road. The design he ended up with is the familiar cast-iron base into which is set the rubber moulding with the little reflectors like torch bulbs which are wiped clean by two pairs of rubber 'eyelids'. Altogether 130 people work in the factory, making every single component in the catseye; the company only buys in the raw materials.

Over the county boundary in North Yorkshire the Pennines unfold to form the Yorkshire Dales, where you can find some of the grandest and most imposing scenery in England. Perhaps the most celebrated of the dales is WENSLEYDALE, made famous by its delicious cheese. On the outskirts of Hawes, which lies at the western end of the dale, we went to Wensleydale Creameries, where they produce hundreds of thousands of these distinctive cheeses in all shapes and sizes.

Over eighty people were working there on the creamery side, using lots of sparkling machinery but also doing a lot of the work manually, I noticed. I saw one of them turning cheeses over by hand to remove moisture in the traditional way, which in the case of Wensleydale cheese stretches right back to shortly after the Norman Conquest, when Cistercian monks arrived at Jervaulx Abbey and began rearing sheep, using their milk to make cheese. Cow's milk is used today, brought in from 120 farms in the surrounding districts.

Getting down to basics, I asked Ian Millward, the Creamery Manager, what the characteristics are of a good Wensleydale cheese. 'It should be moderately firm,' he replied. 'It should be bright, clean-looking, clean-flavoured, a little bit flaky. But principally we're looking for a nice, clean, bright, alert-looking cheese.'

Having been round a number of cheese factories where the cheeses seem to be matured for quite a long time, I was surprised to see these virtually coming in and going straight out again. Most are sold between seven and twenty days old, Ian said. 'If they start to get old, they start to get stale.' They go out in a variety of shapes and sizes, the two commonest being forty-pound blocks, which go to large supermarkets where they packet them themselves, and 400-gram round Dalesman cheeses, of which hundreds of thousands are sold each year.

In the village of BAINBRIDGE, a few miles down Wensleydale from Hawes, I interviewed one of the youngest people we ever met on *Down Your Way*, twelve-year-old Alaistair Metcalfe, who has the very important title of Hornblower of Bainbridge. Alaistair inherited the title and the horn from his uncle, following a tradition which has been in the Metcalfe family for a very long time. Alaistair's uncle taught him the playing technique on a little horn before he graduated to blowing the huge two-foot-three South African buffalo horn. With a circumference at the end of sixteen inches it must take some puff to blow it, but Alaistair gave us a very impressive demonstration with three blasts nearly half a minute long.

The tradition of blowing the horn dates back to the time when the land around Bainbridge was all thickly forested. On winter evenings the horn used to be sounded to indicate to travellers that there was a village nearby where they could rest for the night. Although there can't be many lost travellers these days, Alaistair was carrying on the tradition, blowing the horn three times every evening at nine o'clock between Holyrood (in mid-September) and Shrovetide.

If you follow the river Ure down Wensleydale for thirty miles it will bring you to the ancient cathedral city of RIPON, which has its own hornblowing tradition. Alfred the Great granted the city its first charter in 886, and it was he who instituted the hornblowing and presented the first horn. In those early days the horn was blown at nine o'clock to sound the curfew and set the watch. Once the watch had been set, the people could rest easy in their beds, knowing that the constables and elders were patrolling the streets under the guidance of the Wakeman. If anything happened to their property during the duration of the watch they were entitled to claim back from the Wakeman the value of their property that had been stolen or damaged. The Wakeman's job was a lifelong position which also involved collecting all the taxes, so in the early days they had quite a job filling the post.

On one side of the market square stands a timber-framed house which used to belong to Hugh Ripley, the last Wakeman, who became the first mayor of Ripon. It is said that it is his ghost which looks out of the top window whenever the hornblower isn't doing his duty. The ghost has a good view, too, because by tradition the hornblower must sound his horn at the four corners of the obelisk in the centre of the square at nine o'clock every evening of the year. In days gone by he also sounded it every hour throughout the night, but this has now been reduced to three blasts outside the mayor's house at any time between nine and midnight.

59 The Ripon hornblower.

Ripon has seven horns in all, only three of which can be blown. The one I saw in use was an African ox horn dating from 1865. Then there is the 1690 horn, which was bought to replace the original one given by Alfred the Great, and the most recent of all, bought in 1986 to celebrate the city's 1100 years. (With the arrival of the new one, the 1690 horn was put into retirement to join King Alfred's horn, which now forms part of Ripon's civic regalia.)

Ripon Cathedral may be one of the smaller cathedrals in England, but it is one of the oldest and has a west front which is world-famous. The first stone church on the site was consecrated by St Wilfred on St Peter's Day (29 June) 672, and part of that survives as the little Saxon crypt under the central tower. A substantial Norman church was erected on the site, a third of which has been incorporated into the present cathedral.

Entering from the west door, you see two fonts on the right – one of which looks very old. 'The first is perhaps the original font, part of the Norman church,' said Dr Bill Forster, head verger of the cathedral. 'That was recovered from a nearby garden in Victorian times and was put back in the church. It is not very often used because the one used today by the lovely medieval window is an early Tudor font.' The window he mentioned is thought to be the work of Robert the Glazier, who was active at Oxford Cathedral and York Minster in the early fourteenth century, and down at the bottom of the Ripon window you may notice a mutilated coat of arms, a royal coat of arms which went out of use after 1350, helping to date this lovely bright piece of work.

Ripon Cathedral is virtually cut in half by a stone screen separating the nave from the choir and when I asked Dr Forster why this was he answered that it acted as a medieval sound barrier. The choir was used to hold services for the large cathedral staff and several would have taken place each day. The nave, however, would have been the largest roofed area in Ripon, as the nave of any church would have been in any medieval community. The towns people came here to eat, drink and carry out their business which must have been a pretty noisy affair with all the bartering that would have taken place. So the screen helped to provide some seclusion for the priests at their religious offices.

Down in the crypt there is a magnificent collection of gold and silver plate drawn from all over the diocese, which stretches from pastoral Teesside down to industrial Leeds. This covers a range of dates right through from the sixteenth century to the present day. Dr Forster showed me a lovely little chalice dating from the sixteenth century, at a time when only the priest received the wine, and then compared this with a gigantic flagon which was used in the seventeenth century, when everyone insisted on having a drink of the wine.

We found something in Ripon that we hadn't expected to find in such a beautiful and seemingly tranquil city – a Police and Prison Museum. Downstairs there is a museum of police history, with several interesting bits of equipment that I hadn't come across before. There are large rattles, for instance, which the night watchmen who patrolled towns and cities before the creation of police forces used to summon help. Old helmets are on display there, too, showing that the British bobby's helmet has been copied from a range of sources. The Peeler, the first police constable, wore a top hat made of hard leather for protection. Fairly soon after that the style was changed to copy that of the French military cap, and some time later in the nineteenth century the German military helmet exerted its influence and provided the model for the modern policeman's helmet.

Among the marvellous display of decorated truncheons one little one called a 'tipstaff' caught our attention. These would have been carried by some police officers and by the famous Bow Street Runners in the eighteenth century who kept their warrants in the hollow sections of the tipstaffs. It is said that when they made an arrest they used to tap the miscreant on the shoulder as they charged him with the crime in question.

Over the North York moors from Ripon and the Vale of York stands the picturesque seaside holiday resort and fishing port of WHITBY, lying on either side of the estuary of the river Esk twenty miles up the coast from Scarborough. High up on the east cliff its famous old abbey stands stark and proud, a landmark for centuries to sailors way out in the North Sea. The first Anglo-Saxon monastery was built on this site in 657 under the guidance of the great abbess Hilde, or Hilda to give her her modern name. It was here that the Synod of Whitby was convened in 664 to decide whether the Roman or the Celtic church should be followed in determining the date of Easter. The Roman lobby won the day. Hilde's community was also the home of Caedmon the cowherd, the first English poet, who died in Whitby in 680.

Winds sometimes reaching 110 miles an hour have severely

eroded the remaining sections of the thirteenth-century abbey that still stand. In this century the abbey was attacked by German warships which bombarded Scarborough, Whitby and Hartlepool – the first time that these shores had been damaged by enemy action since the Norman Conquest.

Whitby claims another first from the Second World War, when the first German aircraft to be shot down on English soil came down just outside the town.

Below the abbey the parish church of St Mary is well worth a visit. Inside it still retains its eighteenth-century box pews, including the one for the lords of the manor, who sat with their backs to the altar. They had their own entrance to the church, as well, below which is a most unusual grave. The gravestone records the extraordinary fact that the husband and wife buried beneath were both born on 19 September 1800 and after living eighty years and rearing a dozen children died within five hours of each other, again on the same day.

Nearby stands the cross honouring Caedmon, unveiled by Alfred Austen, then poet laureate, in 1898. Christ and the four apostles are depicted on this, alongside King David the Psalmist, Caedmon and Abbess Hilde. She is shown standing on serpents, a reference to the local legend that when the town was plagued with snakes she cut off their heads and turned them into stone. Apparently this explains the tremendous range of ammonites found in the cliffs around Whitby, some in the museum measuring almost a meter across.

Down the 199 steep stone steps which climb the East Cliff to the church you come into Church Street, and on one corner is a little shop owned by Roy Jay, who advertises himself as a jet-carver – one of the last of his profession, which has shrunk to two or three craftsmen from the 1250 jet-carvers who worked in the town towards the close of the last century. I had to begin by asking the obvious question: 'What exactly is jet?'

'Fossilised resin, millions of years old, much older than coal,' he replied. 'For some reason as yet unexplained, from all accounts, the world's best jet is found in the Whitby area. There is a variety known as Spanish jet, but it hasn't the same quality or hardness as Whitby jet.

Polished jet is always black, and because of this Queen Victoria took to wearing it as mourning jewellery after the death of Prince

Albert in 1861. The fashion caught on, and for the rest of her life the jet-carvers of Whitby were kept well occupied creating similar jewellery for the rest of the nation.

Roy finds his jet ten or fifteen miles each side of Whitby, either cut from the cliff or lying on the beach at high-water mark. Most is found casually by people walking along the shoreline. Roy can tell at a glance whether its real jet or not; his simple test is to rub it on the ground. If it leaves a brown mark it will invariably be jet.

Every Ascension Eve Whitby harbour is the setting for the ancient ceremony of Planting the Penny Hedge, which stems from a local legend that originated in Norman times. In those days the hermit of Eskdaleside was set upon by three Norman nobles and suffered fatal injuries. However, before he died he imposed on them and their successors the penance that a hedge built of branches and twigs should be built in Whitby harbour on the Eve

60 Planting the Penny Hedge
       at Whitby.

of Ascension at nine o'clock in the morning. If they failed to build the hedge, or if the hedge failed to stand three tides, they forfeited their lands to the abbot of Whitby. This custom still takes place today, and has been going on for hundreds of years. At the end of the ceremony an ancient horn, rather like a hunting horn, is sounded and the bailiff of the Manor of Filing delivers the rebuke, 'Out on ye! Out on ye!' repeating the words of the hermit of Eskdaleside at the time of his death.

Whitby has rather eerie associations with Dracula and the novel about him by Bram Stoker. Apparently some of the most exciting and horrific chapters were written after Stoker had eaten a crab supper in Whitby and subsequently had a horrific nightmare. Many visitors ask to be directed to Dracula's grave. As a figment of Bram Stoker's imagination Dracula doesn't have a grave, of course, but up on the East Cliff, just to the seaward side of the parish church, there is a stone seat very similar to one Stoker describes his heroine Lucy sitting on one night while Dracula hovers round in the background in the form of a large dog. Needless to say, this seat has become known as Dracula's seat.

Across the river Esk on the West Cliff stands the statue of Captain James Cook looking over the town to the abbey on the other side. Cook began his sailing life in Whitby, and all his ships – *Resolution, Endeavour, Discovery* and *Adventure* – were built in the port. From Mrs Cordelia Stamp, a biographer of Whitby's famous son and a self-confessed devotee of the lovely little Yorkshire port, I learned that the names of his ships tell a great deal about the man himself. He was a strong disciplinarian when it came to cleanliness on board, she told me. Cook had the ship's quarters regularly smoked out to reduce the risk of infectious diseases, and his greatest success in maintaining health at sea was the eradication of scurvy, which he achieved by adding foods like sauerkraut to the ship's diet. (The hands didn't take to the sauerkraut at first, so Cook had it served to the officers only, which soon altered their opinion. In fact it wasn't long before it became so popular that he had to ration it.)

As anyone interested in railways will know, Stockton-on-Tees around the coast from Whitby, has a unique position in the history of steam trains because it was here that the world's first steam-hauled passenger train completed its first journey in 1825. That train had set out from SHILDON in County Durham, the spot nearest to the coalfields of southern Durham from which a railway could be built to the sea with no uphill gradients, allowing either horses or steam engines to pull an economic load down to the port. This first train was pulled by the *Locomotion* and consisted of one passenger coach and fourteen coal wagons, which ended up carrying six hundred passengers by the time they reached Stockton. At top speed the train reached five miles an hour.

In my ignorance I had always associated George Stephenson with the first locomotives. Standing in Shildon, that was tantamount to sacrilege. Stephenson did indeed build the *Locomotion* – I was right on that point – but the first successful locomotive, that is to say the first that was more economical than a horse, was built in Shildon by Timothy Hackworth. He was the first railway works manager and the first railway engineer of real standing. If you go to Shildon you can visit his house, which has been turned into a very attractive museum near the town's station.

Twelve centuries before the social revolution brought about by the coming of the railways the North-East was already in the forefront of national life, as the old monastic settlement of JARROW on the south bank of the river Tyne proves.

The great monastery at Jarrow was founded in 681 and flourished for two centuries until Viking raiders brought about its downfall. The greatest scholar to have lived at Jarrow was the Venerable Bede, copies of whose books were sent far and wide throughout the Christian world, helping to make his monastery one of the greatest centres of culture and learning in the Western world. In the Bede Monastery Museum there are lots of examples of the skill and craftsmanship the monks possessed. There is a beautiful display of coloured Saxon window glass, which archeologists excavating at the site of the monastery have unearthed and reinstated. In its collection of books the museum includes one of the three great Bibles produced at Jarrow.

The monks here followed the rule of St Benedict, and their days were divided into periods of study and prayer. They also did a certain amount of manual work, all in all living a fairly simple life within their community, as one of the displays shows. Living on the banks of the river, they ate an almost exclusively fish diet, eating lots of cockles and winkles, and you can see some of their Saxon winkles on show, complete with the winkle-pickers that would have been used.

St Paul's Church, which stands a couple of hundred yards from the Bede Monastery Museum, was part of the original Saxon monastery built in the middle of the seventh century. It is still the parish church of Jarrow and has been in use for 1300 years. This was the first of the monastery's buildings to be built and contains features with which Bede and his fellow monks would have been familiar. In the wall is an aumbry, a little cupboard used to keep the elements for the Mass, which they would have used. Bede's chair is there too, made from oak and finished with an adze.

Bede was buried in a new porch on the north side of the church and rested there until two monks from Durham – relic-hunters, as it turned out – stole his bones and took them away to Durham Cathedral, where they were placed inside St Cuthbert's coffin along with Cuthbert himself and St Oswald's head, which for some reason was also locked up there.

Up in one of the walls are three tiny Saxon windows. The one in the middle looks like a porthole and is made from a solid piece of stone with a nine-inch hole cut in it. In 1980 archeologists working on the site of the old refectory found a piece of 1300-year-old glass which was cut to fit this, with the result that the window is the only Saxon window glazed with Saxon glass in existence.

During this century Jarrow has become famous for the march which took place to London in 1936. The media at the time dubbed it a hunger march, which hurt the pride of the towns-people of Jarrow and the organisers, to whom it was always a crusade. From Jarrow to London is 291 miles, and 1200 unemployed men came forward to undertake the walk south. The town made a national appeal for funds, and when £400 had been received it was decided that this was enough to cover the costs for 200 men. The medical officer of health for Jarrow examined the 1200 volunteers until he found 200 fit enough to undertake the journey.

In the early 1930s unemployment among employable men in the town following the closing of the main shipyard was running at 85 per cent, and it was in an effort to stimulate new industries that the walkers took their petition for work to London. This was presented at the bar of the House of Commons by Miss Ellen Wilkinson, MP for Jarrow, and attracted widespread sympathy and support. Among the less well known acts of kindness that resulted was the raising of £45,000 by the people of Surrey, about half a million pounds in today's money.

Just across the Tyne, shipbuilding was still very much alive when we visited the town of WALLSEND on a chilly November day in 1978. Swan Hunter is the principal yard here and next to be launched in its famous line of 1500 ships was HMS *Illustrious*. Ships have been built on the Wallsend site since the mid-1850s, and the yard has always prided itself on its ability to build just about any class of ship: submarines, battleships, cargo ships, floating docks and stately ocean liners, the most famous of which was the *Mauretania*.

The *Illustrious* was due to be launched by Princess Margaret shortly after our visit and I took the opportunity of finding out from Norman Gilchrist, one of the directors, what the procedure was for launching a ship of this size. 'What we're going to do is to slide her down the berth,' he explained. 'We do this on a series of what we call "ways", which are a series of continuous lengths of timber with lubricant between them. The lower lengths of timber are fastened to the ground; the upper lengths are fastened to the ship. Between the two you have the lubricated layer. At the appropriate moment the triggers holding the ship will be released, and because it's built on an incline it will slide down the ways and into the river.' It sounded very simple, but the mechanics have to be judged very precisely.

Norman went on to explain that when Princess Margaret pulled the lever to release the bottle that smashed against the ship's bow, she would also release the cables that held the triggers. When she pulled that lever she would be physically launching the ship. No one but her would be involved.

I asked what type of champagne they would be using for this launch. 'We won't be using champagne on this particular ship,' he corrected me. 'It's established practice at warship launches that you use a British or Commonwealth wine. And I think on this particular occasion we will be using a British wine.'

When we were in Swan Hunter we were shown the end of Hadrian's Wall, or rather a plaque announcing where it was found. The piece of wall was excavated while the yard was being extended to build the *Mauretania*, and since keeping it in its original position wasn't very convenient, to say the least, the major section was transferred to Wallsend Park. The Romans started building the wall in Wallsend in AD 122 and it runs across the country for seventy-three miles to the Solway Firth.

Twenty miles up the river Tyne from Wallsend lies the old market town of HEXHAM, famous for its ancient abbey. Like most visitors, this was our first port of call. The Rev. Timothy Withers Green, bearer of a title new to me, Rector and Lecturer, kindly showed me round his historic building, where, as the plaque outside informs the visitor, 'God's people have worshipped . . . since 674.' That was the year when St Wilfred founded the abbey. He heads the list of 'rulers' of Hexham Abbey, which contains five other saints, giving the Rev. Withers Green a lot to live up to.

The abbey has had a turbulent history and has been attacked numerous times in its 1300 years. The Danes came and set fire to it. So did the Scots. As you look round the bottom of the walls you can see where crashing roof timbers have scorched the stonework, and in places there are traces of lead in cracks in the stone where molten lead fell from the roof when the abbey was burned down by the Scots in 1096.

The builders of the abbey used a considerable amount of Roman stonework which they took from ruined buildings nearby. A tall stone I spotted standing in one of the walls originally served as a memorial to a Roman soldier who served on Hadrian's Wall. The inscription below it tells us quite a lot about him. The Rev Withers Green said that the soldier was twenty-five at the time of his death, that he had been recruited in Spain and that he was the legion's standard-bearer. You can see the standard carved clearly on the stone, bearing the image of the sun and decorated with fine plumes. His horse also carries magnificent saddlery. Beneath the two of them is a crouching figure who the Rev. Withers Green reckons is the ancient Briton who killed the soldier. He looks as if he is hiding in the undergrowth, ready to spring to the attack as the legion passes by. It is a wonderful old stone, giving a vivid, dramatic glimpse of our early history.

In the seventh century St Wilfred was Bishop of York, and it was he who built the abbey. His stone bishop's stool still stands in the choir, and for hundreds of years it was on this that kings of Northumbria were crowned. Later it became a sanctuary stool, providing a safe haven for fugitives from the civil law.

Walking round the abbey, my attention was drawn to a Saxon chalice housed in an alcove. It is the oldest chalice in England and was found in the tomb of one of the monks. Not much bigger than an egg cup, it would have been used to take the communion round to worshippers in the vicinity.

61 The Roman memorial stone in Hexham Abbey.

One of the most amazing features of Hexham Abbey is the crypt. To reach it we went down twelve very steep steps, descending about a couple of feet on each one. In the crypt is a little chapel where the relics of St Andrew, brought to Hexham by St Wilfred, were kept. In early days only the priests and monks would have been allowed in here. Pilgrims visiting the shrine were permitted down into the main part of the crypt to see the relic chapel from the outside only.

The Roman occupation of Britain ended about three hundred years before St Wilfred founded Hexham Abbey, and there must have been many Roman buildings and structures still standing in the surrounding areas. Today Hadrian's Wall is the most obvious reminder of the Roman presence, and there is a good-sized section of it still standing outside the village of Wall, about five miles north of Hexham. This is the Brunton section, complete with a littel turret of the same name. Here I was joined by Tony Macdonald, officer for the Northumberland National Park. We had seen the end of the wall during our visit to Wallsend, and Brunton lies slightly less than halfway along towards the Solway. For most of its distance in Northumberland the Roman engineers and their British slaves used locally quarried stone for their building work. Into Cumbria the stone was less easy to find and initially the wall was built of turf, later replaced with stone brought from further afield.

Standing on the wall, I was about six feet above the ground, though when it was built it was supposed to have been fifteen feet high at the parapet on the northern side. Small forts were built every mile with six or seven larger garrison forts spread out along the wall's length from coast to coast. Between each of the little forts two small turrets were erected, like the one at Brunton, to provide shelter for a small group of troops during the day. On the south side of the wall the Romans built a 'vallum', a line of two parallel banks with a ditch running between them, which is supposed to have delimited the edge of the true military zone. Everything between that and the wall was military territory under the direct control of the military commanders in the area.

MORPETH, the county town of Northumberland which lies some twenty-five miles to the north-east of Hexham, was the home of an eminent English scientist named William Turner, dubbed the Father of English Botany and about whom I'm ashamed to say I knew absolutely nothing until *Down Your Way* went to Morpeth at the end of March 1984. It was only when I met George Chapman, retired headmaster of the King Edward VI School, that I found that I wasn't alone in my ignorance. 'I'm not surprised you know little about him,' George comforted me. 'There appeared to be very little known about him in Morpeth when I came up here in the mid-1960s. He was a Tudor gentleman of considerable influence throughout the reign of Henry VIII, Edward VI and Queen Mary. He was the son of the tanner in the town, spent his boyhood here and then left for Pembroke College, Cambridge. He was a great friend of Nicholas Ridley, Hugh Latimer and William Cecil, later to become the Chancellor of Queen Elizabeth. Turner ended his life as Dean of Wells and the writer of numerous herbals – the first herbals in English which were scientifically accurate. It is for that reason that he is referred to in most quarters, certainly in Europe, as the first man in England to write a scientific account of plants.

'When I first came to Morpeth there seemed to be little known about him, although I enquired, and then someone on the council thought there was a book connected with him in one of the offices . . . We found wrapped in newspaper an old herbal of his which they said they had had an offer of forty pounds for. Now, I wrote to the Linnaean Society and got a letter back which pointed out that it was worth at least one to two thousand! The book's in very good condition, it's been rebound and is now well looked after *in* the safe rather than on top of it.'

The book is well illustrated and tells you where various plants grow both in this country and on the Continent. Turner was also responsible for the first definite identification of 200 to 300 British flora. He is credited with bringing the first mulberry trees into England, and his approach to the use of herbs and medicine in general is very enlightened for its time. In 1949 a British pharmacopoeia recommended the use of coltsfoot for the treatment of dry irritant coughs. Turner recommended the same plant for 'the dry cough and the shortness of wind' in 1531.

For a period of ninety years from the 1870s until the mid-1960s Morpeth was the site of the 'Olympic Games', an annual sporting event which drew competitors from all over the country. Events included the 80 yards, the 110 yards, long jump, high jump, pole-vaulting, as well as competitions for quoits and the Cumberland and Westmorland wrestling world championships – not to mention pitch and toss (a gambling game played with two coins on your hand that had to be thrown up and fall down to show two heads). Unlike the other Olympic Games, the Morpeth ones were run for money. On the Saturday and Monday of August Bank Holiday, when they took place, there would have been a dozen or fifteen bookmakers in the field taking bets, and the competitors themselves weren't amateurs by any means. The 110 yards was the premier event and carried £100 as prize money –

a sizeable sum twenty-five years ago. Prior to that, when the prize money was more like £50, the winner would also be presented with a gold medal.

One Morpeth man who is no stranger to winning athletics medals is the long-distance runner Jim Alder, who held the world and Commonwealth records for the 30,000 metres, and won a gold medal for the marathon at the 1966 Commonwealth Games, not to mention a silver and a bronze on other occasions. Jim had TB when he was a child and was advised to take up sport to improve his health. He played football and cricket, but as he grew into his mid-teens running took over. In those days athletics was demanding in more than physical terms. Jim lost four weeks' wages in order to win his first medal, and throughout the sixteen years that he competed for Great Britain he was also working forty hours a week as a bricklayer. It seemed amazing to me, looking at the life of top athletes today, but there was one occasion when Jim ran four and a half miles to work at seven-thirty one morning, wheeled and laid concrete until lunch time, caught the five o'clock flight to London in the afternoon and at quarter to eight ran the seventh fastest time in the world for the 10,000 metres.

The most northerly town *Down Your Way* ever visited in Northumberland, and the most northerly in England, was BERWICK-UPON-TWEED, that tiny English enclave that lies across the river on the Scottish bank. Berwick has changed hands between the English and Scots at least fourteen times in its history. The first recorded sacking of the city took place in 1173, when the English won it from the Scots. It then changed hands several times over the next three centuries until 1482, when Richard Duke of Gloucester, later Richard III, captured it for the English, who have retained it every since – up to a point, as the people of Berwick are quick to remind you.

The town is ringed by magnificent defensive walls which run for a mile and a quarter around its circumference. Edward I began their construction after capturing the town in 1296. As time went on they were improved by various kings and queens until the reign of Queen Elizabeth. She built a rather shorter circuit, using the latest principles imported from northern Italy. These form the main part of the town walls today. There is nothing else like them in the British Isles. They have 'bastions' and 'flankers' and similar features that aren't found anywhere else outside the continent of Europe. The basic height of the walls is twenty feet, though in places they have been heightened to fifty feet.

The walls are turfed on top, and in the course of walking round them we discovered that for the last few years a series of races called the Running of the Walls have been held on them. Male competitors run five laps, a total distance of six and a quarter miles, while youngsters run a single lap in their events; with its popularity growing every year, the men's race alone attracts as many as 400 competitors.

Berwick is the home of the King's Own Scottish Borderers, who have their headquarters in a splendid set of barracks, the oldest in Great Britain, built by Sir John Vanburgh in 1717. Here they have a smashing regimental museum filled with all sorts of uniforms, weapons, drums and regimental flags. One unexpected item with a nice story attached to it is the Mons tablecloth, which carries the embroidered signatures of at least a hundred officers. They had all just enjoyed a cup of tea in a little coffee shop

62 A reconstructed barrack room of the 1750s in the museum of the King's Own Scottish Borderers at Berwick-upon-Tweed. (The soldier, his wife and child lived in the bunk behind the curtain.)

outside Mons in 1914 when the two elderly ladies who ran it came up and asked if they would autograph the tablecloth, which they duly did. Come the end of the war one of those officers, who had risen from major to brigadier during the four years of fighting (showing just how many had been killed), found himself back in the same coffee shop, where the two ladies produced the table-cloth once again and asked him to sign it a second time. They had spent their war carefully embroidering all the signatures, and once the bigadier's had been embroidered they gave him the tablecloth, which is now among the museum's many treasured possessions.

One of the most imposing buildings in the centre of Berwick is the magnificent Guildhall, which is topped by a splendid spire. The Guildhall has a gaol above it, a big timber gaol with six cells, from where a fair number of prisoners were transported to Australia, all gruesomely branded on the arm with the symbol of the black bear, Berwick's civic insignia.

We had climbed up to the belfry, where Jack Weatherburn, Berwick's Sergeant at Mace, proudly displayed the town's eight bells. Before hearing each of these in turn he explained why there are eight beer mugs lined up on a shelf on the wall. 'Each bellringer has his own pint pot, and these are all filled on special occasions by the mayor,' he told me. 'When they're ringing as a team, if one of them misses his pull on the bell, it puts the whole team off, so he forfeits a pint.'

Until recently there were no bells in Berwick parish church and a tradition evolved that during the service in which each new vicar was installed he had to run from the church down the street to the Guildhall, climb into the belfry, ring the largest bell and then run back to his pulpit. This announced his formal arrival in the parish and as Jack added, it may have helped to keep his sermon short.

Jack then rang the curfew bell, which is sounded every night at eight fifteen and in times gone by used to be the signal that all the townspeople had to be inside the gates before they closed. The 'pancake' bell gets its name from being cracked and having a flat tone, but it is rung every Shrove Tuesday for the quarter of an hour immediately before midday. Then there is the 'freedom' bell, rung whenever anyone is awarded the freedom of Berwick. The 'death' bell used to be tolled to announce a death in the

town, for which the fee was a guinea; families who couldn't run
to that were charged ten and sixpence to have the lighter 'freedom'
bell tolled instead.

The North-West

63 Wansfell, Cumbria.

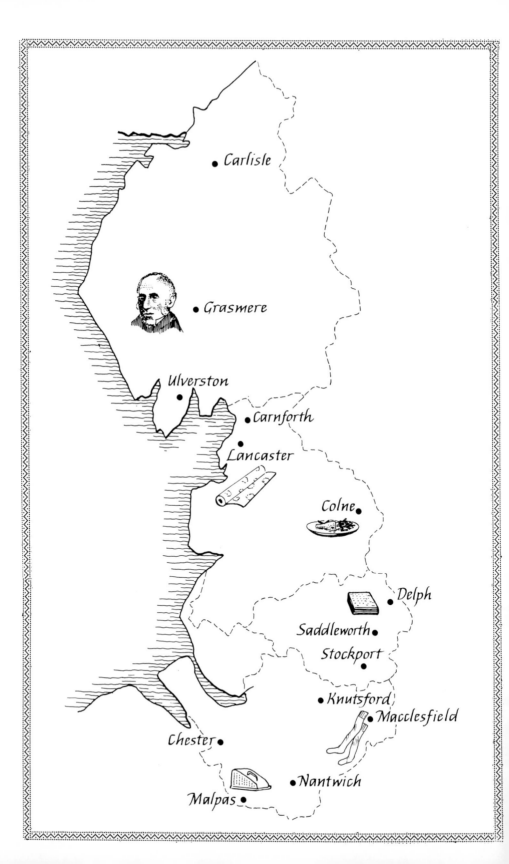

Carlisle

Grasmere

Ulverston

Carnforth

Lancaster

Colne

Delph

Saddleworth

Stockport

Knutsford

Macclesfield

Chester

Nantwich

Malpas

Every August in the 1930s the Eton Ramblers used to have a cricket tour in Cheshire, so I got to know the county well. Black and white magpie houses, lots of woods and meres and cattle grazing in lush green meadows. It was a peaceful, picturesque county with delightful villages and its masterpiece, the old walled city of Chester, with so much evidence of the Roman occupation. The left-handed, or anti-clockwise, racecourse is right in the town, and racegoers get a marvellous view as the horses race round the oval course. Our horse W. G. Greys was leading up to the long final bend, but when the horses came out of it into the home straight, W. G. Greys was nowhere to be seen!

We had a lot of schoolboy fun on these cricket tours. We used to go to Blackpool to sample the fun fairs and the Golden Mile. It was here that we paid sixpence to look through a hole in a barrel. Sitting inside was the notorious Rector of Stiffkey, who claimed to have 'saved' the souls of many London chorus girls. We had a large friend who was secretary of our club. On one of the piers was a talking weighing machine. We were all weighed individually and then it was his turn to get on. 'One at a time, please,' said the voice. I have always loved Blackpool, with its numerous seaside shows, the trams on the promenade, the illuminations and that fantastic Golden Mile with some of the best side-shows in the world. There are miles of sandy beaches, which in season are packed with holidaymakers, many of them regulars every year. Blackpool's industry is to make fun for people. And how well they succeed, with their theme song of 'I do like to be beside the seaside', played for so many years on the organ of the Tower Ballroom by Reginald Dixon. A lovely man. I once did a broadcast of a race he and I had down the Grand National Scenic Railway in the amusement park. There was a double track with each car alongside the other and the winner was the one who was least frightened and therefore braked less. Weight also helped a bit. The awful thing is I cannot now remember who won, though I was certainly heavier than Reginald.

For the Old Trafford Tests we always stay at the Swan Hotel at Bucklow Hill, not far from Knutsford in Cheshire. If not playing golf at Mere Golf Club, I usually have a picnic lunch in Tatton Park, and walk round its many acres of woodland and gardens. Old Trafford itself has changed remarkably since we televised our first Test from there in 1952. We used to have a commentary box high up on scaffolding, and one of the sights of the day for the crowds was Jim Swanton and Roy Webber climbing the rather precarious ladders. We once had to abandon ship temporarily when a gale was rocking the scaffolding; but we felt fairly safe so long as we had Swanton and Webber to act as ballast. It was here in 1955 that Paul Winslow of South Africa hit Tony Lock for six to reach his hundred. It was a steepling drive straight over the bowler's head and went soaring over the top of our commentary position.

It was also from this high perch that we witnessed Jim Laker's incredible feat in 1956, when he took 19 wickets for 90 runs against Australia. That's a record which surely will never be broken. The ground itself now looks a picture with its gaily coloured bucket seats. We occupy a brand-new stand at the Stretford end, and have a superb view as we look down from the roof of the stand.

Lancashire is wonderfully served by motorways, weaving their way round the network of industrial towns, which all seem to be joined up together. Three special favourites of mine are Rochdale, which conjures up clogs, Gracie Fields and the giant frame of Cyril Smith; Wigan, because I now know that it has a pier; and Liverpool, because it is the home of the Grand National at Aintree. I have been twice and watched once from a box in the rather old grandstand, and once down by Beechers. I must say that it is terrifying to watch the horses jumping and galloping at such close quarters. It is only then that one realises how fast they go.

I'm afraid my pre-*Down Your Way* knowledge of the Lake District was confined to Wordsworth, Beatrix Potter and of course the Lakes. But this was all from reading or hearsay. My only sad connection was the tragedy of Donald Campbell in his attempt to beat the world waterspeed record in 1967 on Lake Coniston. He crashed at 328 mph in his famous *Bluebird*, and his body has never been recovered.

I had met him at several sporting functions and found him a delightful companion. He was outwardly calm and self-effacing, but underneath was a spirit of determination, guts and a sense of dedication. He was a man of steel and a tremendous patriot. The record he was seeking was not for himself but for England. He was also a superb driver on land, and I felt very proud during one Monte Carlo Rally that he trusted me to drive his Bentley. I have been to Lake Coniston since, and he is still a folk-hero amongst the Lake people.

Cheshire is for me inseparable from the delicious cheese that bears its name, and it was on a visit to the market town of MALPAS that we had the chance to visit Overton Hall, the home of Mrs Henry Barnett and one of the few farms still making Cheshire cheese in its own dairy. The lovely old timber-framed house has a long and colourful history dating back to the Middle Ages. During the Civil War it was the home of a staunchly royalist family who mortgaged everything to support the cause of Charles I, as a result of which the house was completely plundered by the conquering Parliamentarian forces. Later in 1656, when Cromwell appointed a Major General to rig the county elections, the High Sheriff and the Justices of Cheshire came to Overton Hall and spent three days planning their opposition – an act of defiance that culminated in the Restoration of Charles II in 1660.

Today the three hundred acres of the farm are given over to mixed farming. Although the green pastures were looking pretty parched and arid when we were there, Cheshire and the area around Malpas in particular has some of the richest dairy land in the country, the result of which is the cheese that I and so many other people enjoy.

'There are three types,' Mrs Barnett began. 'The red and the white, and the blue, which is unique and is only made at one farm.' At Overton Hall they make the traditional round red Cheshire which gets its colour from a natural vegetable dye.

Compared with cheddar, for example, Cheshire cheese matures

quickly; you can eat it within a month to eight weeks of its being made. At eight to nine months it achieves its best taste when it is mature and mellow. Mrs Barnett reckoned that they produce upwards of a hundred cheeses a week at Overton Hall. The largest of these look rather like footstools and weigh fifty pounds. Then there is a smaller size like turrets on children's sandcastles which weigh two and a half pounds.

Malpas has one of the finest churches in Cheshire, the lovely 600-year-old St Oswald's, built of mellow red sandstone and decorated with masses of gargoyles. For a couple of centuries it was served by two rectors, a curious state of affairs which arose after a visit made to Malpas by James I. The story I heard went that His Majesty arrived unannounced at a local hostelry called the Lion and, without revealing his true identity, settled down to dine. Since there were no other travellers to keep him company, he invited the rector and curate to join him. After their meal they each paid their share but the rector decided that he wasn't going to stump up for the curate. Whereupon King James revealed who he was and told them that when he got back to London he was going to make the curate equal to the rector, and until 1884 Malpas had two rectors. There is a big black chair in the Lion today as a memento of the visit. It is known as the King's Chair, and by tradition anyone who sits in it has to stand a round.

NANTWICH, lying a few miles to the east of Malpas, has several notable pubs itself. We saw one called the Crown which really looked as if it was about to collapse, though it was made clear to me that a considerable amount of money had been spent to ensure that this venerable building (it is thought to be a thousand years old) remains standing. In Saxon times Nantwich was a major centre for salt-mining in England, and when the industry was at its height the workers on the neighbouring estates and labourers in the town were not paid in money but received their wages in salt. And this may well have given rise to the expression: 'He's worth his salt.'

Alan Chapman, a tailor we visited, told us some of the sayings that are peculiar to Nantwich. For instance, when a neighbour gave him a sprig of honesty from her garden, she handed it over with the caution that it was considered very bad luck to offer it without at the same time saying the Nantwich rhyme:

Honesty is a very rare plant only grown by few.
It's sometimes found in Nantwich, but it's never
found in Crewe.

(But that rivalry between the two towns is another story.)

People born within the town boundary are known as 'Dabbers', Alan went on to tell us, and once a year they receive a sum of money for this privilege, making Nantwich the only town in England which actually pays people to live within its boundaries. The name 'Dabbers' may have something to do with the old practice of sealing bargains in the cattle market many years ago, when one of the parties held out the palm of his hand and the other would lick his forefingers and 'dab' them down on it to fix their bond. Nothing was ever written – that act of 'dabbing it down' constituted their agreement pure and simple.

This part of Cheshire is rich in old timber-framed buildings like the Crown at Nantwich, and less than twenty miles to the east stands Little Moreton Hall, a superb example of a moated Tudor mansion built in the second half of the fifteenth century. It is now owned by the National Trust, which has undertaken extensive roofing and other building work to preserve this marvellous old house. And old it appears. I had to admit to the administrator, Stanley Middlemiss, that bits of it look like the house that Jack built; all the lines are crooked and parts look as if they might well fall down.

'I think this is the unique feature of Little Moreton Hall,' he gently corrected. 'It looks like that, but it isn't. It's very solid, largely due to the timbers which were well chosen by the builders. They have warped and twisted throughout the centuries, and the warping and twisting in fact keeps the building up. If they cracked, the building would come down. But they don't. They stand the strain.'

The house is justly famous for its long gallery. Again, the floor of this slopes at quite an angle, though the National Trust have strengthened it to make it perfectly safe. It is renowned, too, for the designs of its glass-work. Because of the movement in the windows many of the original panes have cracked and been replaced, so only a small amount of the original glass remains, but the designs remain masterpieces to the present day. Up on the roof are stone tiles, the largest of which require two people

to handle them! It has been estimated that the weight of the
roofing materials over the long gallery alone is equivalent to that
of six double-decker buses.

In the parlour you can see examples of early domestic wall-
painting dating from around 1570; these were later covered by
wooden panelling when the fortunes of the Moreton family improved and they could afford this more luxurious internal decoration. In the great hall there is a magnificent dining table which
still has its original oak top measuring thirty feet in length,
showing that it must have been cut from a mighty tree. As great
a treasure is a delightful cupboard of drawers dating from around
the same period, which still open and close easily. This would
have been used by its original owners to store herbs and spices.

MACCLESFIELD is one of several Cheshire towns with a strong
textile tradition based on silk-weaving. In the Rowe Street Sunday
school we met Jill Norris, the director of the Silk Heritage Project,
which had been set up to find out as much as possible about the
history of the industry in Macclesfield. The building where we
met had itself been erected as a result of the silk trade, to provide
a means of educating the children who worked in the mills
and whose only school day was Sunday. In the course of their
research, Jill and her colleagues were finding out how silk was
made and what is still left in the town, as well as asking people
for their memories of an industry which was still active well into
this century.

As a luxury fabric silk was very much subject to booms and
slumps, and mills came and went as the market dictated. It was
also an industry which was very late in being mechanised, and
there were still people in Macclesfield hand-weaving silk at home
between the two wars. One of Jill's visitors was an elderly man
who had called in only the week before to chat about his mother,
who had been a handloom weaver in Paradise Street. He remembered as a small child lying in his cradle while his mother was
weaving away. She had the cradle attached to her loom, so that
the rhythm of her weaving rocked her baby.

Charles Rowe, after whom the street was named, was the first
man to establish a mill for 'throwing' silk, as it was called, in
Macclesfield. That was in the 1740s. Another famous name in the
Macclesfield silk trade is that of John Ryle, who emigrated to
Paterson, New Jersey, where he set up a silk-weaving trade which

lasted until comparatively recently. A lot of Macclesfield people emigrated to Paterson, and continued doing so at least until the First World War. So Jill wrote to the Paterson daily paper to ask if anyone remembered Macclesfield, and had eight replies within a very few weeks.

Much of her research is based on asking lots of questions, and among these was one about the sort of work people might have carried out. Looking down the list of possible occupations there were several I had never come across. What was a 'soaker', for example?

'Those were the people who got the gum off the silk,' replied Jill. 'Raw silk, when it came into the country, was very harsh and unpleasant, and full of gum. This had to be removed very carefully by being boiled off. If you did it too fast you could make your silk yarn very lumpy and nasty.'

Next on my list was a 'tierer'.

'The tierer was the little boy who helped the printers. A lot of the old printing was done by block-printing – hand-printing with an enormous block rather like a potato-cut or lino-cut. The tierer was the little lad who had the job of coming round with a vat of paint into which the printer dipped his block.'

Finally there were three names: 'reeler', 'gatter' and 'up-twister'.

'They were similar,' said Jill. 'They all referred to final stages in the preparation of the silk yarn. The reeler and up-twister wound the yarn to get the actual twist and thickness you needed. You had a different yarn for knitting silk stockings from the one you would use for weaving silk for ties or handkerchiefs.'

Another important point she made was that the majority of the silk-workers were women. The soakers, dyers and printers tended to be men, but the other jobs were usually done by women.

I remember that it was a few weeks before Christmas that the *Down Your Way* team visited KNUTSFORD, the Cheshire town which probably derived its name from a visit made by King Canute in 1017, and provided the setting for Mrs Gaskell's novel *Cranford*. However, our minds were on spring-time festivities when we called at Tatton Antiques at the bottom of King Street, to find out about Knutsford's unique Royal May Day from Joan Leach, something of an authority on the town's history. She told us that this special celebration dates from another royal visit made by the then Prince and Princess of Wales in 1887. They stayed at nearby Tatton Park, so that the Prince could cut the first sod in the construction of the Manchester Ship Canal. Unfortunately, the canal's constructors found that they still hadn't the necessary funds to start the project, so the Prince merely opened a local exhibition. However, when the royal couple came through Knutsford at the beginning of May they were so delighted by the May Day performance laid on for them that they allowed the celebrations thereafter to be called Royal May Days, the only ones in the world.

It isn't only the name of the May Day festivities that is unique; Knutsford is also the only place in the world where the roads and pavements are ceremonially decorated with coloured sand, and to learn about this unusual custom we met Ray Veal, known officially as the Sandman. By tradition he and all the other holders of this office use very fine-coloured sand fed through a funnel to write and draw traditional messages and patterns around the town. 'It's a tradition that goes back to King Canute,' he explained. 'Having forded the river he got sand in his sandals, so he sat on a rock on the other side of the river to shake it out, and while he was doing this a young married couple walked by. Canute wished them as much happiness and as many children as there were grains of sand in his footwear. (I just hope he didn't have too much sand in his sandal.)

On May Day morning Ray is out and about at five o'clock. 'God bless our Royal May Queen,' he writes outside the young lady's house, along with other time-honoured messages around the town. Brides in Knutsford are treated to the same ceremony by the Sandman and, like a chimney sweep at a wedding, Ray reckons that his visit brings good luck. 'In the thirty years that I've been doing it, I haven't known one split up yet,' he announced proudly.

Every year hundreds of thousands of tourists from all over the world flock to the ancient city of CHESTER ringed by its walls that stand on their Roman foundations. Entire medieval streets are preserved, recalling the time in the Middle Ages when Chester was an important port – long before Liverpool was ever heard of. Supreme among the city's buildings is the cathedral, which we approached along St Werburgh's Street under a medieval archway and into Abbey Square, once the courtyard of the medieval monastery founded at the end of the eleventh century by a community of Benedictine monks. On our tour, given by the Dean, the Very Reverend Ingram Cleasby, we saw the magnificent medieval refectory where the monks would have dined and the abbot would have entertained his principal guests on a dais at the end. As the Dean reminded me, hospitality was an important feature of monasteries in the Middle Ages, and this tradition is still maintained in Chester, where the refectory is open to visitors all through the season, allowing them to eat in a building that has served this purpose for over seven hundred years.

64 Ray Veal, the Knutsford Sandman, at work on May Day morning.

In the cathedral itself the choir is regarded by many people as the real treasure. Its wood-carving dates from 1380 and is among the finest to be found in Britain. It is generally thought to have been the work of a team of carvers who carved the stalls in Lincoln Cathedral. Over each of the forty stalls there is an intricately carved canopy or tabernacle, with little figureheads and angels decorating them. Looking around, I saw the unlikely figure of an elephant, made all the more unusual because whoever carved it gave the animal horse's legs, and for a howdah built on its back a little castle with medieval windows.

Nearby I also spotted the picture of the Madonna and Child painted on cobwebs which fascinates thousands of visitors each year, and which inspired an artist we visited in Wales to try her hand at this difficult type of work. The Dean told me that this was painted in the Tyrol at the turn of the eighteenth century, when there was quite a flourishing local craft of cobweb painting.

We ended our visit to Chester just the other side of the city wall at the racecourse, which today stands almost slap in the middle of the town. The Chester race meeting is claimed to be one of the oldest in the racing calendar, with records dating back to 1540. It is a very compact course, accommodating up to sixteen horses, and, as Ray Walls the manager confirmed, it favours a short horse with a good draw at the start. The two famous races held here are the Chester Cup and the Chester Vase, the latter being an official trial for the Derby. Up in the Long Room are the honour boards showing the names of all the winners, which have a rather nice tradition associated with them and one that is unique to Chester: during a race meeting there is always a signwriter standing by to put the name of the winning horse on to the board, with the owner's name, as soon as a race has finished.

Down in the south of Greater Manchester we went to STOCKPORT to visit its 700-year-old street market which is held on Fridays and Saturdays. Almost everything seems to be sold there – I even signed a cricket bat on one stall. As you might expect, a market as old as this has built up dozens of time-honoured traditions over the centuries, including its own special vocabulary. Bill Johnson, one of the stallholders, gave me a taste of some of the words that completely baffled him when he first took a stall at Stockport. To begin with, the market isn't called a market, it's a 'gaff'. Then there's the market superintendent. He's a 'toby'. 'Because he puts you in jug?' I quipped. Profit margins are referred to as 'bats'. And a stall, Bill told me, isn't a stall but a 'joint'.

'Bagataway' was another name I came across in Stockport which I hadn't heard before. It came up in a conversation with Jeff Mounkley, who was going to Los Angeles later that summer with the British Lacrosse Team to take part in a pre-Olympic tournament. I only knew a little about lacrosse, but Bagataway, Jeff explained, was the name of the original game played by North American Indians. If the present game looks perilous (I remember seeing a game at Lord's once, where the players were allowed to hit each other over the head, though that counts as a foul now) the original version sounded positively lethal – and was sometimes. In Bagataway there is no fixed size of field and no fixed number of players; you just start off with the ball and everyone goes hunting for it regardless of who gets in the way.

While we were in Stockport we heard a lot about the local ratcatcher, Ken Edwards, but I hadn't reckoned on meeting some of his quarry when we called at his home to meet him. Ken described being able to take home some of the rats as one of the perks of his job, though I doubt if many others would see it in that light. He keeps about a hundred in cages in his garden, all fully checked by veterinary laboratories and treated with antibiotics, which he trains for various purposes. Ken and his rats appear in horror films like *The Black Death* and George Orwell's *1984*, in which they are trained to attack him. With his assistant, Robin (the two work under the name of 'Ratman and Robin'!), Ken also takes his rats to discos up and down the country, where thirty of them attack him on stage as the last word in what he referred to as 'bad-taste entertainment', a description with which I didn't quibble.

Up in the north-east corner of Greater Manchester, nestling in the foothills of the Pennines, are the group of seven or eight villages collectively known as SADDLEWORTH. This is the name of the parish where the original farms lay around which the villages grew in the Industrial Revolution. In the village of Uppermill we went to see Peter Ashworth, who we had been told was the Squire of the Morris dancers. The Morris team began in Uppermill in the early 1970s, adopting a typically colourful costume with large bowler hats decorated with fresh flowers; red and blue sashes; red, white and blue waistcoats; black breeches; white socks and clogs. In addition to the dancers there is a little band of musicians playing concertinas, accordions, penny whistles, melodions, fifes and drums. There is no shortage of enthusiasm among the team – one member finally retired at the age of seventy-two. The Uppermill Morris men perform four rushcart dances based round a tower of rushes fifteen feet high, which are towed round the villages on a two-wheeled cart – pretty hard going from the sight of the hills. The second Saturday after 12 August, the old wakes day in Saddleworth, is the time

65 Ken Edwards and assistant (alias Batman and Robin)
with some of their charges.

for the rushcart ceremony that lasts over two days. Teams come
from all over the country to take part in the cart-pulling and
braking, and there is one man who each year has the distinction
of riding on top of the rush tower. Once the rush tower has
finished its tour it is dismantled and the rushes are spread out
on the floor of the church in Uppermill, where they are mixed
with sweet-smelling herbs.

Close to the little bridge over the river Tame in the village of
DELPH lives Clara Shaw, who recalled for us the old practice of
making and baking on bakestones which she remembered from
her childhood. The stone I saw was about a foot square and
seemed to be made out of slate. The rock is actually a shale, she
told me, which used to be dug out from a nearby stream where
the stones were worked into their rough shapes before being fired,

a process which hardened them for kitchen use. In their final dressing each stone was given a slight hollow on its base, so that there would be a clearance when it was put in the oven. The main use for bakestones in Delph, Clara recalled, was to make bakestone muffins, big round cakes about three-quarters of an inch thick, which sounded absolutely delicious.

We couldn't leave Delph without paying our respects to mine host at the White Lion, a man known to cricket-lovers the world over and a great friend of mine from thirty or more years ago, Sonny Ramadhin, who with his equally famous partner Alf Valentine pulled off the celebrated West Indies victory at Lord's in 1950. The White Lion is Sonny's third pub, and he took it over in 1962. It is well and truly a cricketer's pub, with players coming from both sides of the Pennines to visit the landlord and while away many happy hours chatting about cricket.

A visit to COLNE in the eastern corner of Lancashire gave us the opportunity to find out about the Pendle witches we had heard such a lot about. The man to whom we went for further information was Edgar Peel, co-author of *The Trial of the Lancashire Witches*. I began by asking the significance of 'Pendle'. 'It's the name of a prominent hill across the valley which has given its name to the district,' he answered. The witches lived in the area in the early years of the seventeenth century. Their case came to light in Colne itself following the death of a pedlar, whom it was claimed died as a result of a spell cast by a teenage member of the coven. This took place on Wednesday, 19 March 1612. The girl was later brought before the magistrate and confessed to the crime, as well as telling a lot of silly stories about her grandmother, other members of the family and neighbours. The result was that a dozen people from in or around Pendle Forest were eventually taken to Lancaster, where they spent the whole of the summer in the dungeons before being brought to trial in August. Although it wasn't illegal in England to be a witch, it was certainly illegal to maim or kill people by witchcraft. For reasons which Edgar admits he can not satisfactorily explain, most of the accused confessed to killing people with their spells, and seven women and two men were found guilty and hanged.

On *Down Your Way* we discovered quite a lot of unusual games, and in Colne we came across a new one to me which made use of a less menacing 'spell' than those of the Pendle witches – the game is actually called Knur and Spell. From Sam Ansell, a former champion and chief referee, I learned that it is a game with similarities to teeing off in golf. The 'knur' is a small ball of porcelain about the size of a gob-stopper; the 'spell' a spring trap used in Yorkshire to flick the knur into the air in order to be struck. The object of the game is to knock the knur as far as possible. The stick used to hit it looked to me rather like a billiard cue fitted with a club head about the size of a playing card. As Sam explained, in Lancashire they use a sort of gallows called a 'pin', from which the knur is suspended, rather than a spell. In either case hitting the ball looked pretty tricky to me, but good players can knock a knur two hundred yards, I gather.

We also discovered three firsts in Colne, mentioned to us with pride by Geoff Crambie, a local historian. Colne, he told us, had the first purpose-built public cinema in Great Britain; it missed having the first in the world by a bare six months. It also had the first fish-and-chip shop in Great Britain, opened by a fishmonger called Joe Harry Pickles at the end of the last century. On a visit to France he noticed the strange shapes in which French cooks served fried potatoes and, on this return home, decided to try serving these with fish fried in batter. His idea caught on, and from it stemmed the fish-and-chip trade. Colne is also the proud owner of the only surviving pair of wheeled stocks in the country, which were also the first to be made – a first and a last, so to speak.

Until the river Lune silted up in the last century, LANCASTER was an important port and, according to local tradition, James Williamson, a painter and decorator in the town, used to watch sailors on the ships preserving their sails with linseed oil and hit on the idea of applying the same technique to waterproof products ashore. The oil-coated fabrics he created became useful table coverings because they could be wiped clean, like the one we used to have in the nursery, and by the time he died in 1879 James Williamson had developed a very successful business. His son took over the company and extended it greatly, moving into the production of linoleum and building his Lancaster-based firm into the largest linoleum producer in the world. Linoleum is also based on oxidised linseed oil, which is mixed with rosin, wood flour, cork and colouring matters – applied to a hessian backing before being hung up for three or four weeks to allow the linseed oil to dry out.

Today the linoleum manufacture is based in the firm's sister company in Scotland. The Lancaster firm, Nairn Coated Products, concentrates on the new generation of vinyl wall coverings. The name 'vinyl' may be very familiar, but I wonder how many people really know what the material is. I certainly didn't until Frank Jefferson, the technical director, explained. 'Vinyl is produced from ethylene, which is derived from petroleum, and hydrogen chloride, which is produced from salt. These are combined to form a substance called vinyl chloride, which is then linked together to form long chains known as polyvinylchloride (PVC). In a liquid state this is mixed with other substances and is applied to its paper backing by a coating machine, after which the two are fused in an oven to produce the flexible vinyl coverings that decorate many walls today.'

Seven miles north of Lancaster, we visited the railway town of CARNFORTH on a bright October day. At one time there were three railway stations in the town: one for the Furness railway coming in from Barrow; one for the Midland railway coming in from Leeds and ultimately from St Pancras; and the third for the London North-Western railway coming up from Euston. The main railway station in Carnforth was the setting for the film version of *Brief Encounter* with Celia Johnson and Trevor Howard. The refreshment room used in the film is now the railwaymen's signing-on point. However, our railway destination was Steamtown, a working steam museum and home to forty privately owned steam engines, including the *Flying Scotsman* and *Lord Nelson*. Several of the engines are run by British Rail on their secondary lines as tourist attractions during the summer months, and Steamtown hires out coaches as well. As a sideline they have developed a restoration centre, where initially the ten Orient Express Pullman cars were restored between 1979 and 1982 for the English leg of that famous run.

Across the A6 towards the sea we came across a very unexpected American connection in the village of Warton, where the village policeman, Graham Parkinson, welcomed us into his house, called, revealingly, Washington House. It was in about 1382 that a John Washington crossed the country from County Durham, where the family originated, and settled in Warton, where his line of the family remained until the middle of the eighteenth century. George Washington, first president of the

United States, never came to Britain (he was born at Mount Vernon in Virginia), but there is a legend that he remembered his English ancestry when the time came to design the American flag.

In 1460 the Washington family had built the tower to the church at Warton, and when this was finished Robert Washington carved a stone shield about two feet high into the stonework, depicting what he claimed to be the family crest. This shows three stars, and underneath them a number of stripes. Apparently this was Washington's inspiration. In 1976 the Washington House in Warton was presented with a full-sized American flag by a visiting US senator, on condition that it is always flown on Independence Day and on George Washington's birthday. Graham admitted that he doesn't have a flag pole, but he makes do with levering it out of one of the upstairs windows, from where it does fly very well, he assured me.

A little way up the road from Warton we called at a hospital for birds of prey run by Alan Oswald, who every afternoon during the summer gives displays of trained eagles and falcons to visitors at Leighton Hall, a stately home nearby. In fact it was from these displays that word got about that Alan knew how to care for birds like this, people started bringing injured birds they had found to be treated by him, and so the hospital developed. There were two tawny owls, a barn owl, a kestrel and an eagle in residence when we met Alan. The kestrel had been in the hospital for two or three months and was due to leave a week later. To help it transfer from the hospital to the wild Alan had it flying in a 'hacking aviary', where it could see open space all round. After three weeks of getting used to that, a hatch is opened to allow the bird to fly out at will and it returns to the hopital to feed for as long as it needs to before gradually fending for itself in the wild.

It was always a pleasure to find one of the old crafts, and in ULVERSTON in Cumbria we discovered a firm which had revived the art of making crystal glass. Martin Johnson, the managing director of Cumbria Crystal, set up business in the old cattle mart, producing an enormous range of wine glasses, decanters, jelly bowls, candlesticks, ash trays and virtually anything else that has ever been made in crystal.

And what is crystal? 'Ordinary glass is basically a mixture of silica sand, potash and soda lime,' Martin explained. 'But back in the seventeenth century it had the nasty habit of crazing and cracking after several years. So a royal commission was given to a chemist called George Ravenscroft to try and formulate a method of overcoming this crazing. In 1676 he discovered, or rather rediscovered because it was known in Roman times, that the addition of lead solved this.' There are various percentages of

66 Glass-making at Cumbria Crystal, Ulverston.

lead, he went on to tell me. Cumbria Crystal uses about 32 per cent. Ordinary crystal would have up to 14 per cent lead; lead crystal up to 24 per cent; and full-lead crystal, which is the best, over 30 per cent. Ironically it is this dense, solid, heavy metal that makes the crystal so clear and brilliant. Apart from this, the lead also softens the crystal, making it easier to cut and engrave.

At Cumbria Crystal the glass is made by teams of three or four men known as 'chairs'. Each is led by a skilled man, the 'chairman', who trains up the local apprentices working with him and for him. Cutting is undertaken in two stages, first by the 'rougher', who rapidly makes the basic cut with a big carborundum wheel, following lines painted with waterproof paints. When he has finished the crystal moves to one of the smoothing wheels, where the cut is finished and smoothed out.

As a lifelong fan of Laurel and Hardy, I was delighted to learn that Stan Laurel was born at Ulverston, and even more delighted to find that there is a little museum in his honour full of cuttings and photographs of the famous pair. There were even a couple of bowler hats hanging up. This collection was the inspiration of Bill Cubin, another devoted Laurel and Hardy fan, who gave me a potted biography of one of Ulverston's most famous sons. Stan Laurel's birth certificate is hanging on one wall, showing that his father was a comedian, and Bill confirmed that there used to be a tented theatre near Argyll Street where Stan had been born and where his father no doubt appeared. Stan made his own stage début in Glasgow, traditionally held to be the comedian's grave-yard. But he survived the ordeal and rose to international fame in partnership with Oliver Hardy, with whom he made 104 films. Lucille Hardy, Olly's widow, gave Bill enormous help when he was gathering material for the museum.

From Stan Laurel's birthplace we went back in time at nearby Swarthmoor Hall, the acknowledged birthplace of Quakerism. This Elizabethan manor house on the southern outskirts of Ulverston was formerly the home of Judge Thomas Fell, his wife Margaret and their family, who were all Puritans and well known for offering hospitality to travelling preachers. In June 1652, while the judge was away sitting at some assizes in Wales, George Fox, a 24-year-old preacher from Leicestershire, arrived at Swarthmoor in search of sustenance. Although he was not an ordained priest, Fox was powerfully moved in his belief that people needed to be led back to the original teachings of Christ. It was at Swarthmoor Hall that Fox received his first really powerful backing. As Margaret Fell wrote in her subsequent letters, she saw the truth of what Fox was saying and knew that she could never deny it. The name Quaker originated as a term of derision, from all accounts. George Fox, up before a judge on one occasion, told him that they should all quake in the fear of the Lord, to which the judge replied, 'Oh, you would have us all Quakers, would you?' and the name stuck ever after.

William Wordsworth described the village of GRASMERE, twenty miles north of Ulverston, as 'the loveliest spot that man hath ever found', and in the ten years during which he made his home here he wrote many of his greatest poems, including the

Prelude which he completed in 1805. Dove Cottage was Wordsworth's first house in the village, and nowadays a favourite destination for 50,000 visitors every year. George Kirby, the curator, impressed on me the poet's passion for walking, 'The mileage was enormous,' he said, 'even by today's standards. It was nothing for him to walk to Ambleside and back twice in one evening.' (That is a distance of twelve miles.) Wordsworth was also keen on gardening – a sort of therapy for him, George reckoned.

Dove Cottage was originally built as a public house, the Dove and Olive Branch, and like many pubs in the Lake District a spring was diverted through the house to flow right through one of the downstairs rooms in order to provide a means of keeping the beer cool. It is still flowing through today. This is actually the only water in the house – there is no loo or bathroom. Wordsworth had a well in the garden of which he was very proud, though his sister Dorothy referred to it as a muddy pond. As George said,

67 Wordsworth's home, Dove Cottage, Grasmere.

'There's little doubt that William dug the well himself. No local man would have tapped a stream that dries up in the summer time.'

Upstairs there is an extraordinary little room with newspapers all round the walls which served as the children's bedroom. It is the only room in the cottage without a fireplace, and in an attempt to keep it warm Dorothy tried insulating it with old papers. They are all dated 1800 or 1802 and make fascinating reading. On the way up the stairs you pass the cuckoo clock which was the subject for one of Wordsworth's poems. 'It's a bit of a nuisance when the children block up the stairs, but it's really one of the most popular exhibits in the cottage,' George admitted.

After the Wordsworths moved into a larger house nearby, Dove Cottage became the home of their friend Thomas de Quincey, who lived here on and off for twenty-one years and, as George told me, wrote his most famous work, *The Confessions of an English Opium-Eater*, during his time in Grasmere.

William and Dorothy are both buried in Grasmere churchyard, alongside William's wife Mary and other members of the Wordsworth family, and we passed their graves when we went through St Oswald's churchyard on our way to Church Cottage. Passing through the lychgate, we were met by a gorgeous smell of ginger, and over the doorway was the notice 'Sarah Nelson's original celebrated Grasmere gingerbread', which today is made in the cottage by Margaret Wilson and her husband. From 1660 to 1854 this tiny cottage was a school catering for about half a dozen children. Then came Sarah Nelson and her family, and the first of the famous gingerbread. 'It's been a secret all these years,' Margaret assured me. 'The recipe's kept in the bank and many people say they've got it – but they haven't. Some of the ingredients in the gingerbread you can't buy over the counter, but we knew where to get them when we bought the recipe.' For over a century the lovely smell has pervaded the cottage, and it seems that even when the shop is closed there is a hint of ginger lingering in the air.

Right in the middle of Grasmere, in Red Lion Square, you will come across another pleasant aroma wafting out of Fragrance House, aptly named because perfumes are made there. Twenty-three frangrances were on the books when we visited, all closely guarded secrets and made behind locked doors in laboratories in the house. As I couldn't find out what went into each of the perfumes, I thought I had better try to discover how you set about matching a perfume to a lady. Mrs Christina Moor, who runs the business with her husband and father, was the obvious person to offer guidance. 'We figure out the colour combination of her face, her eyes, her skin, her hair,' she told me. 'These matter a lot because they give us a clue to her chemical make-up, and this is what the perfume reacts with.' The right perfume on the right skin helps it to last, too – up to twelve hours if the combination is correct.

As well as William Wordsworth, the gingerbread and English Lakes Perfumery, Grasmere attracts visitors to its annual sports, known as the Highland Games of the Lake District. These are always held on the Thursday nearest 20 August and include hound-trailing, various athletic events, Cumberland and Westmorland wrestling (in which the competitors grasp each other round the back and struggle until one loses his grip or falls to the ground), and the famous Guides Race. Competitors in this run to the top of the fell above the field where the sports are held, a height of 1000 feet, and back down again. Going up takes about eleven minutes; coming down just over two, as the runners bound down with jumps of eight or nine yards at a time.

For me the city of CARLISLE has always meant railways, biscuits, state pubs and Carlisle United. We weren't able to include the first or last of these when *Down Your Way* went to Carlisle at the end of May 1981, but we did look into the other two. By a happy coincidence Carr's Biscuits were celebrating their 150th anniversary that year, and the company's history was very much to the fore. As a child I remember the little alphabet biscuits that Jonathan Dodgson Carr, the founder of the firm, is said to have made when he started out as a biscuit-maker. The famous water biscuit, for which the firm is so well known, originated in the days of the old hard tack biscuits which used to be taken to sea. Carr noticed that the ship's captains were starting to appreciate the hard tack, and he developed the more refined table water biscuit, suitable for serving at the captain's table. The ingredients are wonderfully simple: flour, water, a little fat and a few minor ingredients. Today they are made by the million in the modern factory, being cooked at over 450 degrees Fahrenheit as they pass through the ovens on conveyor belts. There are eight

68 Cumberland and Westmorland wrestling at Grasmere Sports.

ovens at the Carlisle factory, which allows eight different types
of biscuit to be baked at any one time. In a week these add up to
450 to 500 tons, and on any one day the factory reckons to make
about twelve million individual biscuits!

The state-owned pubs offered a different type of sustenance.
According to June Barnes, who knows a lot about the history of
Carlisle, the city used to be a very boozy place: 'Practically every
second person appeared to be an innkeeper in Carlisle.' During
the Great War there was a large munitions factory at nearby
Gretna, and the drunkenness of the workers seemingly reached
such a pitch that in order to tighten things up for the war effort
Lloyd George's government bought up all the pubs and put in
state-controlled managers to run them. I looked in vain to see if
I could still find one, but they have all been taken over now by
the large breweries.

On the battlefields of the First World War Cumbria suffered
particularly at the Battle of the Somme. A private battalion raised
by Lord Lonsdale (he of boxing's Lonsdale Belt) on Carlisle race-

course as the 11th Lonsdale Battalion, the Border Regiment, was one of the first over the top on 1 July 1916 when the battle began. Out of a total complement of nearly 800, they suffered 500 casualties and it took a generation for the county to recover.

Records of this and other military campaigns are housed in Carlisle Castle, which acts as the regimental museum for the Border Regiment. There is a melancholy case containing mementos from the Indian Mutiny, including a bloodstained baby's cap found near the well where the massacre of Cawnpore took place. The museum also possesses a set of French drums captured from the French 34th Regiment, the Border Regiment's opposite number during the Iberian campaign in 1811. Each year on the anniversary of the battle, drummers are dressed in uniforms of the Napoleonic wars and the drums are paraded through the battalion.

Scotland

69   Eilean Donan Castle, Wester Ross.

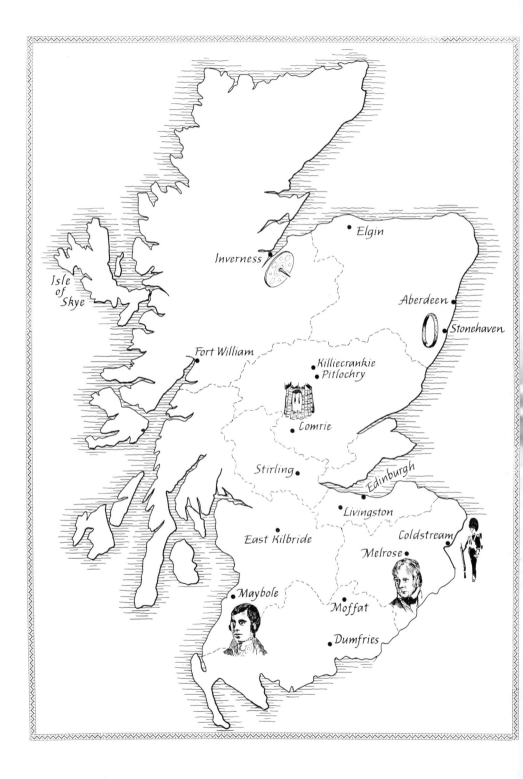

Isle
of
Skye

Inverness

Elgin

Aberdeen

Stonehaven

Fort William

Killiecrankie
Pitlochry

Comrie

Stirling

Edinburgh

Livingston

East Kilbride

Coldstream

Melrose

Maybole

Moffat

Dumfries

I am half Scottish, though which half I'm not sure!

Our family crest is a pair of spurs. The story is that a Johnston was dining with friends when the butler came round with the beef course, a silver beef cover over the dish. He went straight to Johnston and surreptitiously lifted the cover. Underneath, instead of the beef, was a pair of spurs – a pre-arranged signal for: 'Flee at once – the authorities are after you.' Anyway, in spite of this I am very proud of my Scottish ancestors, and on my visits to Scotland sometimes wear my Johnston tartan tie. But not the kilt. I wouldn't risk that – far too draughty, though in fact my second son Andrew often wears it as he is mad keen on Scottish dancing, and an expert at the reels.

I didn't go to Scotland until I was in my early twenties, and then went to the Hirsel near Coldstream in Berwickshire, and Douglas in Lanarkshire. This was at the invitation of my friend William Douglas-Home, whose family homes these were. I always remember my excitement on waking up in a sleeper as we approached Coldstream and I had my first sight of Scotland, up until then a land I had only read about, mostly in history books or Sir Walter Scott novels.

During my stay at the Hirsel I was persuaded to play a practical joke on an uncle and aunt of William's. They had been invited to tea to help entertain an eccentric clergyman who was staying at the house. They were told that he was half blind, totally deaf and very strange in his behaviour. Needless to say, I was the clergyman – disguised with hair parted in the middle, a thick pair of horn-rimmed spectacles, and dressed in dog collar and dark clerical suit.

When we saw their car approaching up the long drive I began

to walk towards them with a mincing gait, holding a Bible. As they passed me I gave them a limp wave and noticed their startled look.

I later joined them at the tea table, where William proceeded to shout at me, and I pretended not to hear. The uncle and aunt did their best but soon gave up. I just sat there nodding and smiling, and I heard them mutter, 'It's hopeless. He's quite mad. Why on earth did you ask us?' Even when William deliberately upset a cup of tea over me, and I let out an unclerical expletive, they still did not realise it was a leg pull.

After tea I moved into the drawing-room, where, pretending I could not see, I 'inadvertently' sat down on the aunt's lap. I then asked her if she would like to come for a walk with me in the shrubbery. By then she was becoming quite hysterical. So we finally let her into the joke. I must say she took it very well.

In 1938 William and I went to a political meeting on Lanark racecourse. William's brother, then Lord Dunglass, was the MP and had asked Sir John Simon, then Foreign Secretary, to address the meeting. He waffled away about the Czechoslovakian crisis and how serious it was. Stabbing the air with his forefinger, he asked, 'Who knows where it will end?' William and I felt that if he, the Foreign Secretary, did not know the answer, it wasn't much good asking us!

Thanks to *Down Your Way* I have been to Scotland many times since. At a rough guess, over fifteen years we must have visited about fifty places, large cities like Edinburgh, Glasgow and Aberdeen, and far distant places like Ullapool and the Isle of Skye. I have never ceased to be amazed at the breathless beauty of some of the rugged scenery. The glens, the lochs, the rivers, mountains and castles – all form part of a pattern which is so different from the rest of Britain. Wherever one goes there is fierce national pride, coupled with a friendly tolerance of the Sassenachs and a warm welcome.

This has often been embarrassing to me, as I dislike the taste of whisky and the welcome has often been accompanied by: 'What about a wee dram?' I must admit that on occasions I have managed to smuggle my tot to Tony Smith in exchange for his empty glass. But to make up for this there have always been some real Scottish delicacies to eat – smokies, bannock or Dundee cake and so on.

I have to admit that I am still not certain why Hogmanay is so called, nor exactly what Scotsmen do or do not wear under their kilts. Perhaps Bud Flanagan knew the answer in his crosstalk act with Chesney Allen. 'I've just been up to Scotland. All the Scotsmen were wearing kilts.' 'Really. Did you see the Trossacs?' 'No. It wasn't windy!'

Some of my happiest hours in Scotland have been spent away from the hustle and bustle of the towns, talking to a gillie on an isolated moor or on the banks of a river with a raging current cascading against the rocks. Wherever you go in Scotland you are soon made aware of their great love and enthusiasm for fishing and golf. There are golf courses and links everywhere, and children start playing at a very young age. I have been lucky to visit many of the famous courses like St Andrews, Troon and Turnberry. When interviewing the professional at North Berwick I actually risked driving a ball off the first tee. It didn't go far, but it was at least straight. Just as well, really, as these delightful links run alongside the sea. At one time cattle were allowed to graze there, and it was a favourite with politicians like Lord Balfour and Sir John Simon. Lord Balfour was once playing in a foursome with the local pro as his partner. Lord Balfour's drive landed slap in the middle of a giant cow-pat. It was the pro's turn next and in order to avoid the inevitable splash he made a deliberate air-shot. 'Sorry, m'lord, about that. I'm afraid it's now *your* shot!'

When *Down Your Way* visited COLDSTREAM, we opened the programme talking to Henry Douglas-Home, Lord Home's brother (now sadly no longer with us), who told us about their family home, the Hirsel, and its estate. Henry was known as 'the Birdman' in Scotland and during the summer he led parties of birdwatchers through the six hundred acres of woodlands and adjoining grounds to see the hundred or so species of birds that nest there each year.

Records of bird sightings go back to 1916, but the Homes' connections with Coldstream go back rather further – to the days of Macbeth. Like many Scottish kings, he found the borders with England rather turbulent and sent down one of his sons to keep order there. He settled into Home Castle, about eight miles from the Hirsel, and took the name Home from it.

The Hirsel itself has always been open to the public, and in summer literally thousands of people visit the grounds and in particular the wood where we were talking, which was a blaze of rhododendrons and azaleas. It is a lovely setting with the lake, the river Tweed on one side and the little river Leet, a tributary of the Tweed, running right through the estate. In the distance you can see the Cheviot Hills in 'the foreign country', as Henry put it.

70 With Henry Douglas-Home, my producer Tony Smith
and our sound engineer in the grounds of the Hirsel.

About four miles to the south of the Hirsel stands Flodden Ridge, the site of the battle in September 1513 which has a particular significance for the Homes. Flodden was a disastrous battle, in which almost all the principal families of Scotland, except for the Homes, were wiped out.

The river Tweed itself has a particular importance for one man at the Hirsel, Alexander Brown, Lord Home's head gillie. When we talked on the programme in 1977 he had been fishing the Tweed for forty-seven years, during which time he had taken 22,000 salmon, more than anyone else on the river. He told me that he held the record for one day's fishing when he had caught no less than twenty-eight salmon. Other outstanding catches included 65 in three days, 76 in another three days and 204 in ten days' fishing. When I asked him what was the biggest he had ever caught, he replied with modesty, 'Not really big – forty-three pounds', adding, 'but I've lost bigger fish: two fifty-pounders and a sixty-pounder, which was caught near Hawick with my fly still sticking in his mouth.'

I knew that Alexander's reputation with salmon went beyond catching the fish, and asked him for his recipe for smoking salmon. This he gave me with perfect candour. 'Take the best of your fish; one that weighs about sixteen or seventeen pounds smokes the best. Fillet it from the tail down to the head, washing it out thoroughly with a hose. Take out all the inside and let it drip dry for ten minutes. Then put the fish in the bath or tub – whatever it is being cured in – and rub it all over with three pounds of demerara sugar and salt. After twelve or twenty-four hours, depending on how you like your fish, take it out, hose it down again and let it drip dry for ten minutes.

'The period of smoking depends on whether you like your fish light, medium or heavy. It needs two days' smoking for light, three for medium and four for heavy, and the smoking takes place in a little wooden hut six feet long, four feet high and a yard wide, inside which all the fish are hung on trays.' Alexander told me that the best woods for smoking the salmon are chips of oak, hawthorn, juniper and apple.

Another method of smoking he described to me used demerara sugar and rum. In this process the fish are cured with salt for twenty-four hours and then hosed down. Back in the tub they are rubbed with three to four pounds of the sugar and half a bottle of rum, and then left to cure in the tub for four days, where they are basted with a pastry brush three or four times a day as the rum dissolves the sugar after about six hours. After this basting the fish go straight into the smoker without being washed down, and the smoking carries on as before. He made it sound absolutely delicious.

Twenty-year-old Donald Maxwell followed another time-honoured tradition in the town in holding the proud office of Coldstreamer, to which he was appointed by tradition in April. As the Coldstreamer it fell to him to represent the town at all the Border festivals during his year of office and to preside over the town's own Civic Week, which begins on the first Sunday in August. At this point the Coldstreamer replaces the sash with

which he was presented on his appointment in April with a new
sash worn throughout Civic Week. This contains the borough
standard, below which appear the names of previous Cold-
streamers. He also wears a rosette with red and white at the centre
to represent the town of Coldstream, and two colours of his own
choice – in Donald's case burnt orange and turquoise.

Civic Week in Coldstream caters for the whole community.
There are children's games, a ball, a grand firework display, even
a tea party for the 'exiles' (anyone from the town who has returned
for the celebrations).

The principal day in the week is the Thursday, when the
Coldstreamer leads a mounted cavalcade from the town across
the border into England to Flodden in an act of commemoration
for their compatriots who fell four and a half centuries ago. One
hundred and forty-five riders followed Donald on the sixteen-mile
ride, which was first held in 1951, making it comparatively recent
when measured against towns like Berwick that have had riding
of the marches' for four hundred years.

I think for most of us the town of Coldstream is best remembered
for the Coldstream Guards, which originated there in the bitter
winter of 1659 when the force that General Monck was leading
south to London to restore the monarchy had to camp in the town
for several weeks until he had gathered enough men to continue
his march south. From that time on they adopted the name of the
town.

General Monck's headquarters were on the site of the town's
museum, which contains a special room devoted to the regiment.
This houses tunics on loan from regimental headquarters (distinguished from those of the other guards regiments by their
buttons, placed together in pairs), and one of the regiment's
bearskins with a red plume on the right-hand side. This is actually
kept in a box to stop it from getting dusty, but I was told by James
Davidson, the chairman of the Community Council, who showed
me round the museum, that cleaning it is fairly simple. All it
needs is a shower of rain to wash away the dust, a chance to dry
and then a good comb.

James Davidson feels a special attachment to the Coldstream
Guards since he was provost when the regiment was given the
freedom of Coldstream on 10 August 1968, which coincided with
Civic Week that year. In addition to the entire regiment and the

full complement of the regimental band, there was a crowd of 3000 people packed into the market square to watch the Conferment Ceremony and see James take the salute on a memorable day in his life and that of the town of which he is so justifiably proud.

A few miles up the Tweed from Coldstream the town of MELROSE has also played a notable part in the centuries of cross-border upheavals between England and Scotland. Its crowning glory is the abbey, probably the finest and most beautiful of all the ruined abbeys found in Scotland. The earliest abbey in the area was constructed a couple of miles away at Old Melrose by monks who arrived there from Iona. The abbey on its present site was founded in 1136 by King David I and was the very first Cistercian monastery to be built in Scotland. It was sacked three times in its history. In 1322 it was wholly destroyed by Edward II and was rebuilt by Robert the Bruce. Richard II destroyed it next in 1385, and its final ruin came about in 1545 at the hands of Lord Hertford during the reign of Henry VIII. Among those buried here are King Alexander II, the only king buried inside the abbey, and Michael Scott the wizard, made famous by Sir Walter Scott in his novel *The Lay of the Last Minstrel* – the man who, according to legend, cleft in three the Eildon hills to the south of the town.

Outside the abbey lies the heart of Robert the Bruce. Robert the Bruce was buried in Dunfermline Abbey in 1329, but before he died he asked that his heart should be buried in the Holy Land. James Douglas was given permission to carry the heart there in a casket, but unfortunately he was killed on the way, fighting the Moors in Spain, and the heart was brought back to Scotland and eventually buried in Melrose Abbey, where its final resting place is marked by a little plaque in the Chapter House.

On the north side of the abbey is a museum housing finds made in all the border abbeys, including stained glass, coins and charts. There is also a Roman Room containing finds made at the Roman fort of Newstead, built by the troops of Agricola in AD 80.

In more recent history Melrose became the birth-place of seven-a-side rugby in 1883. The town has always been an important rugby centre, and its club was in its ninety-ninth year when we visited and was making excited preparations for its centenary. By that time fourteen internationals from Melrose had represented their country, two of them being Chisolm and Hasty, who helped Scotland obtain ten consecutive victories.

Sevens were first played at the club's ground, the Greenyards, in an effort to help raise funds. Seven other teams were invited to compete in the tournament, which was the brainchild of Ned Haig, a local butcher, aided and abetted by a fellow butcher, Davie Sanderson. A century later their inspiration has spread all round the world and the Melrose tournament, held on the second Saturday in April, has attracted as many as 15,000 spectators.

Perhaps Melrose's other great claim to fame is its close connection with Sir Walter Scott, and three miles out along the Selkirk road stands Abbotsford House, built by Scott, who also died in it.

We went there to find out about the house and its owner from his great, great, great granddaughter, Mrs Patricia Maxwell-Scott, who lives there with her sister, Dame Jean Maxwell-Scott. She told us that as a boy Sir Walter had lived in the Borders near Kelso and grew up to love the border country and especially the area around Melrose-on-Tweed. So when he became Sheriff of Selkirk in 1811 he decided to buy some land and a little old farmhouse that had originally been part of Melrose Abbey lands, on which to build a house of his own. He chose the name Abbotsford after the ford over the Tweed, just below the house, which had once been used by the abbot and monks of Melrose.

The house was built by John Smith, a local builder, under the careful direction of Sir Walter, who created Abbotsford in his own baronial style of gothic architecture. He died in the dining-room, looking out on to the Tweed, on 21 September 1832, when he was sixty-one. A year later the house was opened to the public.

Among the other principal rooms are the study, in which we talked to Mrs Maxwell-Scott, and where Sir Walter wrote many of his forty-eight works. This has a little gallery and a door leading up to his bedroom, so that he could come down very early in the morning to work before breakfast. Abbotsford also houses his famous library, which contains between 9000 and 10,000 books, all collected by Sir Walter during his lifetime.

He was a tremendous collector of armour and armaments as well, and he was fascinated by anything to do with battles and military history. In fact he might well have become a soldier himself, thought Mrs Maxwell-Scott, if polio at an early age hadn't left him with one leg shorter than the other. In any event, he was a member of the volunteer forces and the territorials during the Napoleonic wars, and waited with great excitement for the French to invade.

71 Abbotsford House.

Dogs were another of his great interests. Abbotsford has pictures of them all over the place, and he used to like having as many as twelve living with him at a time.

Visitors to Sir Walter's study will notice the gas light over his desk which caught my attention, and I was intrigued to find out that he was one of the first to have gas lighting in his home. In fact he had a complete private gas works which converted gas from oil at one side of the house.

Moving south-west to the valley of the river Annan, we learned something of the hazards that have always awaited travellers in the hill country of Scotland from the author Molly Clavering. She lives in MOFFAT and well knows the magnificent country around it from years of walking and collecting material for books like *Near Neighbours* and *From The Border Hills*.

From her we learned that there is a mountain rescue team in Moffat which is called out far more often than the innocent appearance of the hills might suggest from a distance. She also gave us a fascinating glimpse of some of the rewards that await walkers in the area. There is the Devil's Beef Tub, formerly called the Marquis of Annandale's Beef Stand, because the Johnstones of Annandale used to drive their stolen cattle into the bottom of this immense depression, surrounded by precipitous grass hills.

Nine miles to the east of Moffat, the visitor can find the Grey Mare's Tail, a magnificent waterfall now owned by the National Trust for Scotland, which has a cascade over two hundred feet high. These hills are also the home of a number of birds of prey: buzzards, merlins, peregrines and even the occasional golden eagle – making them a favourite destination for bird-watchers. But as Miss Clavering reminded us, danger is never far away for the unwary.

A hunting horn mounted in a case above the door of what was the Council Chamber in Moffat, and a little memorial stone beside the present road to Edinburgh, are reminders of one such tragedy which befell the guard and driver of a mail coach bound for Edinburgh in February 1831. The two of them left Moffat late in the afternoon as snow was falling heavily. They travelled as far as they could by coach, and then abandoned it to ride through the drifts on horseback. The driver was all for turning back, on all accounts, but the guard, who had once been 'faulted' for failing to deliver the mails, insisted on pressing on, saying, 'Come ye, or bide ye? I gan on.' So on they went together. Eventually the horses couldn't go any further, so they left them behind and struggled on foot. The last thing they did was to tie the mail bags to one of the snow posts alongside the road, where they were found by searchers after the blizzard had subsided. But it was several weeks before the snow melted to reveal the bodies of the two postmen.

Although my surname is spelt differently from that of the 'cattle-thieving' branch of the family, we do claim part of the same crest as the Hope-Johnstons, which is also used by the town of Moffat, having the feathered spur that appears on my signet ring topped with some castellations. This crest decorates the provost's lamps which stand outside the home of Andrew Fingland, provost of Moffat for eighteen years and the town's first and only freeman. It was him I asked whether it was true that there aren't any ears to be seen on the town's famous bronze statue of a ram, because I couldn't find any when I went to have a look. He agreed that no one else had been able to find any either, although to spare the sculptor he added that sometimes the ears can be hidden in the wool of a black-faced sheep!

'What about famous people associated with Moffat?' I asked. John Loudon McAdam, of tarmacadam fame, lies buried in the churchyard, Andrew answered, whilst Robert Burns was a frequent visitor to the town. He told me the delightful story of the time when Burns was standing in the Black Bull Hotel enjoying a drink when he saw two ladies going by outside – one large and gaunt, the other small and petite. Taking his ring off his finger, he wrote on the window pane:

> Ask why God made the gem so small
> And why so huge the granite?
> Because God meant that man should set
> The higher value on it.

These lines are printed on the wall of the hotel today, although rumour has it that the original pane of glass is now behind the Iron Curtain for some reason.

When any Scotsmen think of Robert Burns, however, they think of DUMFRIES, the town where he lived for the last five years of his life, where he wrote 'Auld Lang Syne' and 'Ye Banks and Braes of Bonnie Doon' and many other songs and poems, and where he lies buried today in the Burns mausoleum.

We turned to George McKerrow, a past president of the Burns Federation, to tell us something about Scotland's 'national poet', and met him in the Globe Inn which had been the poet's favourite 'howf' (meaning house or home) in the town.

As a child Burns had to work under very severe conditions on his father's farm in Ayrshire, which undermined his health and led to his early death at the age of thirty-seven. He moved from there to take over the tenancy of three farms on the river Nith, about six miles from Dumfries, and chose Ellisland as his home – a poet's, not a farmer's choice, George commented. As well as his farming, he took up an excise appointment in Dumfries, but his writing was his first love and his wonderful heart and great compassion shines through in over three hundred songs and verses. As one admirer put it, Burns 'took a handful of mud and created a precious jewel'.

Dumfries itself was a good thousand years old when Burns first trod its streets, and it witnessed one of the most important events in the history of Scotland – the killing of the Red Comyn by Robert the Bruce in the church of St Mary of the Greyfriars. Bruce, later King Robert I of course, apparently had a violent quarrel with Comyn, his rival for the throne, when they met there on 10 February 1306, and stabbed him. This action left Bruce with a clear path to the throne, and sparked off the revolutionary war which re-established the kingdom of Scotland and made Bruce king.

The area around MAYBOLE, across the Southern Uplands from Dumfries, saw much of the fighting during the Covenanters uprisings, and the number of hill forts around the town, some of which date back to the Bronze Age, suggest that it has been an important strategic centre for a very long time. Of the surviving fortifications Culzean Castle, standing on the coast a few miles from Maybole, is probably the best known and certainly the most widely visited.

Built by Gilbert Kennedy in the middle of the sixteenth century, Culzean is distinctive with its famous drum tower, which produces round rooms inside on three floors. Its defence associations come right into this century too, for a flat was created at the top of the castle and presented by the Scottish nation to General Eisenhower at the end of the Second World War in recognition of his services in the Allied cause. He was also made a freeman of Maybole, and during his life stayed in the flat on visits to the area on four or five occasions; he also played a round or two of golf at nearby Turnberry. Today the top flat is still out of bounds to visitors to the castle, serving as Scotland's guest flat, available to people involved in the economic and social betterment of Scotland.

Culzean's setting made it an ideal location to become Scotland's first country park in 1971. In addition to the three miles of magnificent coastline, there are seventeen miles of pathways winding through the attractive landscape surrounding it. Every year 300,000 visitors come to Culzean to enjoy its tranquil surroundings, shared with deer, wildfowl and a wide range of birds.

Anyone seriously contemplating walking every footpath in Culzean in a day could do far worse than wear a pair of boots made by Dick Goudie, who we learned is the last maker of heavy boots in Scotland. During his fifty years in the trade he has seen it decline drastically from a once thriving industry. But no matter, he was kept well occupied when we visited his workshop in Maybole to find out just what is a 'heavy boot'.

It is principally a working boot, Dick explained, made for farmers, shepherds, gamekeepers and anyone else who is on his feet walking for most of his working life. The boot we saw him working at on his bench certainly looked sturdy enough, and lived up to its name 'heavy': seven pounds of leather go into each pair Dick makes. In addition 150 hob nails are hammered into the sole, producing a stout pair of boots that will give years of good service if properly looked after.

I was interested in the shape of the sole, which curved up in the front. That is to make it easier walking uphill, Dick told me with a chuckle, adding that there is a three-inch spring that comes from a sole designed like this, which helps take the weight off your feet.

I wanted to know how long it would take to make a pair of these boots, and Dick reckoned he could complete a pair from start to finish in a long day. And how long would they last? A shepherd's boot used on grass would go for four years before it needed any repair, he told me with quiet confidence, whereas a boot worn on concrete would need attention in a quarter of the time. So if you want a pair of the only heavy boots still made in Scotland, Dick Goudie's your man.

In 1946 EAST KILBRIDE was little more than a village with three factories a few miles south of Glasgow. When we visited it the number of factories had grown to 350, in less than forty years. We gathered this information from John Bruce, who pointed out that the settlement itself dates from the distant past. The name East Kilbride comes from the Gaelic, meaning 'the cell of Bridget in the east'. Further back still, it has connections with the pagan goddess Frigga, a deity of childbirth and herds, and it is no coincidence that East Kilbride was an important dairy-farming area before becoming the first and largest of Scotland's new towns.

Not far outside the new town we came across Mains Castle, which originally belonged to the Red Comyn murdered by Robert the Bruce. Mike and Paula Rowan, the present owners who live in the castle today, found nothing standing but the walls when they bought the ruin. The walls were good, though: built on rock and standing sixty feet high, they had moved about an inch since they were erected. Although there wasn't a fragment of wood in the castle when the Rowans bought it, they found beams of the right size and many other building materials through friends also involved in restoring old castles, so that after two and a half years the castle was more or less complete. Apparently the flagstones on the floor had once been a pavement in Wigan!

In LIVINGSTON we met a couple of men with hobbies no less unusual than restoring old castles. The first was Stuart Marshall, a schoolteacher and cartophilist, or collector of cigarette cards, whose collection extended to over 50,000 cards by the time we met him.

Now that cigarette cards have more or less disappeared, I was interested to know when they were in vogue. Stuart said that the first ones appeared in America early in the 1880s, reaching Britain about ten years later. The first manufacturers were a firm called Alan and Ginter, while the first in the UK was a cigarette manufacturer with the brand name of Globe. In most cases the cards ran in sets of fifty, of which Stuart had 500 complete ones. However, some ran to many more, like the Guinea Golden Mammoth series which had 8000 in the set!

Most of the British cigarette cards were printed in or around Bristol. At the peak of their popularity before the First World War there were nine mills involved full-time in printing the cards, and Wills alone had a staff of 5000 involved in their production, over a hundred of whom were designers. The shortage of paper in both world wars brought an end to the cigarette-card production and after the Second World War most manufacturers found that production costs had risen to the point where the cards were no longer viable, so bringing an end to their brief but hectic run of popularity.

Our second Livingstonian, Bob Davis, also had an interest dating from the recent past, and we got a clue as to what it might be when we spotted a yellow motorbike with a sidecar parked outside his house. And inside his garage was another one. They both turned out to be AA motorbikes, complete with all their equipment, which Bob had restored and kept in perfect running order.

He told us that the one we had seen outside was a 1956 ex-AA bike which he had bought for £54 in 1963, when the patrolman had already ridden 100,000 miles on it. Even so, it was in mint condition when Bob became its owner, and by attaching a series of sidecars which increased in size as his children grew, it had run faultlessly with him for a further 240,000 miles at the time of our visit. The other bike, a 1959 model, he had bought to use for spare parts, but since it had never been needed for that, he decided to keep it in its original condition.

72 Bob Davis in AA uniform, astride one of his former AA BSA M21 600 cc motorcycles.

So much for the machines, what about the men who rode them? The AA started using motorcycles with sidecars for the patrolmen around 1920, Bob told me, and, lifting the lid, he showed me what they used to carry inside. Inside the lid itself was a case for carrying maps, handbooks and membership leaflets. Up in the nose compartment there was a shelf where the patrolman put his cap, because they wore safety helmets after 1955, but replaced these with their peaked caps when they were parked on duty at the side of the road. Beneath this was a compartment for water-proof leggings and an oil-skin coat. The main compartment had a section for a one-gallon can of petrol and room for a large tool kit, a tyre pump and a first-aid kit. At one time patrolmen also carried two red warning flags to be used at the scene of accidents.

I reminded Bob that patrolmen always used to salute members they passed on the road, and then for some reason they stopped doing this. I wondered if he knew why. He thought that the increasing volume of traffic in the 1960s made this impractical, as they would probably have been riding one-handed with a permanent salute. I also reminded him that when I started driving in the 1920s, if the patrolman didn't salute you it meant that there was a police trap round the corner to stop you going at over thirty miles an hour.

I remember that it was a fine, clear couple of days in mid-May that *Down Your Way* spent in EDINBURGH on a memorable visit to Scotland's capital. Like many visitors, I imagine, we made our way straight to the castle and the esplanade where the spectacular military tattoo takes place each year. There we met Colonel Leslie Dow, who was in his third year as organiser of the tattoo in which between 500 and 650 men take part. As a spectator it is easy to forget the very careful rehearsing that needs to take place for a display like this to work with such precision, and I was amazed to hear that Colonel Dow and his team only have ten days in which to get everything practised and ready for the first night.

Looking at the esplanade, even my limited military knowledge suggested that it wasn't an ideal parade ground – uneven and sloping down fourteen feet as it is. Colonel Dow agreed, and commented that there is an extra pace marching uphill compared with marching down, which can throw musicians who are not carefully watching the beat. The approaches also restrict the display, with only three narrow entrances. The one over the drawbridge, he told me, can be sheer hell for the pipe bands as they march in, but everyone expects to see them entering from there, so each year the bandsmen and pipers have to struggle through as best they can.

Dating back to the seventh century, the castle is steeped in Scottish military history. Today it is mainly occupied by the headquarters staff of the Scottish Division and the Brigadier's Command. The Scottish War Memorial is here, and so are two famous cannon – one ancient, one modern. Mons Meg is the oldest cannon in the castle, built down in Galloway around 1450.

Records show that it fired a royal salute when Mary Queen of Scots married the Dauphin in France in 1558. It was also fired to salute Charles II in 1680, though unfortunately the barrel split on this occasion and Mons Meg hasn't been fired since. In its heyday it was capable of firing a five-hundredweight stone ball a distance of a mile and a half, and there is a story that Cannon Ball House, below the castle, still holds one of these massive projectiles, fired accidentally from Mons Meg at some stage in her history. The modern cannon is the one which is fired at noon each day across the city.

73   The Tattoo, Edinburgh Castle.

From the esplanade we wound our way up to the top of the castle to King's Lodgings, which stands in the old palace block, and there we went to discover the romantic story that surrounds the Scottish regalia. I must admit that it came as a bit of a surprise to learn that Scotland has its own crown, sceptre and sword of state, and John Wilson, Warden of the Regalia, agreed, saying that even Scots visitors are surprised when they visit the castle.

Our present knowledge of the regalia owes much to Sir Walter Scott, and their story is the very stuff of Scott's own novels. Together, the sword, sceptre and crown form the oldest complete regalia in Europe and the crown is the oldest in the world belonging to a monarchy. This started its long history in 1307 with Robert the Bruce, and was remodelled in 1540 by James V. Everything in the crown is native to Scotland. The four pounds of twenty-four carat gold was mined in the kingdom, the ninety-four freshwater pearls came from the river Tweed and the ten diamonds and thirty-three other precious stones all came from the Cairngorm mountains.

The sword and sceptre also started their royal story with Robert the Bruce and finished it with Charles II in 1651. When Oliver Cromwell invaded Scotland and laid seige to Edinburgh Castle he had hopes of capturing the regalia, but this was smuggled out before the castle fell and was spirited away to Dunnottar Castle on the south-east seaboard. This made Cromwell furious, and he set off after the regalia and laid siege to Dunnottar Castle in turn. There another plot was secretly hatched to rescue the regalia a second time.

It so happened that the wife of the local minister, a Mrs Grainger, was great friends with the wife of the governor of the castle, a Mrs Ogilvy. Mrs Grainger was also fond of collecting flowers, and every morning she could be seen walking along the beach gathering flowers for her husband's church. Cromwell's troops got quite used to seeing her walking through their lines and paid no attention to her. So it was decided that the regalia should be lowered to her from the castle, out of sight of the soldiers, and that she should carry it through the lines in a donkey basket. In order to do this she had to bend the scabbard, the broken parts of which can still be seen and she also had to snap the sword, which carries the signs of its repair to this day. Apart from these necessary measures, the Scottish regalia passed through Cromwell's army without harm, and that night Mr Grainger buried them under the pulpit of his church, where they lay in secret for nine years until the Restoration of Charles II. After his coronation the regalia returned to their home in Edinburgh.

However, although the crowns of England and Scotland were united in 1603, the parliaments did not join until 1707, and the last Scottish parliament were afraid that, as the English crown had been destroyed, the Scottish one might be taken south. To prevent this the three high peers of Scotland had a huge chest made, put the regalia inside it, locked it securely and walled up the room in which it remained hidden from 1707 until 1818.

Now Sir Walter Scott enters the story. While he was researching material for his novel *The Wizard of the North*, poring through old documents in the Signet Library in Parliament Square, he came across a deposition which told the story of the Scottish regalia and identified where it was hidden. Scott was a personal friend of George IV and was given his permission to search the castle. His book describes how the room was entered by a small entrance and how they found the big chest standing in one corner. They broke the padlocks and lifted the lid, and there at the bottom, covered in muslin, tarnished but undamaged, was the Scottish regalia. Today it is on display in that room, lying on the chest in which it was discovered. Ceremonially it is used little now. The sword is used most, being taken from its display case whenever a new knight is invested with the Scottish Order of the Thistle. The only time that the crown leaves the case today is when a new sovereign makes his or her first visit to Scotland and is presented with the crown in a ceremony in St Giles's Cathedral, at which it is accepted by the placing of the monarch's hand upon it.

Down from the castle, along the cobbled street of the Royal Mile, past the Cannon Ball House (which really does have a cannon ball in one of its walls) and on past the outlook tower with its *camera obscura* which offers as fine views of Edinburgh as the one at Dumfries provides of that town, we came to a heart-shaped design in the cobbled pavement. This is the Heart of Midlothian, marking the entrance to the old prison and the scene of the start of Sir Walter Scott's novel of the same name.

At the opposite end of the Royal Mile we crossed the Sanctuary Line and entered the forecourt of the palace of Holyrood House, the Queen's official residence in Scotland. As an abbey this dates back to the twelfth century, when it was founded by King David I in 1128 following a vision. The story goes that some of his courtiers persuaded their royal master to go hunting on the day of the Exaltation of the Cross – a holy day. In those days part of what now forms the Royal Mile was forest, and while King David was hunting here a huge stag rushed from the undergrowth and knocked him from his horse. However, before the moment of

impact he raised his hand to ward off the blow, and between him
and the stag an image of the cross appeared which frightened
away the great animal. That night King David dreamed that he
should found an abbey on the spot where his life had been saved
and should name it after the Holy cross, or Holy rood. As a result
the arms of Holyrood show a stag's head with a cross between
the antlers.

The existing palace was built by James IV for his English
princess Margaret Tudor in about 1503, but Holyrood is probably
best known to most people as the home of Mary Queen of Scots
and the place where Rizzio, her secretary and favourite courtier,
was murdered in her presence by her husband Lord Darnley and
a group of Protestant nobles.

Rizzio was stabbed to death in Queen Mary's Supping Room,
but the main banqueting room in the palace is the Great Hall,
which is surrounded with royal portraits. These were commissioned by Charles II, who engaged the Dutch artist Jan de Witt
to paint his ancestors. Working backwards in time from his royal
patron, de Witt painted 111 portraits going right back to 330 BC.
If you look at the faces in each picture they all share similar
features, in particular the Stuart nose, which isn't surprising –
not that this was a sinecure for de Witt. Charles paid him £110
per annum, which worked out at just over £2 per painting!

High on a crag commanding a view of the crossings of the upper
Forth, where the Highlands meet the Lowlands, stands Stirling
Castle, overlooking the town and the gateway to the north.

We were in STIRLING in the middle of November, and standing
on the esplanade on that bright autumn day we looked out across
the magnificent view, knowing that what we saw was a focal point
in the history of Scotland, stretching back before the Romans.

Beside us was Bob McCutcheon, a local historian, antiquarian
bookseller and guide to Stirling and its castle – an ideal man to
point out the places of historic importance that lay spread out
before us: the battle of Stirling Bridge in 1297; the battle of
Falkirk, to the south, in 1298; the battle of Bannockburn in 1314;
Sheriffmuir in 1715; and the second battle of Falkirk in 1746.

There have been fortifications on the site of Stirling Castle for
the last two or three thousand years, guarding the river crossing,
and today the castle houses the regimental museum of the Argyll
and Sutherland Highlanders. Inside the castle you can also see

74 Stirling Castle.

the chapel royal, built in 1594 specifically for the baptism of Prince Henry, the son of James VI of Scotland, James I of England.

On the way up we saw the statue of William Wallace, who fought his two most famous battles in the area around Stirling. Bob McCutcheon told us that the first proposals to erect a national monument to him were made in 1857, one of its prime supporters being the chaplain in the castle at the time, one Dr Rogers. He started collecting subscriptions and to keep the momentum going, bought the statue that we see today.

He didn't actually have any money with which to buy it, so he immediately approached Sir William Drummond, one of the town's benefactors, who agreed to put up the money and the statue was duly delivered to Stirling. There it provoked great argument in the council and received a very bad press, being described as a 'nuisance' in one article.

As a result of this furore, Sir William Drummond promptly took the statue home and erected it in his front garden. This brought about a swift turnaround in public opinion and the newspapers started referring to the Wallace statue as a 'fine piece of modern sculpture', with the result that it eventually ended up in its present position in the middle of the town. Funds were raised from direct subscriptions and other imaginative measures like bringing the carcase of a whale washed up in the river into the town and charging everyone who wanted to see it threepence for the privilege.

Twenty miles north of Stirling is the village of COMRIE, which has the unenviable reputation of being Britain's earthquake centre. In days gone by the earth tremors were fairly frequent and the most violent ones could bring down gables and chimneys. Donald McNab, a retired garage proprietor, told me that he remembered an occasion in 1964 as he was chatting to a customer outside his garage when there was a distinct boom followed by a thud, and he felt quite a distinct movement under his feet.

I asked what sort of special conditions gave warning of a quake. 'We call it an earthquake day,' he replied matter-of-factly. 'It's a humid, overpowering atmosphere and there's something between the sun and us – an intervening medium that is peculiar and yellowish.

The reason for these alarming upheavals is that Comrie lies on a fault which runs from east to west across Scotland and seems to be at the point where the movement is most clearly felt. I wondered if anyone had ever measured the severity of the tremors, and Donald replied that Comrie had its own special earthquake house built for that very purpose, though when he described it I realised that it might lack some of the scientific refinements we associate with the Richter Scale.

The Comrie Earthquake house is a stone structure with a slated roof, standing ten or twelve feet square. The floor is an outcrop of rock over which there is a covering of sand. Wooden pegs are driven into the sand and the earthquakes are classified according to the tilting of the pegs caused by the tremors. It may not be terribly technical, but Donald assured me that it was very effective – and who knows, it probably means more to the layman than Herr Richter's elaborate formulae.

In Drummond Street in Comrie we found the Museum of Scottish Tartans, which had opened less than eighteen months before our visit. In that time, though, it had already been awarded the Museum of the Year Award – in 1979 – for the best small museum in Scotland. Comrie was an old weaving village back in the seventeenth century and, situated almost right in the middle of Scotland, it is in an ideal location for a national museum of this sort.

The museum records every known tartan – about 1300 at the last count. There are lots of fascinating things to see there, and my eye was caught by a tiny little square of tartan which had been recreated from a piece found in a Roman pot known to date from about AD 250. It is called The Falkirk Tartan, after the place where it was found, and is thought to be the oldest known tartan in existence.

There is no doubt that tartan goes back hundred and hundreds of years. What the museum is struggling to discover is how soon each tartan became associated with its specific clan.

I had never been sure just what the reason was for the kilt, and since Dr Michael MacDonald, our host, was wearing one, I asked him to explain how the kilt originated. He answered that it came about from a huge piece of cloth about two weaving widths wide (roughly fifty-six inches) and about twenty feet long. This was a garment that could be used as a tent, a sleeping-bag, something to wrap yourself in – a unique garment but something very practical for mountain people, even if nothing like the modern kilt.

The museum also has a full-length portrait of the famous John Brown, which I was amused to hear was the original from Windsor Castle. In 1901 Edward VII, who hated John Brown, kicked the picture out of Windsor Castle after his mother had died, and the museum subsequently picked it up for £30; today it is worth over a thousand times that!

After walking through the museum we went out to the back, where Dr MacDonald and his team have recreated, or rather reconstructed, a Highland cottage from the 1720s, which local craftsmen built in three weeks, the same time as it would have taken their forebears. The walls are built from dry stone, the roof is supported on a cruck frame and the roofing material is heather and sod. It wasn't that cold outside when we visited, but the cottage did strike me as being particularly warm and Dr MacDonald mentioned that when all the modern bungalows had frozen up in the previous winter with thirty-five degrees of frost outside, the temperature inside the weaver's cottage was forty-seven degrees warmer, thanks to the thick stone walls and the

very well insulated roof. The cottage struck me as being pretty
small and, bearing in mind that a whole family would have lived
and worked here, it must been very crowded.

75 The Weaver's Bothy at the Scottish Tartans Museum, Comrie.

On the loom in the cottage I saw a piece of tartan being woven
from the wool of the original breeds, the Soay sheep, dyed with
vegetable dyes taken from the museum's own dye garden, so
recreating the lovely colours of the original tartans before, in Dr
MacDonald's words, 'aniline dyes tended to ruin the effect'. So
weaving has come once again to Comrie after disappearing early
in the nineteenth century, and with the museum open every day
of the year I commend it to any visitor.

One of the great delights for me in *Down Your Way* was the
opportunity to meet so many engaging people, and I know that
whenever I think of the Highlands my mind takes me back to the
day we went to PITLOCHRY and visited the croft of Gideon Scott
May. To anyone who has visited Pitlochry during the summer he
will be well known already as the presenter of the Highland
evenings that take place between May and October. In addition
to the pipe bands and Highland dancers, you may be lucky
enough to hear Gideon himself singing songs in Gaelic. In his

time Gideon had been a gamekeeper, which he told me about
with a twinkle in his eye. 'It had its tough ways. I did my spells
of moonlight watching, and I had battles – one real one with
poachers with guns. It was a good life. Down by the Solway I
learned to go out there and swim with the porpoises. I made
friends with them. I learned all about wildlife – I'd always wanted
to do this, all my life. But my father had a big firm and I was
apprenticed to it. During the Depression the firm crashed because
he had over a hundred men and he refused to pay them off. There
was no work for me, so I got this chance to take the job I'd always
wanted to do as a gamekeeper. I had to go back as a director of
the firm about seven years later and then the war came.'

When I met him he was living in a charming little croft with a
glorious view over Loch Tummel towards Schiehallion standing
up in the distance. Unfortunately the mountain was shrouded in
mist when we were there – 'but that's only to hide the fairies,'
Gideon explained. 'Schiehallion is Gaelic for Hill of the Fairies.'
Mind you, you have to be jolly careful when you go out of the
back door of his house: in the garden I saw two enormous
Highland cattle.

The one that struck us, though not literally, I'm glad to say,
was an enormous bull with a horn span of over five feet six inches,
a little bigger than Gideon. 'He's my best friend,' he confided.
'Actually I've had him probably two years longer than I should
have, but – well, you never sell a friend down the river.'

This colossal animal weighed getting on for a ton, and once
cracked a couple of Gideon's ribs when he inadvertently turned
to say hello to his master, who happened to be standing just a
little too close.

I was delighted to see that Gideon had already written a couple
of books about his life in Pitlochry, the most recent of which was
called *The Kilt for Keeps* and describes a lifetime of wearing a
kilt, which has been Gideon's happy lot except for his years in
the RAF. There is a priceless picture on the cover showing Gideon
with his arm round the neck of his massive Highland bull, who
only speaks Gaelic, incidentally! 'I've used my life-blood for ink
in this one,' Gideon assured me, which I reckon must make it a
delightful book if it is half as much fun as talking to him.

Not too far from his home is a famous local beauty spot, the
Queen's View, which offers a breathtaking vista up the loch and

away to the hills beyond. Queen Victoria came here for a picnic once (although the spot was known as the Queen's View long before that, possibly after Queen Mary). The picnic wasn't a huge success, I'm afraid: an extract from her diary says that the kettle didn't boil and John Brown had to go off in search of hot water for the royal tea. However, the area met with greater approval in the reign of King George III when Schiehallion was used by the astronomer royal to calculate the weight of the earth. The mountain was deemed to be so regular in shape that it was ideally suited to his observations. Using a zenith sector and plumb line to observe the force of gravity, he took careful measurements of the mountain and then applied Newton's laws to calculate the weight of the earth – and this all took place in 1744.

For the majority of visitors Pitlochry must be best known for its Festival Theatre lying in a lovely setting on the banks of the river Tummel. There was a rehearsal of *Rookery Nook* going on when we poked our noses inside, which took me back to when I first saw the play in 1928.

Building work on the existing theatre started in 1979, and it was officially opened two years later by the Prince of Wales, who came up for the ceremony three weeks before his wedding. This new theatre replaced the original tent theatre that had been based at Pitlochry ever since John Stewart, a Glasgow businessman, settled on the town as the ideal place to create what might become a Scottish national theatre. Sitting almost in the middle of Scotland, and well served by hotels, Pitlochry seemed the ideal setting. Because of building restrictions in force at the time, the only way of creating a theatre was to put it under canvas. This lasted for two years until storms tore the outer walls and John Stewart was forced to build an asbestos shell round this in order to be able to continue. There it remained until 1980, when the theatre moved to its new site.

The theme of the old theatre has been carried through into the new one. The foyer is lovely and bright like the inside of a tent, and throughout the new building the architects have achieved to a remarkable degree the feel of the original theatre that audiences loved so much. The repertoire is as busy as always. The slogan used to be: 'Stay six days and see six plays', but in 1981 they decided to give the cast a night off once in a while and cut the number to only five. There are also visiting artists during the season, and every other Sunday during the summer the theatre holds musical recitals.

There was an exhibition of hydroelectric power at the dam at the end of Loch Faskally when we were at Pitlochry. We went to see it, though I must admit that I was really rather more interested in the fish ladder that had been created to help salmon climb the dam, fifty to sixty feet high. There are over thirty pools, with three resting pools, running to one side of the dam to help the fish do this. Looking into the observation pool, I saw what looked like an enormous drainpipe leading into the next pool, through which the fish swim to make their way upstream. There is also an electronic counter which records the numbers passing through, both going up and coming down. In an average year between 5500 and 6000 fish are recorded going up the Tummel.

If you follow the river Garry northwards out of Loch Faskally, rather than taking the Tummel, which flows in from the west, it won't be long before you come to the Pass of Killiecrankie and the site of the battle fought there in 1689. The Lowland army and that from the Highlands came to blows over the succession of William and Mary, who were supported by the Lowlanders but fiercely opposed by the Highlanders.

In those days anyone intent on waging war in the Highlands had to struggle up and through the Pass of Killiecrankie, and it took the Lowland army of four thousand and their assorted baggage trains the best part of a day to do this. All the while they were being closely watched by the Highland army half their size, who, unlike the Lowlanders in their red coats, were well camouflaged by their tartans. When the Lowlanders eventually emerged on to the plain above the pass, the Highland army had assembled on the high ground above and commanded an important advantage. Here they waited until sunset, when the light would be in the eyes of their opponents. When the critical moment came, the Highland commander, 'Bonnie' Dundee, ordered the attack and his force swooped down on to their foe, driving them back to the pass, where many were killed.

One who did survive was Donald MacBean who was chased by a couple of Highlanders at sword point until he came to the rocks beside the river. In front was a yawning gap some eighteen feet wide to the rocks on the opposite bank. Beneath was the foaming torrent of the river Garry, and behind lay certain death.

Faced with a choice like this I wonder how many of us would match his bravery and jump? Jump he did, though, and landed safely on the other side to scramble up the slope and escape away over the hills. When you look at the spot, named the Soldier's Leap after him, you realise what a remarkable feat this was, particularly as he had almost no run-up before launching himself over the rushing water. His bravery earned him escape from Killiecrankie, and history relates that he went on to serve under General Wade when he later embarked on his programme of road-building in the Highlands.

The east-coast port of STONEHAVEN witnessed another important development in the history of road transport, though one I am ashamed to say I knew nothing about until, passing through the market square, we spotted a notice above Boots the chemist which suggested that Stonehaven has quite a history of innovation. The sign read: 'The birth place of Robert William Thompson, the inventor of the peneumatic tyre. Born 29 June 1822. Died 8 March 1873.' To be quite candid we had never heard of him. To correct this gap in our knowledge we turned to Fred Stephens, a well known journalist in the area who also happens to be the founder chairman of the Robert William Thompson Memorial Society.

He told us that Thompson invented the tyre in 1845 at a time when the rubber industry couldn't produce rubber in large enough pieces to make a complete tyre. So he developed an ingenious combination formed from an outer casing made of leather and lined with canvas and gutta-percha to seal in the air. Finally he invented a brass condenser for pumping the air into the tyre. Once inflated, the tyres were fitted to a horse-drawn carriage and travelled several thousand miles up and down the country, giving silent and comfortable service and starting the whole process of modern road transport.

Hogmanay in Stonehaven sees the old year out with the Fireball Ceremony which recalls the ancient fire festivals of pagan times. The idea is to chase away the evil spirits of the old year to let in those of the new year. In reality it sounds extremely energetic. The ball itself consists of a basket of wire netting at the end of a length of wire cable, filled with any combustible material. No one reveals just what they put into their own fireball, keeping secret the ingredients which help it to burn longer than anyone else's. In reality most stay alight for a quarter of an hour at the most and, weighing twenty or thirty pounds, that is quite long enough to keep a fireball whirling round your head. The swinging takes place down by the harbour at the bottom of the high street and sounds a fairly risky business, with fireballs occasionally meeting in mid-swing and the twenty or so participants having to keep a careful eye on the arc followed by their companions' flaming brands.

76 Swinging the fireballs at Stonehaven on New Year's Eve.

We also found that Stonehaven is one of the last bastions of the ancient sport of quoiting, with its Dunnottar Quoiting Club the only remaining one of its sort in the north-east of Scotland. The game is played on a pitch eighteen yards long. At each end of the pitch there is a peg standing with its top almost level with the ground and surrounded by clay. The quoits themselves are quite different from their younger cousins made of rope which are used in deck quoits. The original quoits are discs of steel with a hole in the middle so that you can grip them. They weigh anything from two to twelve pounds; the choice of weight rests with the thrower, but the heavier the weight, the better it sticks in the clay and the less chance there is of it being dislodged by an opponent's quoit.

You play the game in roughly the same way as bowls, with players competing in pairs and the winner being the first to reach a score of twenty-one. The perfectly pitched quoit should land with the front edge about half an inch over the peg, but in any event the one nearest the peg wins.

It looked impossibly difficult to me, and as I wasn't a very good underam bowler at school I didn't think I stood much chance of reaching the peg. However, I had a go, picked up the quoit with my fingers pointing upwards through the hole in the middle, stood with my feet together as instructed and then took a step forwards to pitch it. The quoit sailed through the air and landed about seven yards away. I suppose practice makes perfect.

Of all the towns and cities in this part of Scotland to have felt the impact of the North Sea oil industry ABERDEEN is the most significant. Ever since the late eighteenth century it has been an important harbour, following the construction of sea walls and quays, and a large amount of dredging that made it suitable for ocean-going craft. The first boom in the city's maritime past was connected with the Arctic whaling fleets that flourished for the first two decades of the nineteenth century. Trade with the Baltic and North America was always important, and in the middle of the century there was a boom in building clipper ships for the tea trade with China and carrying wool back from Australia – the most famous of these being the *Thermopylae*.

As the sailing-ship era came to an end, herring fishing took its place and Aberdeen achieved its long-standing association with the fishing industry. Early in this century there were nearly two hundred trawlers operating out of Aberdeen. When we were there in May 1981 most of the existing fleet was laid up, although in its place there was a sizeable enough seine-net fleet.

Looking further back into the city's past, we were shown the blade of a guillotine dating from the end of the sixteenth century and discovered that Scotland had actually had the guillotine in use before it found service in France.

Aberdeen is also a great centre for entertainment, of course, and we were lucky enough to visit one of the city's great characters to find out about a traditional form of entertainment known as bothy ballads. John Mearns welcomed us to his lovely house in Deeside and made us comfortable before beginning to describe his life on a farm in Aberdeenshire in the first part of this century.

I wanted to know first of all exactly what a bothy is. 'Ah, well,' he began with a little chuckle, 'a bothy is where the single or unmarried men lived at farms, independent of the farmhouse.' The ballads were written by the farmworkers about their work, and you find that the songs not only dealt with the work, but were written to the *rhythm* of the work. To the beat of a horse plodding along pulling a farm cart John began gently singing a carting song, breaking off to tell me, 'Now there are twenty-four verses to that, so you see you'd just be finished by the time you reached the farmyard.'

Each ballad told a story too. There were those for sewing, those for hay-making, others for lambing and harvesting – songs to take you right round the farming year. There were songs about love, as well – lots of them. I asked John for a couple of lines from one of these and he sang:

Bonnie Bessie Logan, she's handsome young and fair,
The very wind that blows it lingers in her hair,
So lightsome is her footstep when she comes o'er the lea,
But bonnie Bessie Logan is o'er young for me.

That, like all the others I heard, was sung to lovely melodies, traditional tunes to which different workers attached their own words to share their songs with their workmates after their day in the fields. Moving from one district to another, there were dozens of variations and John told me that the largest collection of these folk songs from the north-east of Scotland contained nearly 2500 different bothy ballads.

A few miles to the west of ELGIN, up the A96 from Aberdeen, we discovered another source of unique music in Pluscarden Abbey, an ancient monastery that had fallen into total dereliction before being reoccupied in 1945 and gradually rebuilt by Benedictine monks, who now number twenty-four. The earliest monks came from a small monastery near Dijon in France when the King of Scotland founded the monastery at Pluscarden in 1240. They brought with them their divine office sung in Gregorian chant, and the same Latin chants are still sung by their present-day successors at Pluscarden.

Their days must have been similar too. From the Father Abbott I heard that each day begins at twenty to five in the morning with the monks attending the first of their seven services in the church. They grow all their own fruit and vegetables. There is a guest house to look after, a retreat, and in the summer 17,000 visitors have to be shown round and looked after. With the possible exception of the number of visitors, their routine could not have been very different from that of their medieval forebears.

Now, if I do remember one fact from my school history lessons it is that the last battle fought on British soil was the Battle of Culloden, and driving west from Elgin down the A96 the site of the battle lies a mile or two to your left, six miles short of Inverness. There we found the warden, John McRae, who outlined to us the events surrounding the battle. At the end of the 1745 rebellion Bonnie Prince Charlie and his army had retreated from Derby and, after winning a final victory at Falkirk, found that they had to fall back to the Highlands to recoup and renew their forces. The Duke of Cumberland, in command of the government troops, advanced by sea to Aberdeen and eventually marched westwards to Nairn. At this time the Jacobite army was garrisoned in Inverness, where they had captured and destroyed the army. On the night of 15 April 1746 they made a surprise march to Nairn, hoping to catch the Duke's forces unawares. They did not, however, so they retreated towards Inverness and took up positions on Culloden Moor tired, wet and very hungry – possibly the worst place and the worst condition in which to face Cumberland's attack. To make matters even more disastrous, the general in command, the prince's Irish adjutant general General O'Sullivan, dithered over ordering the fiercesome charge which had won the Jacobite army all its victories. By the time he was finally forced to give the order, two-thirds of his army had been killed or wounded by the Hanoverian artillery.

Heavily outnumbered in any case, the remnants of the Highland army were overwhelmed by the musket fire, and in less than an hour their defeat and massacre was complete. You can still see the burial mounds where they were heaped immediately after the battle, marked with small stones carrying the names of the clans that fought there.

Continuing on our battle theme, we carried on to INVERNESS to find out about what I think must be the most unusual craft I've ever run across on *Down Your Way* – targe-making. If like me you have no idea what a targe is, allow me to explain briefly that they are round objects that look like dart boards, but are in fact shields. The man who makes them in Inverness is James McConnell, who took us to his two workshops in his lovely garden, where he makes the targes, fiercesome-looking Culloden swords and vicious little daggers known as skean dhus.

Targes covered with stag skin date back five hundred years, according to James, though at that time the Highland warriors used almost any materials they could get their hands on. Today he exports many of his targes to very hot climates and consequently has to make them of wood that doesn't warp or split. The animal skins covering the targes are still native to the Highlands and I asked why some still had their animal's hair on. 'As far as I know,' James replied, 'many hundreds of years ago they didn't really know how to cure leather, and the skin was just ripped off the animals and dried in the sun before being nailed on to the disc.'

Unlike any other shield I had seen, the targes in James's workshop all had a nasty-looking spike sticking out from the middle, which he sensibly protected with a cork. This made it both a weapon of defence and one of offence, and on the reverse side was a sheath for the skean dhu, which could be drawn and used in battle when all else failed. James pointed out that the skean dhu, or 'black knife' was clearly designed for killing; as he said, 'It's no use for peeling vegetables!' Nor were the Culloden swords that he also makes. These weigh four pounds and have two brutal edges which suggest that there was no finesse in their swordplay.

Before we left James McConnell and his unique craft he had one further surprise for us. As usual I asked him to choose a piece of music and he picked something that he had heard snatches of but never heard in its entirety, which probably goes for many of us. He chose the national anthem of the People's Republic of China!

Anyone searching for the unusual in Inverness must inevitably be drawn to Loch Ness and the so-called monster thought by many to lurk in its depths. One man who had already devoted ten years of his life to studying the monster when we visited him was Frank Searle, who had established the investigation centre which provides information to Nessie seekers.

In 1969 he set up camp (literally – he lived in a tent for six years winter and summer) and began the process of deciding for himself whether 1400 years of recorded history about the strange creature were right, or whether the beast created by the media was really an object of entertaining makebelieve. And what had he deduced?

77 Loch Ness.

'I found out that these animals do certainly exist,' he began categorically. 'There's a breeding herd of them, and I've seen two small ones together. The animals resemble the prehistoric plesiosaur more than anything I can come up with. They are dark grey in colour, with small heads, long necks, large bulky bodies and flippers, and they are not as big as one might think from their "monster" image – perhaps up to about twenty-five feet long. They are fish-eaters, purely marine creatures – not air-breathing. I think if you saw a Nessie for eight seconds you would have had a very good sighting.'

I must admit, like most other people, that I had always imagined there was only one monster, but it made sense that they had to breed to keep going and, as Frank said, there have been many sightings of two of the creatures together.

I was interested too in these 1400 years of written records; what do they have to say? 'Around the year 600,' Frank began, 'the ninth bishop of Iona, a man named Adamnan, wrote a biography of St Columba and in this he makes several references to people of integrity living around Loch Ness seeing the water monsters.'

All right, but how did the monsters first get into Loch Ness? 'I'm often asked this,' said Frank smiling,' and it's a very simple story. About 7500 years ago, which is a very short time in history if you stop to think about it, Loch Ness was an arm of the North Sea. Then it was closed instantaneously by a local land upheaval in the area where the town of Inverness now stands. So it would seem that these animals were coming to and fro from the sea, using the loch as a feeding or breeding ground, as many sea creatures use the Scandinavian fiords, and some were trapped.'

And they feed on the fish? 'They have to be fish-eaters, because the plankton content in Loch Ness is low,' Frank continued. 'And the fact that they are fish-eaters is maybe why we see them, because 75 per cent of the fish are within ten feet of the surface.'

He went on to indicate the problems of trying to sight these elusive creatures. The water in Loch Ness is peat-stained and filled with tiny particles which makes visibility almost nil. What about dead bodies? These sink to the bottom and rest in the peat sludge apparently; it is an established fact that no corpses ever come to the surface in the loch.

In ten years Frank has made thirty-one definite sightings of Nessies, some from the bank, but more from the surface of the loch because he has spent 32,000 hours out there in an open boat! And after all that his musical choice of 'My Way' certainly seemed appropriate.

Thirty-two miles south-west of Loch Ness, down the A82, you reach the west coast at FORT WILLIAM, at the foot of Britain's highest mountain Ben Nevis. Looking up at the clouds that covered its 4406-foot-high summit (4418 feet if you stand on top of the cairn up there), it seemed incredible to me that a race is run up there every year. But on the first Saturday in September getting on for 400 runners set out on the gruelling ten-mile course that leads round the mountain, up to the summit and back down again. There is obviously a risk of exposure and other injury in a race like this, and the organisers are careful to have the mountain well manned to cope with any emergencies. There are usually two RAF mountain rescue teams up there, the Royal Army Medical Corps and forty doctors drawn from large hospitals in the region.

78 Ben Nevis.

They really are needed too. Some of the runners, particularly the tail-enders, reach the top and have to be physically turned round and pointed in the downward direction. They are so worn out and dazed that if they weren't given a little help there would be a serious risk that they would keep on running over the precipice on the other side.

This sounded a frightful race and I found it hard to imagine anyone wanting to put themselves through so much discomfort, but hundreds obviously do and the record time when we were there in 1982 stood at one hour, twenty-six minutes and fifty-five seconds. This was set up by a runner from the Lake District named David Cannon. The best runners seem to come from the Lake District, where they do a lot of fell running.

Taking the Road to the Isles, or the A830 as it is otherwise known, we made our way from Fort William to Mallaig and crossed the sea to SKYE. Landing at Armadale, the first thing we noticed was Armadale Castle, where we discovered the headquarters of the Clan Donald Land Trust. This was formed in 1971 as the result of a worldwide effort that raised enough money to buy the 15,000 acres now owned by the Trust, which might otherwise have been sold outside the clan. Now, every MacDonald in the world can become a member of the Clan Donald society through a network of branches all round the world.

Armadale Castle also houses a museum that tells the story of the MacDonalds, tracing the genealogy of the different branches of the clan and displaying their various tartans.

At the other end of the island stands Dunvegan Castle, the home of the chiefs of the MacLeod clan for over 700 years. Almost as old as the clan itself is the object of greatest interest to visitors to Dunvegan, the Fairy Flag, an ancient silk banner kept in an air-tight case. Legend holds that this originated from fairies found by one of the clan's nurses crooning over the baby in her charge as he slept in his cot, and over him they had laid this flag as a gift to be used whenever the clan was in need of any kind of help. Charlie Heron, who showed it to me, assured me that in battles fought in 1420 and 1590 between the MacLeods and the MacDonalds victory was only secured for the MacLeods after the arrival of the Fairy Flag.

I didn't like the look of the sixteen-foot pit in which the MacLeods of days gone by used to keep their unfortunate prisoners, but I was very taken with their splendid drinking horn and the legend attached to it. Charlie Heron told me that this was used by the clan chiefs when they came of age as a sign that they would be man enough to lead the clan when their time came. And to prove themselves they had to drink this horn full of claret and finish it without stopping or falling down.

With obvious pride he went on to say: 'That was carried out as recently as when John MacLeod of MacLeod, the present chief, came of age. He carried out the old and original custom in one minute, fifty-seven seconds.'

Now, the horn holds a bottle and a quarter and I wondered what state he was in when he finished. 'I can say this too,' beamed Charlie. 'He was down at the village hall at the great celebration dance, dancing until four o'clock in the morning!'

Just before reaching Dunvegan we turned off down a narrow road and after seven miles driving down the glen we came to the end of the road and Skye Venture Knitwear, a genuine cottage industry run by Barry and Sue Everson. Based in a small crofter's cottage, they produced scarves, sweaters, cardigans and other woollen garments knitted on the premises, or in the homes of outworkers living in the glen. Most of the clothes were produced on ordinary domestic knitting machines, but some of the garments in specialist wools were knitted by hand. As well as using dyed wools, the Eversons also used a lot of natural wools from sheep like Swaledales, Herdwickes and Welsh Mountain Blacks, which provided different shades without needing to be dyed.

The bulk of their work was knitted in fishermen's rib, which they said was very windproof and was excellent for wearing outside either working, or playing golf or fishing.

Beside those who actually knitted the clothes there were lots of others who sewed many of them together and did all the finishing work. As Sue Everson said, it really was a cottage industry, turning the clock back to the days when so much of the employment in the western isles was provided by small enterprises like this.

I thought it was marvellous and typified so many of the inspiring and interesting people and activities we encountered in the course of travelling all over Britain when we went *Down Your Way*.

Index